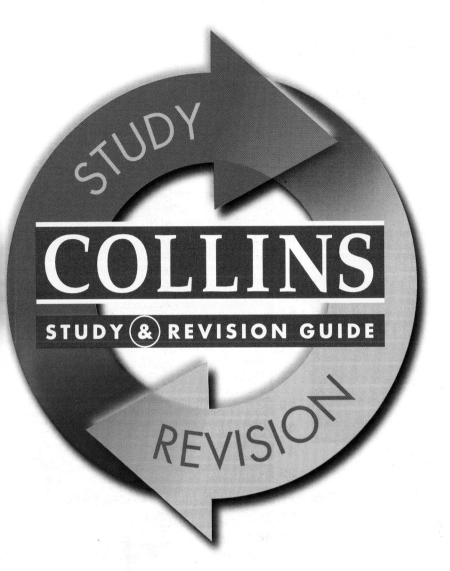

STUDY

COLLINS
STUDY & REVISION GUIDE

REVISION

ENGLISH
GCSE Key Stage 4

▶ Andrew Bennett
▶ Peter Thomas

▶ Series Editor: Jayne de Courcy

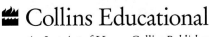

Collins Educational
An Imprint of HarperCollinsPublishers

Contents

How to boost your grade

A Study Guide <u>and</u> a Revision Guide – in one book

You may be starting – or part of the way through – your Key Stage 4 English course. You may be getting close to mock or final exams. Wherever you are in your course, this book will help you. It will improve your skills in Reading, Writing, Speaking and Listening, and will improve your confidence in answering exam questions. These three pages will show you how to get the most out of this book so that you can boost your grade!

An up-to-date book to match your course

This book has been written specifically to match the National Curriculum requirements that are tested in GCSE English exams by all of the Examination Boards. Your teacher will tell you which syllabus you are following and what you will be tested on in the final exam papers. Whatever is not tested in the exams is part of your coursework, and so everything in this book is relevant, no matter which syllabus you are studying!

Short, manageable chapters

Each chapter focuses on one very specific aspect of the Reading, Writing, Speaking and Listening assessment objectives for English.

Chapter headings and introductions tell you clearly what you will be studying. Short chapters mean that you can concentrate on one particular skill before moving on. This also makes it quick and easy to find what you want when you are revising, doing homework or preparing coursework.

Revision hints

- It is a good idea to divide your revision into small, manageable chunks: each chapter in this book is set out to help you do that.

- Use chapter cross-references, e.g. when revising Writing, cross-reference to Reading to see how professional writers achieve their effects.

What makes the grade?

WHAT MAKES THE GRADE?

> For a Grade C, you need to sustain comment on the way an author tells a story, drawing evidence from a range of places in the text.
>
> For a Grade B, you need to develop your comments by showing different uses of narrative and dialogue. If you can explore the likely effects on you or other readers of identifying with the narrator or a character, you will be able to bring in your personal response.
>
> For a Grade A, you need to analyse the narrative structure, showing consistency or variety in an author's approach. You need to evaluate the writing in the context of its own time and today.

At the end of each chapter, a section called *What makes the grade?* tells you how you need to demonstrate the skills you have just learned to move, for example, from a Grade C to a Grade B or a Grade A.

Checking your progress

Check yourself sections let you check your progress quickly and easily. They tell you where you might have gone wrong and how to boost your grade.

At the end of each chapter there is a *Check yourself* section which consists of one or more short questions that will let you see if you have read and understood the chapter properly.

We have purposely placed the answers straight after the questions so that you have a choice. You can **either**:

● Cover up the answers so that you can test yourself properly. When you have written down your own answers, check whether you are right.

or:

● Read through a question, then read through the answer and tutorial. Here you're not using the *Check yourself* as a test; you're using it as an interactive way of revising.

Tutorial help – upgrade your exam result

The examiner has written a *Tutorial* for every question. There are rarely absolutely right or absolutely wrong answers in English but some answers are better than others. The answers given are fair to good. You can compare your own answers with them. The *Tutorials* comment on the answers, give additional hints, and show how these answers – and your own – could be improved following the criteria outlined in *What makes the grade?*

ANSWERS

A1 The writer uses dialogue which is naturalistic. The two characters speak like ordinary people and repeat themselves and say things that don't always follow on from the last thing. You can't tell what each of them thinks because Davies seems to be agreeing with Mick, but Mick eventually turns on Davies for saying what he's been saying himself. Perhaps this means he doesn't think Davies has the right to criticise his brother, but then he shouldn't have asked for his opinion in the first place if he was going to act like this. I think he's quite a sly bloke because he gets Davies to say something and then tells him off for it. Davies is not really sure what to say. He seems a bit nervous, but he gets a bit more confident when Mick seems to trust him. In the end Mick is sharp with him and he (Davies) probably wishes he hadn't said anything.

TUTORIALS

T1 This shows good grasp of Mick's cunning and Davies' uncertainty. These points could be made more convincing by quoting the lines where Davies 'seems a bit nervous' and 'gets more confident'. There is some willingness to explore meaning in 'Perhaps he …' and some personal response in 'but then he shouldn't have asked' and 'I think he's quite a sly bloke'.

For a Grade B, the comment on Davies' uncertainty could be sustained by looking at several moments where he pauses, asks a question or repeats what Mick has said. This would show more use of textual evidence. The comment on Mick's slyness could be developed by referring to moments where he seems to be leading Davies on. For example, he seems reluctant to say any more: 'you see … his trouble is …' and 'It's not a very nice thing to say …' His apparent trust in Davies at the start of the extract could be explored for its motives and its effects on Davies. This could involve analysis of his methods to trap Davies into an opinion about his brother.

There is a brief comment on the author and his use of naturalistic dialogue but not much. There needs to be some reference to the writer's dramatic purpose, referring to its likely effect on the audience. It is a passage which creates interest and tension by not revealing characters' motives, so that the audience is kept uncertain. This is writing in which the drama is in relationships rather than plot. For a Grade A, there could be exploration of the language as something evasive, ambiguous and misleading, rather than for honest communication.

Every answer is accompanied by helpful advice in a *Tutorial*.

Planning your revision time

Use the *Check yourself* questions to plan your revision time. Close to exams, use them as tests. They'll tell you which skills you're weakest at and so will help you identify the chapters you need to spend more time reading. It's tempting to spend lots of time on the skills that you feel confident with already, but you should concentrate on improving your weaker areas.

Revision hint

● Be active when you revise! Write summaries of the main points in chapters, including key words or ideas.

Practising real exam questions

At the end of the book you will find five exam papers.
Each paper contains:

- one question on responding to Reading: either fiction, poetry, non-fiction or media.
- one question that calls for a particular form of Writing:
  - writing to explore/imagine/entertain
  - writing to inform/explain/describe
  - writing to argue/persuade/instruct
  - writing to analyse/review/comment

Whichever syllabus you are studying, these questions will give you invaluable practice in answering exam questions.

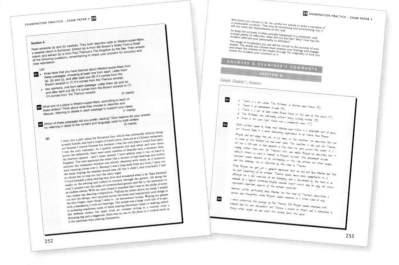

Examiner's comments – upgrade your exam result

For all the exam papers we have provided real students' answers with examiner's comments, pointing out where the answers could be improved to achieve a higher grade, or what makes the answers particularly good as they are.

You can try answering the questions for yourself and can then compare your answers against the sample answers given. The examiner's comments will show you where your own answers can be improved.

Feeling confident

Using this book will help you to enjoy your course because you'll understand what is going on. You'll feel confident and ready to take your exams. And remember –

for every topic and every question, there are Answers, Tutorials and Examiner's comments, so you're never left without help!

GCSE English

About your English course

All Examination Boards have to test the same skills or 'assessment objectives' in relation to Reading, Writing, Speaking and Listening. Because each chapter in this book focuses specifically on one aspect of these assessment objectives, every chapter is relevant to your course.

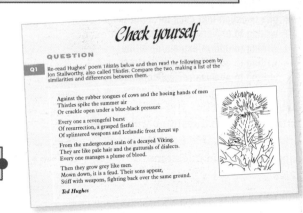

Examination Boards try to vary the texts they use on exam papers, but you are unlikely to be taken by surprise if you have tried all the *Check yourself* sections and sample exam questions.

Exam papers

All GCSE English exams test your skills of Reading and Writing. Speaking and Listening are teacher-assessed in your coursework.

All syllabuses require you to sit two exam papers. Each paper tests both Reading and Writing, although the proportion of marks for each will vary on different papers.

The instructions on the front of each exam paper will tell you what is being tested and what proportion of the total mark is allocated to Reading and Writing.

Many exam boards issue pre-release reading materials in the form of a booklet or anthology, which you are allowed to study and annotate in class and take into the exam with you. Hints on preparing pre-release materials, and other exam tips, are given in *Chapter 35, Examination technique*.

Questions that test your response to reading

Most syllabuses require you to answer reading questions on two types of texts in the exam: fiction texts and non-fiction or media texts.

The specific texts will vary from one Examination Board to another. To test your response to fiction, one may ask you to respond to a passage of prose, while another may ask you to compare two poems. Non-fiction or media texts used on exam papers may be advertisements, leaflets or extracts from writing such as diaries or travel books.

This book gives you practice in responding to the full range of fiction and non-fiction reading (except Shakespeare which is assessed by coursework).

Questions that test your writing skills

For Writing, most Examination Boards will ask you to produce two different pieces of writing on the two papers; for example, one might be an imaginative or personal piece, and the other a descriptive or argumentative piece.

Again, you will find it helpful to work through all the writing questions in this book, as the skills are easily transferable from one task to another once you have mastered them.

To make sure that it is really your writing that is tested, and not your general knowledge, most Examination Boards link at least some of the writing tasks either to reading materials on the exam paper or to pre-release materials that you will have studied in class.

Syallabus coverage

Although the exam papers at the end of this book do not reflect any one Examination Board's exact model, the questions are designed to cover the range across all the different syllabuses to provide you with valuable practice. Your teacher will tell you about the particular requirements of your syllabus, and the exact format of questions on the papers that you will take.

SECTION I
Reading

- In this chapter, you will develop your reading response to characters and to writers' skills in creating them.
- If you can discuss what characters are like and what they do, you will show engagement and familiarity. If you can explain how a character has been made believable and interesting, you will show insight into the writer's methods.

INTRODUCTION

Some readers like books with lots of action in them; others prefer books with characters who are interesting. Authors usually try to keep both kinds of reader happy. As readers, we may not know much about the places, events or actions in a story, so we are likely to trust and believe what the author tells us about them. But when it comes to characters, we all know people in real life, and think we know how they react and what makes them tick. Making readers believe in a book's characters is not easy, so making them interesting is a vital part of a writer's skill.

TELLING

Authors have different ways of making characters seem real on the page. Sometimes, they may give information about them directly as part of the story.

> He was a bad-tempered, ungrateful man who hated children and only showed feelings for his cats.

This is **explicit** information, telling the reader what to think about the character. Writers often use appearance to suggest character, without referring to what the characters do and say. The effect on the reader depends on the choice of vocabulary, which may be positive or negative, as you can see from this extract from *Martin Chuzzlewit* by Charles Dickens.

> The mistress of the Blue Dragon was in outward appearance what a land-lady should be: broad, buxom, comfortable, and good looking … She had still a bright, black eye, and jet black hair, was comely, dimpled, plump and tight as a gooseberry.

The words used to describe the landlady make her seem friendly and good company because they are to do with smiling and good eating. She is not skinny, bony and bad-tempered, but 'buxom', 'dimpled' and 'plump', which makes us think that she smiles a lot and would be good for a cuddle.

SHOWING THROUGH ACTION

An author can, however, convey the same information about a character by describing behaviour and letting the reader form a judgement about the person based on what he or she does. In other words, the writer shows character through action.

1

He gave no thanks for the help and scowled at the boys who had returned his cat, going inside, speaking softly to the wet animal.

In this case, the writer is implying something through action, and it is for the reader to understand by inference. He 'scowls' at the boys who have done him a favour, rather than thank them. This is a negative signal, though the fact that he speaks 'softly' to the animal shows tenderness, and perhaps that he feels more for the animal than for the boys, or that its condition has made him too upset to remember his manners. Whatever the reader's judgement of the man, it is based on narrative detail of what he *does*, rather than what the author tells us explicitly.

Look at the passage below from *Great Expectations*, where Charles Dickens uses the simplest of domestic activities to suggest the attitudes, manner and personality of Pip's older sister, who is his foster-parent. Which details of her manner and movement give you clues to her personality?

My sister had a trenchant way of cutting our bread-and-butter for us, that never varied. First, with her left hand, she *jammed* the loaf hard and fast against her bib – where it sometimes got a pin in it, and sometimes a needle, which we afterwards got into our mouths. Then, she took some butter (not too much) on a knife, and spread it on the loaf, in an apothecary kind of way, as if she were making a plaister – using both sides of the knife with a slapping dexterity, and trimming and moulding the butter off round the crust. Then, she gave the knife a final smart wipe on the edge of the plaister, and then *sawed* a very thick round off the loaf; which she finally, before separating from the loaf, *hewed* into two halves, of which Joe got one, and I the other.

The words in italics make you think of force and physical exercise. They are not words that would normally come to mind when making a snack, because they seem more appropriate to jobs done by people who work out of doors, such as lumberjacks. The verb 'jammed' suggests fierce and violent movement with a purpose. The verbs 'sawed' and 'hewed' suggest physical activities you would associate with a strong, labouring man. The vocabulary suggests that, although she is doing something domestic, she attacks it with fierce and unfeminine energy.

The verbs 'trimming' and 'moulding' suggest exact, almost scientific precision, as if she brought the care of a surgeon or chemist (an apothecary) to the task. She does not allow them 'too much' butter, which suggests meanness, and she gets pins into food, hinting that she is not very soft-hearted or careful about their comfort. The fact that she always cuts a loaf this way suggests that she is not changeable or adaptable.

SHOWING THROUGH SPEECH

Another way authors can create character without simply describing them is to let the reader judge them from what they say.

> 'Yes, that's my cat,' he said irritably.
> 'She's wet and hungry,' said Robert.
> 'I can see that myself,' he snapped, 'I don't need a nosy kid to tell me that!'
> 'I hope she'll be all right.'
> 'Yes. Now clear off.'

The writer uses speech here to show attitude and manner. This writer puts in further prompts about the character in the choice of speech-verb ('snapped') and adverbs ('irritably'). Other writers think this makes it too obvious, and let the reader pick up what they can from the speech alone. In this case, the boy's speech indicates concern about the cat's welfare, so the reader's sympathy is less likely to be with the man.

In the following extract from *Emma*, Jane Austen creates an impression of Mrs Elton by recording only what she says, adding no direct narrative comment or guidance to the reader. The reader has only to follow her talk to realise that she starts off full of enthusiasm, giving everyone the benefit of her superior opinions, then gets tired and ends up contradicting everything she has said previously. Jane Austen does not even have to record every word of what Mrs Elton says – she just gives us 'sound-bites'.

The whole party were assembled, excepting Frank Churchill, who was expected every moment from Richmond; and Mrs Elton, in all her apparatus of happiness, her large bonnet and her basket, was very ready to lead the way in gathering, accepting, or talking. Strawberries, and only strawberries, could now be thought or spoken of. 'The best fruit in England—everybody's favourite—always wholesome. These the finest beds and finest sorts. Delightful to gather for one's self—the only way of really enjoying them. Morning decidedly the best time—never tired—every sort good—hautboy infinitely superior—no comparison—the others hardly eatable—hautboys very scarce—Chili preferred—white wood finest flavour of all—price of strawberries in London—abundance about Bristol—Maple Grove—cultivation—beds when to be renewed—gardeners thinking exactly different—no general rule—gardeners never to be put out of their way—delicious fruit—only too rich to be eaten much of—inferior to cherries—currants more refreshing—only objection to gathering strawberries the stooping—glaring sun—tired to death—could bear it no longer—must go and sit in the shade.'

Most writers mix telling and showing, using the narrative to tell the reader what the character is like, and then developing this by letting the reader appear to overhear the character in speech. Here is Dickens doing both things when he introduces Sarah Gamp into his novel, *Martin Chuzzlewit*. What impression of Sarah Gamp do you get from Dickens' narrative description, and from her speech?

She was a fat old woman, this Mrs Gamp, with a husky voice and a moist eye, which she had a remarkable power of turning up, and only showing the white of it. Having very little neck, it cost her some trouble to look over herself, if one may say so, at those to whom she talked. She wore a very rusty black gown, rather the worse for snuff, and a shawl and bonnet to correspond. In these dilapidated articles of dress she had, on principle, arrayed herself, time out of mind, on such occasions as the present; for this at once expressed a decent amount of veneration for the deceased, and invited the next of kin to present her with a fresher suit of weeds*: an appeal so frequently successful, that the very ghost of Mrs Gamp, bonnet and all, might be seen hanging up, any hour in the day, in at least a dozen of the second-hand clothes shops about Holborn. The face of Mrs Gamp – the nose in particular – was somewhat red and swollen, and it was difficult to enjoy her society without becoming conscious of a smell of spirits. Like most persons who have attained to great eminence in their profession, she took to hers very kindly; insomuch that, setting aside her natural predilections as a woman, she went to a lying-in or a laying-out* with equal zest and relish.

* mourning-clothes

* preparing the body for a funeral

'Ah,' repeated Mrs Gamp; for it was always a safe sentiment in cases of mourning. 'Ah dear! When Gamp was summoned to his long home, and I see him a-lying in Guy's Hospital with a penny-piece on each eye, and his wooden leg under his left arm, I thought I should have fainted away. But I bore up.'

If certain whispers current in the Kingsgate Street circles had any truth in them, she had indeed borne up surprisingly; and had exerted such uncommon fortitude as to dispose of Mr Gamp's remains for the benefit of science. But it should be added, in fairness, that this had happened twenty years before; and that Mr and Mrs Gamp had long been separated on the ground of incompatibility of temper in their drink.

'You have become indifferent since then, I suppose?' said Mr Pecksniff. 'Use is second nature, Mrs Gamp.'

'You may well say second nature, sir,' returned that lady. 'One's first ways is to find such things a trial to the feelings, and so is one's lasting custom. If it wasn't for the nerve a little sip of liquor gives me (I never was able to do more than taste it), I never could go through with what I sometimes has to do. "Mrs Harris," I says, at the very last case as ever I acted in, which it was but a young person, "Mrs Harris," I says, "leave the bottle on the chimley-piece, and don't ask me to take none, but let me put my lips to it when I am so dispoged, and then I will do what I'm engaged to do, according to the best of my ability." "Mrs Gamp," she says, in answer, "if ever there was a sober creetur to be got at eighteen pence a day for working people, and three and six for gentlefolks – night watching,"' said Mrs Gamp, with emphasis, '"being a extra charge – you are that invallable person." "Mrs Harris," I says to her, "don't name the charge, for if I could afford to lay all my feller creeturs out for nothink, I would gladly do it, sich is the love I bears 'em. But what I always says to them as has the management of matters, Mrs Harris"' – here she kept her on eye Mr Pecksniff – '"be they gents or be they ladies, is, don't ask me whether I won't take none, or whether I will, but leave the bottle on the chimley-piece, and let me put my lips to it when I am so dispoged."'

You may have noted that Dickens' narrative gives us the impression of someone who is:

- not sentimental about her dead husband (she sold his body for medical research);
- quick to turn situations to financial advantage (she tries to get second-hand clothes passed on to her, and then sells them);
- fond of drink (red nose, smelling of spirits).

Mrs Gamp's speech gives the impression that she is:

- very fond of drink, even though she pretends it's only to help her do her work;
- craftily careful to set out her charges, especially for any extras;
- long-winded and repetitive;
- keen to impress people with her honesty and sincerity.

The dialogue section of the extract amplifies the preceding information given in the narrative, using a more naturalistic method of making the reader feel that he or she has been on the receiving end of Mrs Gamp's tongue. This use of speech is similar to the way that it is used in plays, and it is often called a dramatic method of characterisation; it's as if the character steps forward and takes over from the author.

Mrs Gamp.

SHOWING THROUGH THE UNSPOKEN

Sometimes it's what's **not** spoken that tells you more about the character's mood, manner or motive.

Are you quite sure?'
'Well … yes … I mean … I, er, I'm sure, I am really.'

Hesitations suggest doubt and uncertainty, and although what the character says **explicitly** is that she *is* sure, the **implied** message is the opposite. A pause or a hesitation can be as meaningful as a statement. The reader needs to ask the question 'Why is the speaker hesitating?' then find a motive which explains the behaviour.

The knack of suggesting something about a character and his or her motives without being explicit is something that can be picked up from listening to people talk in real life.

'How do you like these new trousers?'
'They're … er … very nice.'

Here the hesitation is not because of a speech defect, or not having an opinion, but reluctance to offend. It is a sign that the second speaker is afraid to speak the truth or too kind to say something that will hurt.

USING A MIXTURE OF TECHNIQUES

Most writers use a mixture of all of these different methods, and you can show how well you read by picking out examples of the different methods and commenting on them in detail.

In the next example, another extract from *Emma*, there is hardly any explicit information from the author. Jane Austen allows a character to speak uninterruptedly to bring out her personality. She uses no speech adverbs, so that the reader has to imagine the tone from what is being said. (Remember that it is always easier to get a sense of how a character speaks if you read the passage aloud.) Mrs Elton, invited to Hartfield on a first visit, wants people to know that she moves in better society, is used to a finer house and is familiar with people who own the latest luxury status-symbol, a top-of-the-range horse-drawn carriage called a barouche-landau. When you read through the passage, keep these questions in mind:

- How does Mrs Elton try to impress everyone with her connections and familiarity with the good life?
- How many times does she give offence to the people who have invited her to Hartfield?
- What impression do you get from Emma's speech and the moments when she says nothing?

The very first subject, after being seated, was Maple Grove, 'My brother Mr Suckling's seat;' a comparison of Hartfield to Maple Grove. The grounds of Hartfield were small, but neat and pretty; and the house was modern and well-built. Mrs Elton seemed most favourably impressed by the size of the room, the entrance, and all that she could see or imagine. 'Very like Maple Grove indeed!' She was quite struck by the likeness!—'That room was the very shape and size of the morning-room at Maple Grove; her sister's favourite room.' Mr Elton was appealed to. 'Was not it astonishingly like?— She could really almost fancy herself at Maple Grove.'

'And the staircase.—You know, as I came in, I observed how very like the staircase was; placed exactly in the same part of the house. I really could not help exclaiming! I assure you, Miss Woodhouse, it is very delightful to me to be reminded of a place I am so extremely partial to as Maple Grove. I have spent so many happy months there! (with a little sigh of sentiment). A charming place, undoubtedly. Everybody who sees it is struck by its beauty; but to me, it has been quite a home. Whenever you are transplant-ed, like me, Miss Woodhouse, you will understand how very delightful it is to meet with anything at all like what one has left behind. I always say this is quite one of the evils of matrimony.'

Emma made as slight a reply as she could; but it was fully sufficient for Mrs Elton, who only wanted to be talking herself.

'So extremely like Maple Grove! And it is not merely the house; the grounds, I assure you, as far as I could observe, are strikingly like. The laurels at Maple Grove are in the same profusion as here, and stand very much in the same way,—just across the lawn; and I had a glimpse of a fine large tree, with a bench round it, which put me so exactly in mind! My brother and sister will be enchanted with this place. People who have extensive grounds themselves are always pleased with anything in the same style.'

Emma doubted the truth of this sentiment. She had a great idea that people who had extensive grounds themselves cared very little for the extensive grounds of anybody else; but it was not worth while to attack an error so double-dyed, and therefore only said in reply—

'When you have seen more of this country, I am afraid you will think you have over-rated Hartfield. Surrey is full of beauties.'

'Oh! yes, I am quite aware of that. It is the garden of England, you know. Surrey is the garden of England.'

'Yes; but we must not rest our claims on that distinction. Many counties, I believe, are called the garden of England, as well as Surrey.'

'No, I fancy not,' replied Mrs Elton, with a most satisfied smile. 'I never heard any county but Surrey called so.'

Emma was silenced.

'My brother and sister have promised us a visit in the spring or summer at farthest,' continued Mrs Elton; 'and that will be our time for exploring. While they are with us, we shall explore a great deal, I dare say. They will have their barouche-landau, of course, which holds four perfectly; and therefore, without saying anything of *our* carriage, we should be able to explore the different beauties extremely well. They would hardly come in their chaise, I think, at that season of the year. Indeed, when the time draws on, I shall decidedly recommend their bringing the barouche-landau; it will be so very much preferable. When people come into a beautiful country of this sort, you know, Miss Woodhouse, one naturally wishes them to see as much as possible; and Mr Suckling is extremely fond of exploring. We explored to King's-Weston twice last summer, in that way, most delightfully, just after their first having the barouche-landau.'

A barouche-landau.

- Mrs Elton mentions Maple Grove eight times, each time finding Hartfield, at best, like it, but not as impressive. She mentions the barouche-landau three times and name-drops Mr Suckling whenever she can.

- Her praise of features of Hartfield is only in terms of its likeness to Maple Grove. She refuses to accept Emma's opinion that other counties may be called the Garden of England. She explains that when Mr Suckling arrives, she will be exploring and have little time for other people. She does not listen or give others a chance to speak. She does not ask them what they think or give them cues to share in the talk.

- Emma's only attempt to interrupt the flow of Mrs Elton fails, and she 'is silenced'. She listens patiently either out of tact and patience or because she can't get a word in edgeways! Her silence throughout the scene is part of the writer's technique to put the reader in Emma's position.

Finally, when you read, remember that you are looking at the *characters* – for what they are like – and at the *characterisation* – for the writer's skill in creating them.

WHAT MAKES THE GRADE?

For a Grade C, you need to be able to sustain your comments on character, showing that you can find supporting evidence for a comment from a number of places, not just one.

For a Grade B, you will need to develop your comments, showing that one comment may not be enough to fit all the evidence. You also need to show that you can make apt inferences from implied meaning, as well as from explicit detail. This means trying to explore what you read for possible motives and possible reader reactions to them.

For a Grade A, you need to refer in detail to aspects of language, structure and presentation, to analyse dialogue for characteristic features of attitude and feeling, and to explore the author's range of characterising devices in dialogue and narrative.

Check yourself

QUESTIONS

Q1 What do you learn about Jenny from the following?

'Now tell me honestly, and don't try to hold anything back. Were you there when the police arrived?' Jenny studied her shoes intently.

Q2 What is the author suggesting about Fothergill in the following sentence?

Fothergill picked his way carefully between the two swaying bag-ladies, drawing his coat-collar tight and flicking some dust off his sleeve.

Q3 What impression do you get of these two characters from what they say and how they say it?

'With respect, Mr Cornwall, may I humbly suggest that your memory of the event may not be entirely perfect, and that you may have practised some economy with the facts?'
'I, er … that is … I, certainly not! I have told you everything as accurately as I can!'

Q4 Look at the passage on the right from William Golding's *The Lord of the Flies*. What do you learn about Ralph and Piggy:

a) from what the author tells you directly?
b) from what the author shows you of their behaviour?
c) from what is shown by what is spoken and unspoken?

The fat boy lowered himself over the terrace and sat down carefully, using the edge as a seat.

'I'm sorry I been such a time. Them fruit—'

He wiped his glasses and adjusted them on his button nose. The frame had made a deep pink V on the bridge. He looked critically at Ralph's golden body and then down at his own clothes. He laid a hand on the end of a zipper that extended down his chest.

'My auntie—'

Then he opened the zipper with decision and pulled the whole wind-breaker over his head.

'There!'

Ralph looked at him side-long and said nothing.

'I expect we'll want to know all their names,' said the fat boy, 'and make a list. We ought to have a meeting.'

Ralph did not take the hint, so the fat boy was forced to continue.

'I don't care what they call me,' he said confidentially, 'so long as they don't call me what they used to call me at school.'

Ralph was faintly interested.

'What was that?'

The fat boy glanced over his shoulder, then leaned towards Ralph.

He whispered.

'They used to call me Piggy.'

Ralph shrieked with laughter. He jumped up.

'Piggy! Piggy!'

'Ralph, please.'

Piggy clasped his hands in apprehension.

'I said I didn't want—'

'Piggy! Piggy!'

Ralph danced out into the hot air of the beach and then returned as a fighter plane, with wings swept back, and machine-gunned Piggy.

'Sche-aa-ow!'

He dived in the sand at Piggy's feet and lay there laughing.

'Piggy!'

Piggy grinned reluctantly, pleased despite himself, at even this much recognition.

'So long as you don't tell the others—'

REMEMBER! Cover the answers if you want to.

ANSWERS

A1 Jenny is not a person who is fascinated by her shoes! She is looking at her shoes because she does not want to look her questioner in the face. This may be a sign of her guilt or sorrow, or unwillingness to show any emotion.

TUTORIALS

T1 *This is very clear, stating that her motive for looking at her shoes has nothing to do with shoes! This answer looks for a motive to explain the lack of face-to-face contact. Offering some possible explanations shows ability to explore a text for implied meaning and a range of alternative interpretations.*

ANSWERS

A2 Fothergill is fussy and uneasy about the people he has encountered. His gesture shows either that he takes care over his appearance or perhaps shows fear or mistrust of the bag-ladies, securing himself against contact with them.

A3 The questioner is confident and poised, carefully using words to avoid directly saying that Mr Cornwall is lying.
Mr Cornwall is nervous, and his emphatic denials are perhaps a sign that he is bluffing, and has been caught out.

A4 a) Piggy is fat and has to wear glasses. He trusts Ralph ('confidentially') and he is a bit nervous ('with apprehension'). Ralph is more sun-tanned from being in the open ('golden body') and isn't really interested until Piggy tells him about his nickname.

TUTORIALS

T2 *Again, this answer looks for reasons for the behaviour. Offering 'either … or' interpretation shows willingness to explore. There could be more sustained close reference to details such as 'picked', 'carefully', 'tight' and the odd habit of flicking dust off his sleeve. Pointing out that 'picked' and 'carefully' suggest choosiness and caution would tie the comment to the evidence, and the reference to 'tight' suggests that he wants to keep himself covered up, protected from people or from dirt.*

T3 *This is clearly stated, but there is no sustained close reference to the words which create the impression. 'Respect' and 'humbly' are words used by the questioner, but the questioner is actually more confident, and not as humble, as the other person. The relationship between the two could be explored. The speaker seems to be using these words ironically, as he does when he says that the man 'may not be speaking the 'entire' truth, rather than accuse him outright. Reading for his motives, this comment could be developed. It is as if he is making it easy for him to confess that he has lied a bit. He seems skilful at this. Note that it is quite all right to say in your examination answer that a gesture may 'perhaps' mean something or other - it is perfectly in order to venture a possible explanation, as we are dealing with interpretation, not just facts!*

T4 a) *This is mainly factual description, showing understanding and some judgement about Piggy and his feelings. For a higher grade, comment needs to be sustained by charting the detail throughout, showing how it adds up to a consistent impression of being unconfident. Explaining the effect of adverbs and adverbial phrases denoting mood ('critically', 'confidentially', 'reluctantly', 'faintly', 'with decision' and 'in apprehension') will show appreciation of the way the writer has selected language to help the characterisation. Comment can be developed by showing that, although he is mainly unconfident, he is willing to accept any notice, even if it is not the kind he was looking for, grinning 'reluctantly, despite himself'. Piggy's possible past experiences could be explored from hints in the passage. This shows that, although he has suffered from being mocked in the past, he will accept being mocked now, if it's the only form of notice that is offered. Adding a comment about the sadness of this would show personal engagement.*

ANSWERS

A4 b) Piggy is a bit slow-moving and timid ('lowered himself … sat down carefully') and seems nervous about being overheard ('glanced over his shoulder') and keen to be liked (Ralph doesn't react to what Piggy says, as if he's not interested in him, so Piggy has to try harder to get a response).

c) Piggy is the one who keeps trying to make conversation. He makes some practical suggestions, but they don't work, so he decides to share something private. The fact that he says 'Them fruit', not 'Those fruit' suggests he is not very educated in his speech. Ralph seems childish because of his repetition of 'Piggy' and making aircraft noises.

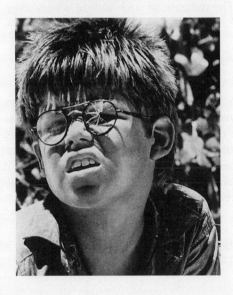

TUTORIALS

T4 b) There is sustained comment on details here, and some insight in the comment on the implicit meaning of 'glanced over his shoulder'. The reference to his timid caution could be sustained by referring to his slowness to take any clothes off, and his feeling of triumph when he does: 'There!'. This could be developed by referring to Piggy's gestures of 'looking round', as if he expects unfriendly people to be about, and of 'clasping his hands', which suggests a deep fear causing him to make a sign of praying.

c) This looks carefully at details of language as a feature of character (idiom/grammar) and at language as an expression of social relationships. To achieve a higher grade, there needs to be sustained comment on Piggy's attempts to start conversation, tracking his speech through the passage, and showing that he keeps trying to get Ralph to talk by starting a conversation: 'I'm sorry …', 'My auntie …', 'I expect …', 'I don't care …', etc. This comment can be developed by demonstrating that each new attempt to start a conversation shows him trying different ways of getting Ralph's interest, starting with an apology which is ignored, then a practical suggestion which is also ignored, then a confidential statement showing trust, which finally gets Ralph's interest.

Comment on Piggy could be developed by looking at his feelings in the course of this dialogue, referring to Piggy's weak complaint 'I said I didn't want …', which is lost as Ralph continues. He doesn't seem to have enough confidence to object to Ralph's mockery, even though it hurts him. Again, reference to what is unsaid after 'My auntie …' could suggest what thoughts may have been going through his mind before he decided to take some clothing off. Exploring the reasons for hesitating in speech, or not completing a speech, will show your ability to read for more than surface meaning.

- In this chapter, you will develop your reading response to settings and the way that writers use them.
- If you can explain what makes a setting vivid and interesting, you will show appreciation of a writer's choice of words. If you can explain how a setting is used in a passage, you will show awareness of an author's purpose and method.

INTRODUCTION

If a writer's purpose is to describe a setting in a literal way, then the description will be mainly factual, containing impersonal details of the place.

> It was a white-walled room with a window overlooking a garden containing shrubs and flowers. There was a TV in one corner, a bookshelf in another and a picture of the Lake District above the blue sofa on the wall facing the gas-log fireplace.

If a place is being described for information only, it is likely to list dimensions, facilities or features as **facts**. The purpose of such writing is to convey objective information, and this information is presented without trying to influence the reader's thoughts, feelings or opinions. The writer's role is to step back and allow the setting to present itself, as in the following description of a town called Winsome:

> This little town (population 5,200) has narrow streets, some of them cobbled, and the central square contains a sixteenth-century church, a pub which serves lunches in the summer months, a post office/newsagent's and a bakery. The railway station was closed in 1967. Since the by-pass was built, there are few cars other than local ones and traders. Market day is Friday. The nearest cinemas, hospitals and national-chain supermarkets are in the neighbouring towns of Shardley and Darnton.

To describe a setting for a particular purpose, the facts can be made less neutral. In the following paragraph, the purpose is to make the same town more attractive:

> Nestling quietly in the rural landscape between the over-developed commercial centres of Shardley and Darnton, the picturesque village of Winsome offers the traveller a retreat into a bygone age. The quaint charm of the ancient cobbled streets and the Friday market which has been held here for centuries gives an authentic flavour of Olde Englande. No supermarkets or express trains mar the tranquil peace of this unspoilt setting. The visitor can while away an hour or two enjoying traditional country fayre provided by mine jovial host at the Ferret and Moleskin.

Here, the writer acts as a guide, steering the reader and trying to influence the reader's impression. Words like 'nestling', 'quaint', 'authentic' and 'traditional' are chosen to flatter Winsome and produce a favourable response. Equally, the same setting can be described in a way that creates a less flattering impression:

> The main problem with Winsome is that it's boring at the best of times. Visitors pass it by, and there's very little public transport allowing locals to get to essential services such as hospitals and supermarkets. There's only one pub and a crumbling church, with nothing for the youngsters, and a tatty tourist market once a week. The unsurfaced streets make cycling difficult and play havoc with car suspension. It's no wonder people prefer to live in Shardley and Darnton.

What makes the second and third paragraphs different from the first is that they do not present literal information. They are coloured by attitude and value, and use language to influence the reader's impression, rather than equip the reader with information. The writers are not saying 'This is Winsome', but 'This is Winsome as I see it'. In this sense, they are more **literary** than **literal**. Literary descriptions of settings usually have a purpose in establishing a mood, creating a meaning, or revealing character. In fiction, the role of the setting is important because it is usually an active force in the unfolding story.

USING SETTING TO CREATE A MEANING

Read the following description of a country scene in Dorset, taken from *Return of the Native* by Thomas Hardy.

> The sombre stretch of rounds and hollows seemed to rise and meet the evening gloom in pure sympathy, the heath exhaling darkness as rapidly as the heavens precipitated it ... The place became full of a watchful intentness now; for when other things sank brooding to sleep, the heath appeared slowly to awake and listen.

This description is not the kind of factual geographical account you would expect to find in an information book. Hardy makes the environment seem like a living thing by choosing words which we normally associate with animals, not places. 'Rise' and 'meet' suggest the ability to move, and 'exhaling' is a feature of living creatures. 'Watchful', 'awake' and 'listening' are all things which animals do, and not things which are usually associated with landscape. In this way, Hardy **animates** the environment. He makes it seem as if it has actions, feelings and intentions, like a living thing.

Hardy made the setting active and powerful because he believed that the natural environment is an influence on human behaviour. It is rather like a character always in the background of his novels.

USING SETTING TO REVEAL CHARACTER

An author may use the description of setting in order to convey something about the character observing it. In this extract from Charles Dickens' *Great Expectations*, a small boy is shown gazing over the landscape near his home.

Ours was the marsh country, down by the river, within, as the river wound, twenty miles of the sea. My first most vivid and broad impression of the identity of things seems to me to have been gained on a memorable raw afternoon towards evening. At such a time I found out for certain that this bleak place overgrown with nettles was the churchyard; and that Philip Pirrip, late of this parish, and also Georgiana, wife of the above, were dead and buried; and that Alexander, Bartholomew, Abraham, Tobias and Roger, infant children of the aforesaid, were also dead and buried; and that the dark flat wilderness beyond the churchyard, intersected with dykes and mounds and gates, with scattered cattle feeding on it, was the marshes; and that the low leaden line beyond was the river; and that the distant savage lair from which the wind was rushing was the sea; and that the small bundle of shivers growing afraid of it all and beginning to cry was Pip.

This account of a setting is as much concerned with the observer as with the setting being observed. The scene is presented through the eyes of the child, and mingled with his feelings. As his gaze travels further and further into the distance, away from the comfortable closeness of his familiar home, it becomes quite frightening to the child, as if the wider world is hostile and menacing, making the child suddenly feel vulnerable and afraid.

In the next extract, from *The Darkness Out There* by Penelope Lively, a girl is doing a job in the garden of an old lady.

There was a cindery path down the garden, ending at a compost heap where egg shells gleamed among the leaves and grass clippings. Rags of plastic fluttered from sticks in a bed of cabbages. The girl picked her way daintily, her toes wincing against the cinders. A place in the country. One day she would have a place in the country, but not like this. Sometime. A little white house peeping over a hill, with a stream at the bottom of a crisp green lawn and an orchard with old apple trees and a brown pony. And she would walk in the long grass in this orchard in a straw hat with these two children, a boy and a girl, children with fair shiny hair like hers, and there'd be this man.

The writer uses the setting to reveal the character's dislikes and dreams. There is a contrast between the character and the setting; the girl dislikes dirt and roughness, and dreams about living an ideal life free of such unpleasantness. The harshness of the setting suggests not only the discomfort she feels ('wincing') but also the difference between the real world and her dreams.

USING SETTING TO REFLECT A CHARACTER'S MOOD

A person's character may be basically stable and consistent, but there can be changes in his or her mood, depending on what is happening in the story. In this extract from *Jake's Thing* by Kingsley Amis, Jake is in a bleak mood, on his way to see his doctor about a worrying problem.

The bus passed between the tiled façade of Mornington Crescent station and the roughly triangular paved area with the statue of Cobden near its apex, pitted and grimy and lacking its right hand, Richard Cobden the corn-law reformer and worker for peace and disarmament, too famous for his Christian name and dates to be needed in the inscription. Almost at the foot of the plinth what looked like the above-ground part of a public lavatory, black railings draped with black chicken-wire, bore a notice saying London Electricity Board– Danger Keep Out and gave a limited view of a stairway with ferns growing out of it and its walls. Two bollards painted in rings of black and white were to be seen not far off, their function hard even to guess at. Weeds flourished in the crevices between the paving-stones, a number of which had evidently been ripped out; others, several of them smashed, stood in an irregular pile. Elsewhere there was a heap of waterlogged and collapsed cardboard boxes and some large black plastic sheets spread about by the wind. Each corner of the space was decorated with an arrangement of shallow concrete hexagons filled with earth in which grew speckled evergreen bushes and limp conifer saplings about the height of a man, those at the extreme ends crushed by traffic and the greenery run into the soil along with aftershave cartons, sweet-wrappers, dog-food labels and soft-drink tins. Turning south, the bus stopped at its stop across the road from Greater London House, through the windows of which fluorescent lighting glared or flickered all day. It stood on ground filched from an earlier generation of dwellers in the Crescent who had woken one morning to see and hear their garden being eradicated.

Fifteen minutes later Jake was walking down Harley Street, buffeted by damp squalls as he went.

The details of this setting reflect the way Jake feels about life. It is described in a way which emphasizes all the depressing and gloomy aspects. The purpose is to reflect the jaded view of the character observing it. As in real life, what people notice about a scene reflects the positive or negative way they feel about life and themselves.

Here is a description of a setting in L. P. Hartley's novel, *The Go-Between*. It is the first time that Leo sees this place, early in his visit to Norfolk, when he is excited by visiting a new place.

Above the sluice, by which we stood, the river came out of the shadow of the belt of trees. Green, bronze and golden, it flowed through weeds and rushes; the gravel glinted, I could see the fishes darting in the shallows. Below the sluice it broadened out into a pool that was as blue as the sky. Not a weed marred the surface.

Later, Leo goes back, in a different mood, to the same place. Things have started to worry him, and he feels alone and anxious. As you read through the extract, look for details that create an impression of ugliness and decay, making a contrast with the earlier description.

> I climbed the stile into the water-meadow and at once the sun caught me in its fierce embrace. What strength it had! The boggy pools that fringed the causeway were almost dried up; the stalks that had been below the water-line showed a band of dirty yellow where the sun had scorched them. And standing on the sluice platform, I saw almost with dismay how far the level of the river had sunk. On the blue side, the deep side, I could see stones at the bottom that had never been visible before; and on the other side, the gold and green side, the water was almost lost to view beneath the trailing weeds which, piled one on another, gave a distressing impression of disarray. And the water-lilies, instead of lying on the water, stuck up awkwardly above it.

In this passage, the sun's warmth is described as 'fierce', with a destructive effect. It has 'scorched' and 'dried' the pool. The place is 'boggy', 'dirty' and in 'disarray'. The river has 'sunk' and the life that is left is 'awkward'. All of these words suggest discomfort and destruction.

As the story unfolds, Leo discovers that the people he had admired so much have been using him, and he feels that his innocence has been betrayed. On a further visit to the place described above, he feels that the ugly side of life has triumphed over his imagined ideals and sense of beauty.

Now read one further extract from later in the story where, again, the details of the setting suggest Leo's state of mind. Which details match Leo's feelings of being disappointed and defenceless in a hostile environment?

> I looked down at the water. It had sunk much lower. The surface of the pool was still blue, but many more boulders than before showed ghostly, corpse-like, at the bottom. And on the other side, the shallow side, the change was greater. Before, it had been untidy. Now, it was a scene of mad disorder: a tangled mass of water-weeds, all high and dry, and, sticking out from them, mounds of yellow gravel, like bald patches on a head. The clusters of round, thin grey-green rushes, whose tufted tops had made me think of an army of spearmen with pennons were now much taller than a man; and for a yard or more above the water line they were coated with a grey deposit – mud. But many had fallen over, let down by their native element, back-broken under their own weight: they lay pointing this way and that, all discipline gone. The army of spearmen had been routed. Their companions-in-arms, the grass-green reeds that tapered to a point like swords, had escaped the blight and kept their colour, but they too were bent and broken.

The disorder has increased. Everything seems chaotic, 'mad' and illogical, 'tangled' and confused, without 'discipline' or control. Ugliness has given way to death – the place is 'ghostly' and 'corpse-like'. The plants that in the boy's imagination had seemed like strong, proud soldiers are now defeated.

We will explore this sort of analysis further in Chapter 7, 'Reading beneath the surface'.

In summary, setting is not just background. It can be something which reflects or has an effect on the character or the mood. When reading about a setting, ask yourself if it's there to explain what happens, or to reflect what's happening: is the description a cause or a result of what a character has done?

 **WHAT MAKES THE GRADE?**

For a Grade C, you need to sustain comment on the importance of the setting to develop character, mood or ideas.

For a Grade B, you need to develop your comments, showing how different settings have different roles, exploring ways in which language is used to make settings vivid.

For a Grade A, you need to analyse the devices and purposes which give significance to settings, and evaluate alternative interpretations and responses to them.

Check yourself

QUESTION

Q1 Here is a description of a setting, taken from Laurie Lee's *Cider with Rosie*, which is used to give more than literal, factual information. How is the reader given a sense of the observer and not just the place?

Radiating from that house, with its crumbling walls, its thumps and shadows, its fancied foxes under the floor, I moved along paths that lengthened inch by inch with my mounting strength of days. From stone to stone in the trackless yard I sent forth my acorn shell of senses, moving through unfathomable oceans like a South Sea savage island-hopping across the Pacific. Antennae of eyes and nose and grubbing fingers captured a new tuft of grass, a fern, a slug, the skull of a bird, a grotto of bright snails.

From the harbour mouth of the scullery door I learned the rocks and reefs and the channels where safety lay. I discovered the physical pyramid of the cottage, its stores and labyrinths, its centres of magic, and of the green, sprouting island-garden upon which it stood. My mother and sisters sailed past me like galleons in their busy dresses, and I learned the smells and sounds which followed in their wakes, the surge of breath, carbolic, song and grumble, and smashing of crockery.

The scullery was a mine of all the minerals of living. Here, I discovered water – a very different element from the green crawling scum that stank in the garden tub. You could pump it in pure blue gulps out of the ground, you could swing on the pump handle and it came out sparkling like liquid sky. And it broke and ran and shone on the tiled floor, or quivered in a jug, or weighted your clothes with cold. You could drink it, draw with it, froth it with soap, swim beetles across it, or fly it in bubbles in the air. You could put your head in it, and open your eyes, and see the sides of the bucket buckle, and hear your caught breath roar, and work your mouth like a fish, and smell the lime from the ground. Substance of magic – which you could wear or tear, confine or scatter, or send down holes, but never burn or break or destroy.

Here too was the scrubbing of floors and boots, of arms and necks, of red and white vegetables. Walk in to the morning disorder of this room and all the garden was laid out dripping on the table. Chopped carrots like copper pennies, radishes and chives, potatoes dipped and stripped clean from their coats of mud, the snapping of tight pea-pods, long shells of green pearls, and the tearing of glutinous beans from their nests of wool.

REMEMBER! Cover the answers if you want to.

ANSWER

A1 This is not so much a description of a place as an account of the way a child sees the environment around him. The setting is described from a child's point of view, making ordinary things seem quite exotic and unusual as if experienced for the first time. Water, for example, is something that adults take for granted, but the child sees it as magic.

Also making this seem like a child's observation is the detail of things found at ground level, perhaps not noticeable to an adult. Things which an adult may not notice are made to seem exciting and interesting – the hole in the wall where snails gather is described as a 'grotto', which is usually a place where treasures are found.

Another thing which makes this description of a place suggest the mind of a child is the way that the senses are used – smell and touch, for example – and the exploration of the environment is physical, rather than just visual – putting his head inside the water.

TUTORIAL

T1 *This answer is very successful in showing how the setting works to illustrate a child's discovery of the environment. It could develop the idea of discovery by showing that it is ugliness, not just beauty which the child encounters, and that this is an inevitable part of the experience of venturing outside the safe 'haven' of the home. There could be sustained comment on other words which suggest 'voyaging', such as 'oceans', 'harbour-mouth' and the sisters who seem to 'sail' past. A child's sense of growing power is suggested by 'captured', making the world beyond exciting but also a little bit menacing because of the reference to death. If you included this, you would demonstrate close attention to the writer's choice of language.*

The child's way of finding out about his environment is amusing because it is play, but it is also a sort of scientific testing of the properties of things around him. The description of water is like an analysis of its properties. The close observation of the insides of broad-bean pods and the comparison of carrots with coins shows a child's attempts to categorise objects in his universe. Exploring this description as typical of childhood development, not the unique experience of one child, would show your ability to make generalisations and appropriate comment on style and meaning.

See page 148 for the way this passage uses language figuratively.

- In this chapter, you will develop your understanding of ways in which authors tell a story.

- If you can explain how a narrative works, you will show your ability to make appropriate comment on style and structure and appreciate authors' purposes. You will also be able to evaluate a writer's use of narrative conventions.

INTRODUCTION

Usually the narrative of a story is written in the kind of language you expect an educated author to use – third person, past tense, Standard English.

> Reginald Fanshaw was twenty-three and feeling older. It was a wet Wednesday in Widnes, and Reginald held in his hand the latest in a long line of rejections from a publisher, together with the dog-eared copy of the masterpiece that was to make him rich and famous.

There are, however, various other narrative techniques that can be used.

FIRST-PERSON NARRATIVE

An author may choose to write in the style of an invented character, especially if this makes the writing more inviting to a particular kind of reader. The purpose is to make the author seem invisible, and make the reader feel they are being spoken to by someone who is not a professional writer, but someone just like themselves. Here is the beginning of a teenage novel, *Push Me, Pull Me* by Sandra Chick. As you read it, try to decide what makes it seem informal and natural.

> Everyone likes Christmas Eve. I don't. Would never admit it, though. Wouldn't be fair on the others to play selfish and dampen the spark. Truth is, I get jealous of the fun everybody else is having. Only like the presents, just pretend to enjoy the rest. Can't stand pushing myself forward, I s'pose. You know, stupid games, dancing, that kind of thing. Makes me feel clumsy and embarrassed, makes my cheeks flush and a sort of cramped sensation belts me in the stomach. I wish I didn't feel that way. I'd like to join in, be the one who's always there, in the centre, but I can't force myself. The more people try to encourage me, the bigger idiot I feel. Prefer my Own company – quite happy but in a different way.
>
> It was chilly out, still had my jacket on, collar turned up to cover my ears, hands pushed up inside the front – didn't have pockets or gloves. I let my tongue taste the clearness that crept down on to my lip from my nose, cold and itchy – always do that and hope no one ever sees. When it's really freezing my eyes go funny, and they were sort of stiff from the bitter wind.

The informality and naturalness of this passage come from the way it is written as if it were conversation. It uses the present tense and sentences are incomplete. The writer doesn't always start a sentence with 'I'. There's a tone of intimate confession about private habits that seems to take the reader into the writer's confidence.

NARRATOR AND PERSONA

This device of adopting the persona of a main character as the tale-teller uses an autobiographical style for fictional purposes. In *The Catcher in the Rye*, an adult writer, J. D. Salinger, writes the book as if it is told by the main, teenage, character. As you read the beginning of this novel, think about how the author makes it seem that a believable teenager is telling the story. Is it the author's choice of idiom (type of expression), the attitudes or the tone in which he addresses the reader that makes you see and hear the character?

> If you really want to hear about it, the first thing you'll probably want to know is where I was born, and what my lousy childhood was like, and how my parents were occupied and all before they had me, and all that David Copperfield kind of crap, but I don't feel like going into it. In the first place, that stuff bores me, and in the second place, my parents would have about two haemorrhages apiece if I told anything pretty personal about them. They're quite touchy about anything like that, especially my father. They're nice and all – I'm not saying that – but they're also touchy as hell. Besides, I'm not going to tell you my whole goddam autobiography or anything. I'll just tell you about this madman stuff that happened to me around last Christmas before I got pretty run-down and had to come out here and take it easy. I mean that's all I told D. B. about, and he's my brother and all. He's in Hollywood. That isn't too far from this crumby place, and he comes over and visits me practically every weekend. He's going to drive me home when I go home next month maybe. He just got a Jaguar. One of those little English jobs that can do around two hundred miles an hour. It cost him damn near four thousand bucks. He's got a lot of dough, now. He didn't use to. He used to be just a regular writer, when he was home. He wrote this terrific book of short stories, *The Secret Goldfish*, in case you never heard of it.
>
> © J. D. Salinger, 1945, 1946

The writer uses informal, youthful words such as 'lousy', 'crumby', 'goddam' and 'crap'. The tone is personal, directly addressing the reader as 'you'. This is written as conversation, with corrections of meaning added – 'I'm not saying that' – that make it sound spontaneous. Because it's written in the first person, it addresses the reader as second person, giving an intimate tone.

The attitudes expressed are disrespectful to adult literature such as David Copperfield, and critical of parents, using an exaggeration to suggest how they over-react to his opinions.

MIXING DIALOGUE WITH NARRATIVE

Some authors feel that writing in the third person can be more immediate if they use a lot of dialogue and make the narrator an unidentified part of the events. This can make the writing seem immediate and authentic, as if overheard directly, not reported, but without having to use 'I' or make the narrator take part in the events, as shown in the following extract from *The Commitments* by Roddy Doyle.

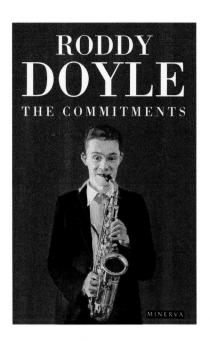

—We'll ask Jimmy, said Outspan. —Jimmy'll know.
Jimmy Rabbitte knew his music. He knew his stuff all right. You'd never see Jimmy coming home from town without a new album or a 12-inch or at least a 7-inch single. Jimmy ate *Melody Maker* and the *NME* every week and *Hot Press* every two weeks. He listened to Dave Fanning and John Peel. He even read his sisters' *Jackie* when there was no one looking. So Jimmy knew his stuff…
The last time Outspan had flicked through Jimmy's records he'd seen names like Microdisney, Eddie and the Hot Rods, Otis Redding, The Screaming Blue Messiahs… groups Outspan had never heard of, never mind heard. Jimmy even had albums by Frank Sinatra and The Monkees. So when Outspan and Derek decided, while Ray was out in the jacks, that their group needed a new direction they both thought of Jimmy. Jimmy knew what was what. Jimmy knew what was new, what was new but wouldn't be for long, and what was going to be new. Jimmie had *Relax* before anyone had heard of Frankie Goes to Hollywood and he'd started slagging them months before anyone realised that they were no good. Jimmy knew his music.

USING TWO OR MORE CHARACTERS AS NARRATORS

An author may present a story through the eyes and voices of two (or more) of the characters in it. What they think, feel and say about a situation they have both been in may vary enormously, just as your account of a concert or match you have been to may differ from a friend's.

The following two extracts are alternate chapters from *Daz 4 Zoe* by Robert Swindells, written as if by the two main characters. Daz is a Chippy, living in a squalid, run-down slum, and Zoe is a Subby, living in a respectable, well-off area fenced off from Chippyville. Normally, these two would not meet because of their different social backgrounds. As you read through the extracts, think about the impression you get from how they speak and what they say. Do you get a sense of their backgrounds as well as their personalities?

Zoe

What happened was, Larry saw this girl. Chippy girl. She was with another girl and two guys. She was pretty and he was smashed and he caught her eye and smiled and started making signs for her to leave the others and come on over. The girl kept smiling, but it was the sort of smile people put on when they're embarrassed and don't know what else to do. I could see that, but not Larry. Oh no. He thought she fancied him and redoubled his efforts.

At first the two guys ignored him. Chippies don't like people from the sub-urbs and they'd as soon smash a Subby to pulp as not. But there's always big trouble with the police when something like that happens, so unless they're members of Dred or very drunk, they'll usually bend over backwards not to get involved. In the face of their seeming indifference, Larry's antics became increasingly gross, until finally he yelled at the top of his voice 'Come on over, honey – you know you're wasted on that trash!' It was just our luck that this outburst coincided with a break in the music. There was this awful silence while everybody in the room turned to look at us, and then one of the two guys – the one who was with this girl I guess – got up and grabbed his chair and came at Larry like he meant to splatter his brain. He probably would've done it too, if two beefy guys hadn't burst on the scene and put themselves between him and us. They must've been lurking somewhere discreetly, watching the trouble build. When the guy saw he wasn't going to reach Larry he let out a roar and flung the chair. Larry threw up his arms to fend it off, and it bounced off him on to the floor. Meanwhile, the two heavies had grabbed the other guy and were wrestling him towards the door.

Larry was hunched over, moaning and holding his arm. There was still no music, and everybody seemed to be watching us. The atmosphere of resentment was unmistakable: there was a sort of murmur, and I had the distinct feeling that the crowd was closing in on us. I was fuddled with the drink, I guess, but I remember thinking, this is it. We'll never make the door. We're gonna die. Tomorrow they'll find the car, and maybe a shoe.

Then I saw him – the guy I'd been looking at all night. I never saw him arrive, but suddenly there he was and he said, 'You better leave with me. Now.' He didn't pause but sort of walked through us, slipping his arm through Larry's on the way past, helping him along.

We didn't hang around.

Daz

So this crash com and Cal's away i open the door a crack and luck owt and its wot i fought. Subbys. i knew ther be trubble tonite wiv them in. Stanstareeson dunnit.

i luck and i fink, sod em. They blew it 4 me. Let em get topped. Then i seen the girl. The 1 i bin watching. She luck scairt. 2 hunnerd peeple want me ded, i luck scairt. i seen her and i cant let em do it. The uvvers i dont give a monkeys abowt but i cant let em top her.

Its a tuff 1 cos the peeples real mad and i gotta be cool. i go over nice and easy. i tork soft. i tell em you better leave wiv me now, nor i dont stop neever. i grab this fin Subby wots hurting and shov frou going hello Pete, hows fings Miz Stanton, givin em the big smile.

And all the time i'm finking, we not gonna make it.

Somfing gonna snap but nofing does and it seems a longtime and then were at the door.

I let go the fin Subby. Run, i sez. i know thay gorra motor near. Thay run. 3 of em. Not her. Run, i sez 2 her. Peeples coming, I sez Lucking 2 her, 2 them, 2 her. Fanks, she sez, and she kiss my cheek quick and runs. I want 2 say somfing back but I dont know wot. People shoving me. I showt somfing. You nice. I like you. Somfing like that, but i dont fink she hears me. A motor starts. Dazzlers corn on, moving. Shes away.

After, I cant beleeve i don it. Wot am i, a Subby or somfing? I got bags ov time 2 fink about it anall, cos i sure cant go back in the Blew Moon now. Peeple stairing and muttering. Mick. He give me this luck like i kick him in the teef and then he turns and gos back in. Evry 1 else gos in 2.

i'm on my Todd. i luck arownd 4 Cal but no chance. i'm not in Dred, our mam.

That's nice, Daz.

i seen this Subby girl, our mam.

Forget her, Daz.

Not easy, our mam. Not easy.

Robert Swindells has made the two narrators very distinct by using different speech, pronunciation and writing patterns. Zoe regards the Chippies as people from another dimension, but she notices Daz. Daz does not speak Standard English, and in his speech he does not sound all syllables, as in his rendering of 'It stands to reason, doesn't it?' – notice how Swindells uses non-standard spelling and punctuation to convey this. He has also made them different in their attitude to danger and the community; he conveys the difference in social attitudes by Larry's reference to a Chippy as 'trash', and by Daz's willingness to let the Subbies 'get topped' except for the girl.

DIALOGUE AS DRAMATIC NARRATIVE

Jane Austen, 1775–1817.

Drama scripts contain dialogue only, with some stage directions. You do not expect the playwright to introduce a scene with a description and a summary of what's been happening. Novelists and short-story writers, on the other hand, have the choice of reporting events in narrative form, or mingling dialogue with narrative. However, some writers have a gift for using dialogue to create character and replace explicit narrative. In this extract from *Emma*, Jane Austen gives the reader a vivid sense of being in Miss Bates' company by recording her conversation. As you read through, try to remember how many people she talks to, and talks about, and if you know what they are doing as Miss Bates arrives at the Ball at the Crown.

Every body's words were soon lost under the incessant flow of Miss Bates, who came in, talking, and had not finished her speech until many minutes after her being admitted into the circle at the fire. As the door opened she was heard—

'So very obliging of you!—No rain at all. Nothing to signify. I do not care for myself. Quite thick shoes. And Jane declares—Well! (as soon as she was within the door), well! This is brilliant indeed! This is admirable! Excellently contrived, upon my word. Nothing wanting. Could not have imagined it. So well lighted up! Jane, Jane, look! did you ever see anything? Oh, Mr Weston, you must really have had Aladdin's lamp. Good Mrs Stokes would not know her own room again. I saw her as I came in; she was standing in the entrance. "Oh, Mrs Stokes," said I—but I had not time for

more.' She was now met by Mrs Weston. 'Very well, I thank you, ma'am. I hope you are quite well. Very happy to hear it. So afraid you might have a headache! seeing you pass by so often, and knowing how much trouble you must have. Delighted to hear it indeed.—Ah! dear Mrs Elton, so obliged to you for the carriage; excellent time; Jane and I quite ready. Did not keep the horses a moment. Most comfortable carriage. Oh! and I am sure our thanks are due to you, Mrs Weston, on that score. Mrs Elton had most kindly sent Jane a note, or we should have been. But two such offers in one day! Never were such neighbours. I said to my mother, 'Upon my word, ma'am.' Thank you, my mother is remarkably well. Gone to Mr Woodhouse's. I made her take her shawl,—for the evenings are not warm,—her large new shawl, Mrs Dixon's wedding present. So kind of her to think of my mother! Bought at Weymouth, you know; Mr Dixon's choice. There were three others, Jane says, which they hesitated about some time. Colonel Campbell rather preferred an olive.—My dear Jane, are you sure you did not wet your feet? It was but a drop or two, but I am so afraid: but Mr Frank Churchill was so extremely—and there was a mat to step upon. I shall never forget his extreme politeness. Oh, Mr Frank Churchill, I must tell you my mother's spectacles have never been in fault since; the rivet never came out again. My mother often talks of your good nature: does not she, Jane? Do not we often talk of Mr Frank Churchill? Ah! here's Miss Woodhouse. Dear Miss Woodhouse, how do you do? Very well I thank you, quite well. This is meeting quite in fairy-land! Such a transformation. Must not compliment, I know (eyeing Emma most complacently)—that would be rude; but upon my word, Miss Woodhouse, you do look—how do you like Jane's hair? You are a judge. She did it all herself. Quite wonderful how she does her hair! No hairdresser from London, I think, could.—Ah! Dr Hughes, I declare—and Mrs Hughes. Must go and speak to Dr and Mrs Hughes for a moment. How do you do? How do you do? Very well, I thank you. This is delightful, is not it? Where's dear Mr Richard? Oh, there he is. Don't disturb him. Much better employed talking to the young ladies. How do you do, Mr Richard? I saw you the other day as you rode through the town. Mrs Otway, I protest! and good Mr Otway, and Miss Otway, and Miss Caroline. Such a host of friends! and Mr George and Mr Arthur! How do you do? How do you all do? Quite well, I am much obliged to you. Never better. Don't I hear another carriage? Who can this be?—very likely the worthy Coles. Upon my word, this is charming, to be standing about among such friends! And such a noble fire! I am quite roasted. No coffee, I thank you, for me; never take coffee. A little tea, if you please, sir, by and by, no hurry. Oh, here it comes. Everything so good!'

This clever piece of writing doesn't only bring out Miss Bates' garrulous character, but it also allows the reader to know who is in the room and what they are doing. Also, it makes the reader imagine what those people think and feel as Miss Bates sweeps through, asking and answering questions, interrupting people and making sure she is the centre of attention.

Jane Austen uses the flow of talk to make the reader supply details of the other characters' responses to Miss Bates. For example, when she spots the young Mr Otway chatting up two young ladies, Miss Bates says he mustn't be interrupted, and then promptly interrupts him; the reader can imagine the effect on him and what his response might have been!

At other points we can see how she starts to compliment Emma on her hair, but can't resist giving more compliments to her niece for *her* hair. Throughout the non-stop talk, we get an impression of the whole company of people being inspected by Miss Bates, chatted to and then passed on for the next. All that we can imagine about their reaction comes from what Jane Austen **implies**, not what she states.

PUTTING THE READER IN THE CHARACTER'S SHOES

In the case of *The Catcher in the Rye*, it is easy to identify with the character because he seems to be telling us the story confidentially, as if it's an autobiographical account. The reader here is in the narrator's shoes, and sees the story from the narrator's point of view throughout. Sometimes, though, there is a distinct narrator who wants the reader temporarily to identify with a character, and this can be done very subtly by making the reader feel as if he or she is in the position of one character facing another. Jane Austen does this in an episode involving the ghastly Mrs Elton when she comes to visit, taking it on herself to advise Emma about improving her social life. As you read through the passage, think how you would feel if you were on the receiving end of Mrs Elton's opinions and advice.

'You have many parties of that kind here, I suppose, Miss Woodhouse, every summer?'

'No; not immediately here. We are rather out of distance of the very striking beauties which attract the sort of parties you speak of; and we are a very quiet set of people, I believe; more disposed to stay at home than engage in schemes of pleasure.'

'Ah! there is nothing like staying at home, for real comfort. Nobody can be more devoted to home than I am. I was quite a proverb for it at Maple Grove. Many a time has Selina said, when she has been going to Bristol, "I really cannot get this girl to move from the house. I absolutely must go in by myself, though I hate being stuck up in the barouche-landau without a companion; but Augusta, I believe, with her own goodwill, would never stir beyond the park paling." Many a time has she said so; and yet I am no advocate for entire seclusion. I think, on the contrary, when people shut themselves up entirely from society, it is a very bad thing; and that it is much more advisable to mix in the world in a proper degree, without living in it either too much or too little. I perfectly understand your situation, however, Miss Woodhouse (looking towards Mr Woodhouse), your father's state of health must be a great drawback. Why does not he try Bath?—Indeed he should. Let me recommend Bath to you. I assure you I have no doubt of its doing Mr Woodhouse good.'

'My father tried it more than once, formerly, but without receiving any benefit; and Mr Perry, whose name, I daresay, is not unknown to you, does not conceive it would be at all more likely to be useful now.'

'Ah! that's a great pity; for I assure you, Miss Woodhouse, where the waters do agree, it is quite wonderful the relief they give. In my Bath life I have seen such instances of it! And it is so cheerful a place that it could not fail of being of use to Mr Woodhouse's spirits, which, I understand, are sometimes much depressed. And as to its recommendation to *you*, I fancy I need not take much pains to dwell on them. The advantages of Bath to the young are pretty generally understood. It would be a charming introduction for you, who have lived so secluded a life; and I could immediately secure you some of the best society in the place. A line from me would bring you a little host of acquaintance; and my particular friend, Mrs Partridge, the lady I have always resided with when in Bath, would be most happy to show you any attentions, and would be the very person for you to go into public with.'

Jane Austen's chooses not to write a dialogue in which the two characters clash and show their feelings, but to put the reader at the receiving end, imagining how Emma must feel about Mrs Elton's patronising advice and comments. If the reader begins to feel desperate or furious, or wants to get a word in, he or she will sympathise with Emma. At this point Jane Austen wants the reader to take Emma's side. Elsewhere in the story, she wants the reader to see Emma's faults, which she describes in the narrative mode:

The real evils indeed of Emma's situation were the power of having rather too much of her own way, and a disposition to think a little too well of herself.

If the author makes you sometimes identify with the hero and sometimes feel against him or her, the hero is being treated in a lifelike way. In real life, we can get cross with our friends, and sometimes see good points in people we don't like. Writing which makes the reader have mixed feelings is usually more realistic than writing which always shows the hero in a flattering light. Also, if we know that Emma usually has her own way and thinks highly of herself, we react to the scene with Mrs Elton with mixed feelings – it's about time she met some opposition, but Mrs Elton is an awful person. In this way, we are kept changing and balancing our view of Emma. The author is making us feel undecided or ambivalent about her, just as we may do about people in real life.

Finally, remember that with fiction, the characters can be made up, the action can be made up – and the narrator, too, can be made up. The teller is sometimes part of the fiction, so you do not have to share the teller's point of view.

WHAT MAKES THE GRADE? ▶

For a Grade C, you need to sustain comment on the way an author tells a story, drawing evidence from a range of places in the text.

For a Grade B, you need to develop your comments by showing different uses of narrative and dialogue. If you can explore the likely effects on you or other readers of identifying with the narrator or a character, you will be able to bring in your personal response.

For a Grade A, you need to analyse the narrative structure, showing consistency or variety in an author's approach. You need to evaluate the writing in the context of its own time and today.

Check yourself

Q1 An author can use narrative and dialogue to undermine the reader's first understanding. He or she may create a character who is not quite what the reader expects. Some writers want to make humans simpler than they are; others want to explore their complexity. Penelope Lively is a writer who wants to look under and behind the appearance of things. What she reveals is less ideal and simple than the reader may want to find. In this extract from *The Darkness Out*

There, the character appears to be a sweet old lady, but there is more to her than we think at first reading.

a) Which *narrative* details make her seem sweet and cosy?

b) Which *dialogue* details make her seem sweet and cosy?

c) What narrative hints are there that she may be something else?

She seemed composed of circles, a cottage-loaf of a woman, with a face below which chins collapsed one into another, a creamy smiling pool of a face in which her eyes snapped and darted.

'Tea, my duck?' she said. 'Tea for the both of you? I'll put us a kettle on.' The room was stuffy. It had a gaudy lino floor with the pattern rubbed away in front of the sink and round the table; the walls were cluttered with old calendars and pictures torn from magazines; there was a smell of cabbage. The alcove by the fireplace was filled with china ornaments: big-eyed flop-eared rabbits and beribboned kittens and flowery milkmaids and a pair of naked chubby children wearing daisy chains.

The woman hauled herself from a sagging armchair. She glittered at them from the stove, manoeuvring cups, propping herself against the draining-board. 'What's your names, then? Sandra and Kerry. Well, you're a pretty girl, Sandra, aren't you. Pretty as they come. There was – let me see, who was it? – Susie, last week. That's right, Susie.' Her eyes investigated, quick as mice. 'Put your jacket on the back of the door, dear, you won't want to get that messy. Still at school, are you?'

The boy said, 'I'm leaving, July. They're taking me on at the garage, the Blue Star. I been helping out there on and off, before.'

Mrs Rutter's smiles folded into one another. Above them, her eyes examined him.

'Well, I expect that's good steady money if you'd nothing special in mind. Sugar?'

There was a view from the window out over a bedraggled garden with the stumps of spent vegetables and a matted flower-bed and a square of shaggy grass. Beyond, the spinney reached up to the fence, a no-man's-land of willow herb and thistle and small trees, growing thicker and higher into the full density of woodland. Mrs Rutter said, 'Yes, you have a look out, aren't I lucky – right up beside the wood. Lovely it is in the spring, the primroses and that. Mind, there's not as many as there used to be.'

ANSWERS

A1

a) Mrs Rutter seems like a typical lonely old lady. She seems friendly and cosy because of descriptions which make her harmless, like 'cottage-loaf', 'creamy, smiling pool of a face'. She smiles a lot, which is friendly. She likes little rabbit ornaments and offers the visitors tea, so she is kind and homely. Her garden is overgrown and untidy, so perhaps she isn't fit enough to look after it or she hasn't got a husband to do it.

b) She uses friendly phrases, like 'my duck' and 'dear', and she says nice things to the visitors, such as 'You're pretty', and she is concerned about getting the jacket messy. She asks questions and takes an interest in her visitors and is a bit of a gossip, remembering Susie from last week.

c) Her eyes 'snapped and darted', which makes them seem quicker and more active than the rest of the description. Although her smiles 'folded' into each other, her eyes above the smile, 'examined' him, which make you think she knows what she is doing. Her face seems to be doing two things, and perhaps this means she is 'two-faced'.

TUTORIAL

T1

a) *There is good use of details. There could be sustained reference to roundness, which seems cosier than something linear or with angles. There could also be more sustained and developed comment on her smiles, which come so quickly that one 'folds into' the next, as if her face is always moving. She seems very concerned to make them at home – offering sugar, for example. The comment could be developed by using her surroundings and her possessions as clues to her nature. She doesn't have expensive tastes – some of the things she has kept are not worth much but seem to have sentimental value to her. There is a good attempt to explore the implications of the untidy garden, offering two possible interpretations.*

b) *This is apt and makes use of details, but for a higher grade there would need to be sustained comment on her tone and language, for example referring to the inviting way she promises to make 'us' a cup of tea. She talks fondly about the flowers in the wood. This adds to the impression given by the ornaments that she likes pretty things and is a peaceful, homely person. For a high grade, there is scope for exploring what she means by saying that working in a garage is all right 'if you've nothing special in mind'. Is she being kind and making him feel it's worthwhile, or is she saying it's not much of a prospect?*

c) *This answer makes good use of material to show contrast. There could be more sustained comment about the eyes being as 'quick as mice', and how she 'glittered' at them, which could be developed by showing how the detail counteracts the cosy sleepiness of the rest of the impression. Penelope Lively uses many of the words which immediately create a stereotype of a dear old harmless biddy, but she writes this story to show that not everyone is quite what they seem if we trust to stereotypes. There is an attempt in this answer to explore contrasts and make meaning from the details.*

CHAPTER 4

POETRY – SOUND EFFECTS AND IMAGERY

- In this chapter, you will develop your reading response to technical skills in the language of poetry.
- If you can explain how poets use sound and imagery to convey ideas, feelings and levels of meaning, you will show insight into the craft of writing poetry.

INTRODUCTION

The good thing about reading poetry is that it's usually shorter than most prose pieces. This means that you have time to give detailed attention to its language and meaning.

It is important to notice technical features like metaphor, simile, alliteration or onomatopoeia, but most of the time you can treat poetry the way you treat prose – as something communicating thought and feeling in language. Focus on how and why the poet chooses words and how and why you react as a reader, and you will write more successfully than someone who labels techniques or translates 'hidden meanings'.

SOUND AND SENSE

You should remember that poetry started long before prose – and certainly long before schools and examinations existed! It began as public performance for listeners, not readers, at a time when books didn't exist – it was entertainment for people who didn't need to be able to read. Today, we tend to read silently, but some poems *need* to be read aloud. Whether we read silently or aloud, poets can influence our feelings by appealing to our sense of hearing.

Alexander Pope got very annoyed with poets who tried to write beautiful, soft-sounding, soothing poems and who ignored other moods and sounds. He thought that poems should be noisy and violent sounding if they were about noisy and violent events, as well as smooth and calm if they were about smooth and calm things. In *An Essay on Criticism* he wrote:

> 'Tis not enough no harshness gives offence,
> The sound must seem an Echo to the sense:

Here is his example of words chosen to match mood and situation, describing firstly a stormy scene and a Greek hero struggling physically to throw huge rocks, and then another describing a fairy-like creature moving across the fields and sea:

> But when loud surges lash the sounding shore,
> The hoarse, rough verse should like the torrent roar.
> When Ajax strives, some rock's vast weight to throw,
> The line, too, labours, and the words move slow;
> Not so, when swift Camilla lightly scours the plain,
> Flies o'er th' unbending corn, and skims along the main.

Alexander Pope: 'The sound must seem an Echo to the sense'.

EXPLOITING SOUND EFFECTS

CONSONANTS

In Pope's six-line lesson in choosing words for their sound effects, notice how he chooses words with 's' and 'sh' sounds in the first line, to make the reader's lips work at the hissing noises of the sea, then words with 'r' sounds in the second line, making the reader's throat do some rasping work. These are forceful, vigorous sounds for a physically violent scene.

When he wants to create a calmer effect, he uses words which contain 'm' and 'n' sounds, produced by letting air out through the nose, not working the throat or the lips, or the tongue and teeth. These sounds are more soothing and mellow, fit for a description of gentle lightness.

Tennyson, wanting to recreate the drowsy heat of a summer day in his poem *In Memoriam*, wrote of:

> The moan of doves in immemorial elms
> And the murmuring of innumerable bees

He could have chosen other birds, trees and insects, as well as different adjectives and a verb. Would it have had the same effect if he had written the following?

> The croak of crows in timeless oaks
> And the buzzing of hundreds of wasps

W. H. Auden, writing about the view from a cliff top in his poem *Seascape*, chose sibilant ('s' or 'sh') sounds to reproduce the noise of water splashing:

> And the shingle scrambles after the sucking surf

Because 's' sounds are made by forcing air across the teeth and over the lips, they are very forceful. Wilfred Owen used sibilants to make hissing sounds for a hostile scene in *Exposure*:

> merciless iced east winds

and again to describe a dying soldier in *Dulce et Decorum Est*:

> Obscene as cancer, bitter as the crud
> Of vile, incurable sores on innocent tongues

Making repeated use of chosen consonants is called *alliteration*.

Alliteration helps to make a phrase memorable, a feature that advertisers often exploit: 'Kwiksave Kuts Kosts' and 'Beanz meanz Heinz' (Heinz baked beans) are examples of this.

VOWELS

The main vowels are 'a', 'e', 'i', 'o' and 'u', but 'w' and 'y' can also sometimes act as vowel sounds. Vowels are all made with an open mouth, but they can each be pronounced in two different ways, called short and long. Short vowels together tend to give pace to a line, producing a hurrying effect. Long vowels can slow a line down, or make it sound more sad and weary. Each of the five main vowels can be short and long, as in the following examples:

| SHORT | c**a**t | g**e**t | f**i**t | b**o**x | g**u**t |
| LONG | st**a**ple | b**e** | f**i**ne | n**o**se | **u**se |

If a writer wants to suggest sadness and grief, long vowels help:

> Oh, woe is me, with hurt I moan and cry
> Life holds no more, I'll surely die

If a writer wants to suggest brisk, light-hearted energy, short vowels will help:

> I'm back, and glad, no longer in the pits
> Yippee, I'm chuffed and thrilled to bits

Play on vowels is called *assonance*.

VOWELS AND CONSONANTS TOGETHER

Gerard Manley Hopkins combines long vowels and repeated 'l' sounds in this line from *Spring* which suggests flowing growth:

> When weeds, in wheels, shoot long and lovely and lush

Long vowels can slow down a line of verse, especially if the line ends with a vowel. This gives a lingering finish to the line, unlike a finish created with a consonant like 't' or 'd'. Look at this example from *Call Not to Me* by Ruth Pitter:

> While under the willows the waters flow
> While willow waxes and waters wane
> When wind is slumbrous and waters slow
> And woodbine waves in the wandering lane

Mixing short vowels and using consonants which are produced at the back of the mouth ('g' and 'c') or exploded as compressed air from shaped lips ('p' and 'b' sounds, which are called 'plosives') help to suggest violence and ugliness in this description from the poem *Dandelion* by Jon Silkin:

> Slugs nestle where the stem,
> Broken, bleeds milk.
> The flower is eyeless: the sight is compelled
> By small, coarse, sharp petals,
> Like metal shreds. Formed,
> They puncture, irregularly perforate
> Their yellow, brutal glare.
> And certainly want to
> Devour the earth.

Shakespeare made fun of writers who overdo these sound effects when, in *A Midsummer Night's Dream*, he wrote a speech for a character who doesn't know when to stop using one technique for effect:

> Whereat, with blade, with bloody, blameful blade,
> He bravely broached his boiling, bloody breast.

Verbal sound effects help to create mood and suggest character. When you read a poem or write about it, remember to look for ways in which the poet repeats sound patterns or chooses words for sounds which match the sense.

IMAGERY

Anyone asked to explain or describe something new to someone else will usually begin by comparing it with something the other person knows or can easily imagine. Saying that the sea is 'as calm as a pond' helps the listener by making a comparison with something familiar. Saying that someone moves as elegantly 'as a pig on ice' helps the listener by making a comparison with something that can be imagined. Linking by likeness creates an image in the reader's head, drawing on something in that reader's memory or experience. The simplest form of linking by likeness is *simile*.

SIMILE

A simile is a stated likeness, using 'like a' or 'as ... as a ...' to make a comparison. Similes are a common part of everyday speech, such as when people refer to 'shaking like a leaf', being 'like a fish out of water' or 'ike two peas in a pod'.

Rupert Brooke wanted to suggest that going off to war was as invigorating and refreshing as diving into fresh water:

> like swimmers into cleanness leaping

Wilfred Owen used a simile to compare the feeling of what it was like to be caught in the brutality of war with the helpless sensation of being burnt by either flames or quicklime:

like a man in fire or lime

Seamus Heaney uses a simile in *Trout* to make an explicit comparison of the rapid fish-movement with something shot from a gun:

darts like a tracer-
bullet back between the stones

METAPHOR

Imagery is not something you find only in poetry; we all use it in everyday speech. It's a way of using expressions to give a bit more meaning to what we're talking about by referring to something everyone is familiar with – perhaps from work or leisure. Imagery appeals to a memory of some other experience by using a word which suggests or recalls that experience.

Imagery can come from all areas of life: from athletics, we get the expression 'toe the line'; from swimming, we get 'jump in at the deep end'; from music and entertainment, we get the expressions 'playing second fiddle' and 'getting your act together'; war and soldiering have left us with 'sticking to your guns', 'keeping a low profile' and 'putting your head over the parapet'.

Because we are using expressions which belong literally to something else, using them in a different context means they cannot be literally true. There is no 'deep end' in an argument for us to jump into. We call these expressions *metaphors*. What we refer to metaphorically does not have to be literally true; the strength of a metaphor lies in its suggestiveness.

When Wilfred Owen described the dawn on the day of an attack during the first world war, he wrote that:

dawn masses in the east

This suggests that dawn is like a hostile army, 'massing' itself ready for an attack. Tony Harrison described his family as a unit held together with a kind of electric energy, but this stopped when he broke away from his parents:

I'd be the one to make that circuit short.

Gareth Owen writes of a rocket launch like this:

Out of the furnace
The great fish rose
Its silver tail on fire

Seamus Heaney, in his poem *Trout*, makes the creature seem powerful and dangerous by using words connected with gunfire and weaponry:

Where water unravels
over gravel beds he
is fired from the shadows
white belly reporting

flat; darts like a tracer-
bullet back between the stones
and is never burnt out
A volley of cold blood

Ramrodding the current

ANIMATING AND PERSONIFYING

In the previous poem, a living creature was compared with mechanical objects, inanimate things, to create a specific impression. Metaphorical language can also create vivid effects by making inanimate objects seem as if they are alive.

If the writer chooses words which are usually associated with animals or human beings, it can make a place or object seem to come to life. Hardy's description of the heath on page 13, or Dickens' description of the wind on page 14 were examples of animating a scene in prose. It's not just in literature that we give a thing a life of its own. We may speak of a cold wind as 'vicious' or we may describe a missing pen as 'lurking' in the bottom of the bag, suggesting that it was the pen's fault for not being available, rather than ours!

Read the lines on page 32 which come from Jon Silkin's poem *Dandelion*. Notice as you read it how he chooses words which give it some of the qualities we associate with animals or humans. It is described as tough and determined to survive. Silkin uses phrases which attribute intention or conscious plans – 'want to devour the earth' – and a physical power over other plants – 'they take hold' of tamer, more civilised 'pert, domestic' plants. Verbs like 'puncture', 'perforate', 'devour' and 'infest' all make the plant seem an active and destructive creature, but the things it destroys aren't made attractive, only 'pert' and 'weak'. Also, the dandelion is described as 'bleeding', as if wounded and having to fight for its existence.

Thomas Hardy thought that human beings were helpless creatures suffering under the cruel play of Time. He was used to living in the country, where he saw pheasants hatched and raised by a gamekeeper ready for the shooting season. This gave him a metaphor for Time as something that seems to be on our side, but has its own purpose:

> Sportsman Time but rears his brood to kill

Giving human intentions to something abstract like Time humanises it. This is usually called *personification*. Inanimate things can be made to seem alive by using verbs and nouns which suggest feeling, or mood, or an intention or attitude. In his poem *Portrait of a Machine*, Louis Untermeyer uses nouns like 'flank' and 'muscle' for parts of a machine, making them seem like bits of a living body. The verb 'purring' suggests a cat-like sound and 'dripping' oil suggests physical effort and sweat. 'Obedient' is an adjective suggesting mood and attitude, things which need a mind and ability to choose, and 'nudity' is a word we would normally use of people rather than things.

> What nudity as beautiful as this
> Obedient monster purring at its toil;
> Those naked iron muscles dripping oil
> And the sure-fingered rods that never miss?
> This long and shining flank of metal is
> Magic that greasy labour cannot spoil

EXTENDED METAPHOR

A poem can be full of all sorts of different images, or it may play with one image, which becomes an *extended metaphor*, where the poet deliberately tries to work the comparison as far as it will go. In his poem *Mastering the Craft*, Vernon Scannell shows that poetry and boxing have lots in common, not only because they both need practice and skill, but because both can involve a surprising knockout:

> To make the big time you must learn
> The basic moves: left jab and hook,
> The fast one-two, right-cross; the block
> And counter-punch; the way to turn
> Opponents on the ropes; the feint
> To head or body; uppercut;
> To move inside the swing and set
> Your man up for the kill. But don't
> Think that this is all; a mere
> Beginning only. It is through
> Fighting often you will grow
> Accomplished in manœuvres more
> Subtle than the text books know:
> How to change your style to meet
> The unexpected move that might
> Leave you open to the blow
> That puts the lights out for the night.

> The same with poets: they must train,
> Practise metre's footwork, learn
> The old iambic left and right,
> To change the pace and how to hold
> The big punch till the proper time,
> Jab away with accurate rhyme;
> Adapt the style or be knocked cold.
> But first the groundwork must be done.
> Those poets who have never learnt
> The first moves of the game, they can't
> Hope to win.
>   Yet here comes one,
> No style at all, untrained and fat,
> Who still contrives to knock you flat.

35

Another writer may want us to see a metaphorical connection only after we have come to the end of the poem. In *Wires*, Philip Larkin seems to be writing about how cows behave. It's only at the end that the reader sees that he has used the description of animals learning as a metaphor for the way human beings learn, too.

> The widest prairies have electric fences,
> For though old cattle know they must not stray,
> Young steers are always scenting purer water
> Not here but anywhere. Beyond the wires
>
> Leads them to blunder up against the wires
> Whose muscle-shredding violence gives no quarter.
> Young steers become old cattle from that day,
> Electric limits to their widest senses.

Imagery is a literary device, not a literal one, because it helps to convey meaning without having to be strictly – literally – true. When you are reading, or writing about poems, look for examples of imagery, and say why the imagery is appropriate and how the linkage is effective for you.

WHAT MAKES THE GRADE? ▶

For a Grade C, you need to do more than explain what the poem is 'about'. You need to sustain comment on how the poet treats the subject and how the language suits the purpose. A personal response to words and their associations will help.

For a Grade B, you need to develop your comments on language, showing how meaning and feeling are influenced by the sound and suggestiveness of words. You should also explore the poet's concerns and attitudes, showing how they affect you. This may mean disliking or disagreeing with what you have read.

For a Grade A, you need to analyse patterns of sound and imagery in close detail. You should also be able to evaluate alternative responses or interpretations.

Check yourself

QUESTION

Q1 Read the following poem, *City Jungle* by Pie Corbett.

   a)   How does the poet use sound effects and imagery to make a city scene seem jungle-like?

   b)   What does it make you feel about a city at night?

Rain splinters town.

Lizard cars cruise by;
Their radiators grin.

Thin headlights stare –
shop doorways keep their mouths shut.

At the roadside
Hunched houses cough.

Newspapers shuffle by,
hands in their pockets.
The gutter gargles.

A motorbike snarls;
Dustbins flinch.

Streetlights bare
Their yellow teeth.
The motorway's
cat-black tongue
lashes across
the glistening back
of the tarmac night.

REMEMBER! Cover the answers if you want to.

ANSWER

A1 a) A city is full of buildings and lots of people, a place which is civilised. Night time is when everyone's indoors and it's quiet, but the writer makes it full of life, but not happy life. Everything in this poem is violent. He makes cars and motorbikes seem like animals in the jungle. In the night, ordinary things around the streets are afraid of the savage creature around them. Objects are like people being picked on – they 'cough' and 'flinch' as if nervous and afraid of all the nasty things around.

b) It makes me think that there's more going on than I see, or perhaps there's more than I want to see. I think some of the poem is amusing – I liked the idea that a dustbin could be frightened and that an old newspaper could want to get away from the hassle and bother.

TUTORIAL

T1 a) This is a good statement about the mood of ferocity and fear. For a higher grade, there could be more sustained comment on language which animates or personifies the scene. Even the rain is shown as something sharp and destructive – it 'splinters' – and cars are not only compared with living creatures in the metaphor 'lizard cars', but they seem to have feelings too, enjoying their own power (suggested by 'grin'). The motorbike sounds like a jungle creature, and the lights, which should make things less like a jungle, are also part of the savage scene, described as 'staring', looking boldly or 'baring their teeth'. The effect of all this savagery is to create fear and nervousness so strong that even buildings feel it, as suggested by the metaphorical description of a house being 'hunched' and coughing. The description of litter makes even this seem nervous and glad to get away, 'shuffling' off with its hands in its pockets. This detail could be developed into an account of the poem as an extended metaphor.
There is scope to refer to the sounds of words chosen here: it is a violent scene, and there are rough sounds in words like 'cars cruise', 'hunched', 'cough', 'gargle', 'snarl' and 'lash'. Short vowels in 'Dustbins flinch' and 'cat-black tongue lashes across' make things seem abrupt and sudden.

b) This adds some personal feeling in response. Although one comment is about a serious aspect of the poem's thought, there is also comment on something which the reader found amusing. For a higher grade, there could be further exploration of the humour or seriousness of the poem, and of the view it gives of urban life.

CHAPTER 5

POETRY – PURPOSE, TONE AND ATTITUDE

- **In this chapter, you will develop your reading response to poets' purposes and ideas.**
- **If you can explain how poets use language to convey ideas, feelings and levels of meaning – and respond to these – you will show engagement and understanding in your reading.**

PURPOSE

The writer Samuel Johnson once said that good writing had the ability to make the new seem familiar and the familiar seem new. Many poets think it is their business to surprise the reader, to say 'Hey – look at this!' They try to take away the dulling effect of familiarity, and show us something interesting about things we take for granted, giving everyday objects an exotic makeover. And what does the poet rely on to pull off this trick? Just words.

Ask someone what they think poetry is, and they may say something about 'flowery' writing, meaning that poetry is decorative, fancy and ornamental. This is a very inaccurate view of poetry. There aren't many poems about flowers in English, and most of them aren't 'decorative'. Look again at Jon Silkin's poem *Dandelion*, about a plant that most people would call a weed:

> Slugs nestle where the stem,
> Broken, bleeds milk.
> The flower is eyeless: the sight is compelled
> By small, coarse, sharp petals,
> Like metal shreds. Formed,
> They puncture, irregularly perforate
> Their yellow, brutal glare.
> And certainly want to
> Devour the earth.

The poem uses animating language to give us a fresh view of a familiar object. It 'bleeds' when it is broken, and is described as something active, because it 'punctures' and 'perforates'. And it seems to have a mind, too, because it wants to 'devour the earth'. The poet wants to make it seem valuable because it's got a fierce spirit, and is a survivor; he is making the dandelion seem something which deserves respect, so that we see it in a new way.

The following poem, *Fishing Harbour Towards Evening* by Richard Kell, shows a violent side to nature, rather than a pretty, picture-postcard view. It uses words which suggest violence in a scene which, from the title, may have been a picturesque one. There is a contrast between the 'snugged' boats along the wharf and the sky above, which is not blue with fluffy clouds, but violent, where the clouds appear wounded ('slashed') and 'leaking' as if bleeding, with winds 'abrasive' like a kitchen cleaner, sweeping gulls away.

> Slashed clouds leak gold. Along the slurping wharf
> The snugged boats creak and seesaw. Round the masts
> Abrasive squalls flake seagulls off the sky:

Many poets want to change the way we see things, so they choose to write about familiar objects or events in a way that gives a new perspective. When you read poems, or write about them, look for words, comparisons and ideas which change a common view, or challenge a cliché or stereotype.

TONE

The tone of someone's voice in speech will tell you whether they are wondering, denying, accusing, preaching, confessing or whatever. Equally, the tone, or how the writer addresses the reader, is what marks the attitude of the writer to the reader.

Some poems are written as if the writer is speaking confidentially to their reader. Others may be very direct in telling the reader what needs to be said. In his poem *Weeds*, Norman Nicholson takes a direct approach to telling the reader what he thinks:

> Some people are flower lovers. I'm a weed lover.
>
> Weeds don't need planting in well-drained soil;
> They don't ask for fertiliser or bits of rag to scare away birds.
> They come without invitation;
> And they don't take the hint when you want them to go.
> Weeds are nobody's guests:
> More like squatters.

Like Jon Silkin's *Dandelion* poem, this one declares a personal preference in the tone of someone who says, 'This is what I think'. Some poems may have the tone of telling the reader what to think. Dylan Thomas writes as someone urging the reader to listen and take advice about coping with old age. He is being instructive, telling his reader how to behave:

> Do not go gentle into that goodnight. Old age should rage against
> the dying of the light

In the last stanza of *Dulce et Decorum Est* (part of a Latin phrase which roughly translates as 'It is a good thing to die for your country'), Wilfred Owen personally accuses his reader, challenging his or her thinking by directly addressing the reader, insisting that seeing what Owen has seen would change the reader's ideas:

> If in some smothering dreams you too could pace
> Behind the wagon that we flung him in,
> And watch the white eyes writhing in his face,
> His hanging face, like a devil's sick of sin;
> If you could hear, at every jolt, the blood
> Come gargling from the froth-corrupted lungs,
> Obscene as cancer, bitter as the cud
> Of vile, incurable sores on innocent tongues,—
> My friend, you would not tell with such high zest
> To children ardent for some desperate glory,
> The old Lie: Dulce et decorum est
> Pro patria mori.

ATTITUDE

Poets do not always write their poems from their own point of view. They may adopt a persona, just as prose writers may let a character speak directly, as we saw with Jane Austen on page 23. In the following poem, *Dress Sense* by David Kitchen, the poet creates a character unlike himself, giving the character speech to make a point about parental attitudes:

You're not going out in that, are you?
I've never seen anything
More ridiculous in my whole life.
You look like you've been dragged
Through a hedge backwards
And lost half your dress along the way.

What's wrong with it?
You're asking me what's wrong with that?
Everything: that's what.
It's loud, it's common,
It reveals far too much of your …
Your … well your 'what you shouldn't be revealing'.

No, I'm not going to explain;
You know very well what I mean, young lady
But you choose to ignore
Every single piece of reasonable helpful advice
That you are offered.

It's not just the neckline I'm talking about
– And you can hardly describe it as a neckline,
More like a navel-line
If you bother to observe the way that it plunges.
Have you taken a look at the back?
(What little there is of it.)
Have you?

Boys are only going to think
One thing
When they see you in that outfit.
Where on earth did you get it?
And don't tell me that my money paid for it
Whatever you do.

You found it where?

Well, it probably looked different on her
And, anyway, you shouldn't be going through
Your mother's old clothes.

Poets don't always write what they personally think, or show an event from their own point of view. They may find it better to create a *persona* to show a point of view, or express an attitude. Some may mimic or parody ideas and attitudes in order to make them more obvious. When you read poems or write about them, ask yourself if the 'I' of a poem is really the author, or someone invented – a persona.

For a Grade C, you need to sustain your comments on why the poet chose to write about the subject and how his or her feelings and ideas can be seen in the choice of words and phrases. A personal response to feelings and attitudes will help.

For a Grade B, you need to develop your comments by referring to variations in tone and attitude as a sign of development or complexity. You could also explain how tone and attitude are reflections of the poet's own feelings or those of a persona. You need to explore the poem's concerns and attitudes, showing how they affect you and how different readers may respond.

For a Grade A, you need to analyse the language for signs of persuasion, irony, argument or amusement which may influence a reader's attitudes and feelings. You need to evaluate the success of the poem in meeting its purpose, and in the context of its own time and now.

Check yourself

QUESTIONS

Q1 Read the following poem, *Thistles* by Ted Hughes.

a) How does Ted Hughes try to make the reader see thistles afresh?

b) What attitude does he have towards these plants?

c) What do you think about *Thistles* now you have read it?

Q2 Read *Dress Sense* by David Kitchen again. As you read it, do you think this is the author speaking, or has the author created a character to speak? How does this poet use a persona to make a point about relationships?

Against the rubber tongues of cows and the hoeing hands of men
Thistles spike the summer air
Or crackle open under a blue-black pressure

Every one a revengeful burst
Of resurrection, a grasped fistful
Of splintered weapons and Icelandic frost thrust up

From the underground stain of a decayed Viking.
They are like pale hair and the gutturals of dialects.
Every one manages a plume of blood.

Then they grow grey like men.
Mown down, it is a feud. Their sons appear,
Stiff with weapons, fighting back over the same ground.

ANSWERS

A1 a) Ted Hughes compares these plants to fierce warriors – Vikings etc. They are like warriors because if they are attacked, they fight back and grow again (or their sons do). When he says that they have 'weapons' he could be thinking of their prickles, which are used to defend themselves and hurt people who come too close.

b) He makes out that they are rough plants, not nice like flowers, but they are still special in their own way. They are strong enough to stand up to cows and men, so he thinks you should respect them for being tough.

c) I think the poet is right when he says thistles are rough. They live on waste ground and they don't have flowers or fruit – they're just weeds and they can hurt if you try to pull them up. I suppose he's got a point about them being like soldiers because humans try to get rid of them and they have to stand up for themselves.

TUTORIALS

T1 a) *This response makes a valid point about the similarity between weapons and prickles. To obtain a higher grade, there could be more sustained comment on words which link the plant with warriors and weapons. Some of the words he uses are intended to suggest human qualities of human mood and intention, such as 'revengeful'. Verbs like 'spike' and 'crackle' give a sense of roughness and activity. There are lots of harsh consonant sounds in this poem, making the plant seem as primitive-sounding as the old Icelandic warriors whose voice was 'guttural'. Metaphors link the plant with violence, such as the description of 'a grasped fistful' and 'blood'. It could develop this point by explaining the use of animating and personifying language.*

b) *This makes a good point about the poet's attitude of respect. There could be more sustained comment on the language that suggests respect, such as 'resurrection' and 'feud' which make the plants seem magically re-born after a long-lasting battle. Discussion of the poet's attitude could be developed by explaining that plants are usually valued for their beauty or what we get from them, but Hughes is finding something to value in the plant in its defiance of humans, its ability to withstand harshness by being tough itself. There could be an attempt to explore Hughes' use of the plant to make us think of human qualities that we should admire.*

c) *This is an honest response, but it is more about thistles than the poem called* Thistles. *To obtain a higher grade, you need to pick out some features of the writing that helped you grasp the poet's ideas, such as the surprising admiration for a weed, or the use of animating or personifying language.*

ANSWERS

A2

Dress Sense is all speech, and it's supposed to be the girl's father talking. He says all the things that parents say to daughters, like not showing too much leg and giving the wrong impression. I don't think it's the writer, David Kitchen, saying all this, because it changes at the end, and I don't think the writer would want to show how he changes his attitude like this when he realises what he's said. He's made the speech like a typical Dad telling off his daughter as if she's too young to know what she's doing, and he forgets that he was young once and his wife wore things like this. I think the writer wants us to see that adults think they know best, and they forget that young people have got to live their lives and make their own mistakes. He's a bit of a hypocrite, really, the person speaking in this poem, because he thought it was all right for his wife to wear clothes like that, but not his daughter. But perhaps it's because he fancied his wife in it and he doesn't want other men fancying his daughter. It makes you see he's got a point, because he's worried about her, but he should realise that you can't just tell people what they should do.

TUTORIALS

T2

This is good in its description of what's going on in the poem. There is insight and exploration in the last part where the answer looks at the father's motives. There is an engaged personal response shown in the opinions about what fathers are like and what they should do. However, the answer is mostly about what happens in the poem, rather than about the author's approach to writing the poem and making a point.

For a higher grade, there would need to be sustained comment on the things which make the persona believable – phrases such as 'you look like you've been dragged through a hedge' and 'you know very well what I mean, young lady'. There could also be more developed comment on the father's attitude, exploring his feelings at the end. Does he feel that he's got it wrong? Does he feel rather foolish? Is he trying to find something else to criticise now that he can't blame the clothes? There could also be comment on the implied feelings and attitudes of the daughter. The father's feelings are explicitly stated, but we have to guess at the daughter's. Sustained comment on what she has presumably said, because the father echoes some comments – 'What's wrong with it?', 'Why don't you explain?' 'Is it the neckline?' etc. – would show reading for her feelings and attitudes, and from implied sources. This would allow developed comment on the questioning and challenging of the daughter, who doesn't get a look in because the father doesn't listen.

There could be comment on the writer's attitude rather than the father's. Is the writer confessing something he's said, or representing what some parents do? Whose side is the writer on – the father's or the daughter's? Look back at points made about telling a story in prose and you will see that some points relate to poetry as well.

CHAPTER 6

RESPONDING TO DRAMA

- **In this chapter, you will develop your reading response to play scripts.**
- **If you can show how dramatists use dialogue to create character and interest an audience, you will be able to evaluate writing that is intended for performance, whether on stage, screen or radio.**

INTRODUCTION

Your reading of drama text must show understanding of how it works for an actor and for an audience. This means reading for cues to the mood and nature of characters, and then for effects upon an audience that makes the play interesting to watch on stage or screen. Some of these cues will be explicit, but most will be implicit in dialogue.

In a novel, a narrator can explain why a character behaves in a particular way, and give details about how other characters react to speech. You may find something like:

> 'The situation was getting nastier by the minute. Jenson knew that any hint of fear would be fatal, so he smiled at his interrogators and said in a calm, pleasant voice …'

This is explicitly directing the reader's understanding of situation and motivation. The narration tells us the character's mood, intention and method of dealing with a situation. In a drama script, there may be some very brief guide to a character's mood or tone given as stage directions, such as '(*suspiciously*)' or '(*becoming impatient*)' or '(*irritably*)', but a character's thoughts are not given, only speech. If thoughts are not provided, the reader has to guess what a character is thinking and feeling in between bits of speech and ask themselves why a character says something. Of course, plays are meant to be seen and heard, not read, so in the theatre there will be visual help to understand feelings and motivation.

READING FOR MEANING

As you read a script, you make judgements and choices like those a director makes in bringing a play to life.

In the theatre, decisions about casting, movement, pace and appearance will be taken by the director, who works out with the actors the best way to signal feelings and intentions by gesture and tone of voice. As you read a script, you make judgements and choices like those a director makes in bringing the play to life. Like a director, you will form impressions from reading the lines, and from reading between the lines. Your understanding and response will be affected by explicit features of the script such as:

- what characters say;
- what they do;
- what the author writes in stage directions;

and implicit features such as:

- how they speak – manner and mood;
- why they say what they do – motivation, feeling and attitudes;
- what the author's purpose is – to make us laugh, make us sad or make us think.

You will probably need to read the whole script before many of these aspects emerge.

WHAT THE WRITER WANTS US TO SEE

Some dramatists are very keen to make sure that their play will be performed exactly as they wish. They may even add details about what characters look like, what they wear, how they move and speak. Writers like this provide detailed stage directions, not only at the beginning of the play, but throughout.

SCRIPTED ACTION

Look at this extract from Bernard Shaw's *Pygmalion*: as you read through, notice how Shaw provides narrative and descriptive detail as well as dialogue.

The Film My Fair Lady *was based on Bernard Shaw's* Pygmalion.

FREDDY	Oh, very well: I'll go, I'II go. [He opens his umbrella and dashes off Strand-wards, but comes into collision with a flower girl who is hurrying in for shelter, knocking her basket out of her hands. A blinding flash of lightning, followed instantly by a rattling peal of thunder, orchestrating the incident].
THE FLOWER GIRL	Nah then, Freddy: look wh' y' gowin, deah.
FREDDY	Sorry [he rushes off].
THE FLOWER GIRL	[picking up her scattered flowers and replacing them in the basket] Theres menners f'yer. Te-oo banches o voylets trod into the mad. [She sits down on the plinth of the column, sorting her flowers, on the lady's right. She is not at all a romantic figure. She is perhaps eighteen, perhaps twenty, hardly older. She wears a little sailor hat of black straw that has long been exposed to the dust and soot of London and has seldom, if ever, been brushed. Her hair needs washing rather badly: its mousy colour can hardly be natural. She wears a shoddy black coat that reaches nearly to her knees and is shaped to her waist. She has a brown skirt with a coarse apron. Her boots are much the worse for wear. She is no doubt as clean as she can afford to be; but compared to the ladies she is very dirty. Her features are no worse than theirs; but their condition leaves something to be desired; and she needs the services of a dentist].
THE MOTHER	How do you know that my son's name is Freddy, pray?
THE FLOWER GIRL	Ow, eez ye-oou san, is e? Wal, fewd dan y' d-ooty bawmz a mather should, eed now bettern to spawl a pore gel's flahrzn than ran away athaht pyin. Will ye-oo py me f'them?

Shaw has a clear idea of how he wants his play to be seen and heard on stage. His use of stage directions is very detailed – there are about seventeen lines of stage direction and about ten of dialogue in this extract – and he also creates a distinctive character through the speech of the flower seller, not just by what she says, but also how she says it. He wanted to reproduce the sounds of a Cockney accent as accurately as he could, showing how dialogue should be spoken.

SCRIPTED NARRATION

Other dramatists may use a chorus or a narrator on stage. This device was used in Greek tragedy and sometimes Shakespeare used it, but it has largely disappeared in this century. Arthur Miller adapts the narrator role in A *View From the Bridge*, using the lawyer Alfieri as a commentator on what is happening, but he also makes him part of the events, so that the audience sees him switch between the roles of narrator and participant:

> [Lights out on them and up on ALFIERI, seated behind his desk.]
>
> ALFIERI It was at this time that he first came to me. I had represented his father in an accident case some years before, and I was acquainted with the family in a casual way. I remember him now as he walked through my doorway –
>
> [Enter EDDIE down right ramp.]
>
> His eyes were like tunnels; my first thought was that he had committed a crime,
>
> [EDDIE sits beside the desk, cap in hand, looking out.]
>
> but soon I saw it was only a passion that had moved into his body, like a stranger.
>
> [ALFIERI pauses, looks down at his desk, then to EDDIE as though he were continuing a conversation with him.]
>
> I don't quite understand what I can do for you. Is there a question of law somewhere?
>
> EDDIE That's what I want to ask you.
>
> ALFIERI Because there's nothing illegal about a girl falling in love with an immigrant.

Using Alfieri as a commentator allows Miller to put some of the play's message into his mouth. Many playwrights use a character as a mouthpiece for their own views without turning them into a narrator. J. B. Priestley, for example, makes the message of his play, An *Inspector Calls*, come through the character Inspector Goole. Priestley gives him the speech that summarises his views about society and responsibility:

> INSPECTOR We don't live alone. We are members of one body. We are responsible for each other ... if men will not learn that lesson, then they will be taught it in fire and blood and anguish.

PLAY SCRIPT AND DIFFERENT MEDIA

Bernard Shaw was particularly keen to add lots of explicit direction because he knew how he wanted his play to look and sound. Some writers have a need to be explicit in scene-setting or in direction because of the medium the script is written for. This is especially true of plays written for radio and television.

RADIO DRAMA

Scripts for radio need to supply all the details which stage or screen can give the eye. Dylan Thomas wrote *Under Milk Wood* as a play for radio which features very detailed descriptions by the narrator who carefully tries to work on the listener's ears and eyes, making a theatre of the mind. As you read through this extract, notice the use of sound patterns, and of visual details which bring the scene to life.

Dylan Thomas.

It is night in Donkey Street, trotting silent, with seaweed on its hooves, along the cockled cobbles, past curtained fernpot, text and trinket, harmonium, holy dresser, watercolours done by hand, china dog and rosy tin teacaddy. It is night neddying among the snuggeries of babies.
Look. It is night, dumbly, royally winding through the Coronation cherry trees; going through the grave-yard of Bethesda with winds gloved and folded, and dew doffed; tumbling by the Sailors Arms.
Time passes. Listen. Time passes.
Come closer now.
Only you can hear the houses sleeping in the streets in the slow deep salt and silent black, bandaged night. Only you can see, in the blinded bedrooms, the combs and petticoats over the chairs, the jugs and basins, the glasses of teeth, Thou Shalt Not on the wall, and the yellowing dickybird-watching pictures of the dead. Only you can hear and see, behind the eyes of the sleepers, the movements and countries and mazes and colours and dismays and rainbows and tunes and wishes and flight and fall and despairs and big seas of their dreams.
From where you are, you can hear their dreams.

TELEVISION DRAMA

Dennis Potter wrote specifically for television and used the medium as part of the setting, not just a device for recording his play. In this opening to *Lipstick on Your Collar*, he is writing a screen script, prescribing all the sound and visual effects for every second of the action. Here is one-third of the lead-in to the first speech from a character

The cinematic titles take us into a real cinema, in 1956, where there is a newsreel showing a revolving globe, black and white, with banal, predictable newsreel 'dramatic' music, and the caption: 'New York's realistic air-raid drill'.

Busy streets, New York. The gabble-gobble newsreel voice begins.
NEWSREEL VOICE: *New York in the rush hour. Eight million
people in a hurry. But the very first civil defence exercise pulls them up with a
jerk. And the streets very soon become deserted.*
Sirens sound. People run.
Pulling back from the newsreel to its audience, in a typical, big, slightly
rococo 1956 cinema.
Blue cigarette smoke curls and twists in the dancing, flickering projection
beam. The newsreel voice continuing:
*Buying and selling on the Stock Exchange reaches zero. And with a scare like this
on, no wonder.*
On the screen, dealers scramble for every exit, leaving abandoned litter.
Leaning against the wall of the auditorium, at the edge of the glistening
flickers, an attractive young woman, Sylvia, has her arms folded: torch
held languidly in hand, jaws desultorily chewing gum. She gives no
attention to the screen, as the voice gabbles on.

Notice that Potter scripts the sounds and sights of a newsreel to fill the
screen, then directs the camera to pull back to show the audience in a
cinema. He includes directions not only for what is performed, but also for
how it is to be filmed. Sylvia is an important character, but Potter does not
give her any dialogue: he chooses instead to show her in a context where her
reactions – or lack of them – tell us something about her.

Potter's skill as a television dramatist is that he scripts pictures, words and
sound effects as part of the dramatic setting and important components of
modern life, where we act out our real lives in a constant surround of
television, pop song and advertising jingles.

When you read a play script, remind yourself of the medium it is written for –
stage, TV, radio or film – and think about any ways in which the writer has
adapted writing for that medium.

THE POWER OF DIALOGUE

Not all dramatists include explicit information, or a character who adopts the
role of narrator or voice of the author. There may be no scripted action to
help you visualise the scene – just the dialogue, of which there are various
different types.

STYLISED DIALOGUE

Oscar Wilde wrote plays about wealthy people to amuse a sophisticated city
audience. His characters have none of the tongue-tied clumsiness or untidiness
which is typical of most people's unrehearsed speech. In his plays, conversation
is much more fluent and polished than you would find in most everyday situations.
Many of his characters appear to be mouthpieces for Wilde's own witty remarks:

All women become like their mothers. That is their tragedy. No man does.
That's his.

We are all in the gutter, but some of us are looking at the stars.

Oscar Wilde, the master of the witty one-liner.

NATURALISTIC DIALOGUE

During the second half of the twentieth century, dramatists tended to use more realistic speech from characters who were not educated or from the aristocracy. Ordinary people were more likely to appear as characters, using dialect or colloquial speech. This shift from writing about upper-class people to ordinary people in ordinary environments was known as 'kitchen-sink' drama, or 'naturalistic' writing.

READING THE SILENCES

Making speech seem natural means reproducing the rhythms, idiom and fillers of everyday talk, including, hesitations, incomplete sentences and clichés. Harold Pinter writes speech with all the flaws and quirks of everyday use. He also thinks of speech as something we use to conceal our thoughts, rather than reveal them, as a defence mechanism; he sees conversation as a ritual in which people don't always say what they mean, or mean what they say. We therefore have to read between the lines to understand what's going on.

Pinter offers very little explicit direction. He may write in a 'pause', but he does not tell us that the pause is because of reflection, or doubt, or anger. The reader needs to think about what is happening in the spaces between the speech, in other words to 'read the silences' for meaning.

As you read through the following passage from Pinter's *The Caretaker*, ask yourself what Davies and Mick are each trying to do. Is Davies (as he says) someone who can't be pushed around? Is Mick (as he says) impressed with Davies? And what do you think each of them is thinking and doing in the moments of pause?

MICK   Eh, you're not thinking of doing any violence on me, are you? You're not the violent sort, are you?

DAVIES (vehemently) I keep myself to myself, mate. But if anyone starts with me though, they know what they got coming.

MICK   I can believe that.

DAVIES You do. I been all over, see? You understand my meaning? I don't mind a bit of a joke now and then, but anyone'll tell you ... that no one starts anything with me.

MICK   I get what you mean, yes.

DAVIES I can be pushed so far ... but ...

MICK   No further.

DAVIES That's it.

[MICK sits on junk down right.]

What you doing?

MICK   No, I just want to say that I'm very impressed by that.

DAVIES Eh?

MICK   I'm very impressed by what you've just said.
[Pause.]
Yes, that's impressive, that is.
[Pause.]
I'm impressed, anyway.

DAVIES You know what I'm talking about, then?

MICK   Yes, I know. I think we understand one another.

As the reader, you have to decide whether to take Mick's repeated 'impressed' as sincere, or as ironic. At the end of this, you may think that Mick understands Davies better than Davies understands Mick! There are hints in this passage that Mick is a step or two ahead of Davies – finishing his sentence for him, for example. Davies is suspicious and not confident, so the pause moments can be tense situations where each one is sizing the other one up, wondering how to continue. Moments of silence on stage can create suspense and curiosity in the audience, so this extract shows a dramatist using dialogue to characterise two individuals and make the audience interested in the relationship between them. What involves the audience most is the lack of specific narrative information.

Pinter is a dramatist who thinks that some of the most tense and dramatic moments in real conversations are when people say nothing. He uses pauses in his scripts where embarrassment, awkwardness, hesitation or anger may cause a character to say nothing. Silence on stage – and in life – can be as eloquent as speech. Think of those moments when you want to say something but dare not trust yourself in case you say too much, or those moments when you handle questioning by silence, or show resentment in 'dumb insolence'.

DRAMATIC IRONY

By reading dialogue carefully, you can comment on an author's skill in structuring a scene or the play as a whole. It may be necessary to let the audience see something in one scene which will be important for what they are to see later. Preparing an audience for a later scene is an important part of the playwright's craft.

Dramatic irony is when the audience knows something that a character doesn't, and is able to watch the character say or do something that he or she would not do if he or she knew what the audience knows. It is a powerful device for creating suspense or a comic situation. It needs no explicit statement or direction, as long as the dialogue gives the audience necessary information.

As you read through the following excerpt from an episode of *Fawlty Towers*, written by John Cleese and Connie Booth, notice how Basil's late entry into the scene creates a comic situation. He enters only after his wife has met their guests, Colonel and Mrs Hall. The audience already knows two things about Colonel Hall which Basil does not: that he has a facial twitch and that he has (very boringly) talked about the weather. Basil blunders by reacting to the Colonel's odd head movements, unaware that he has a twitch. Determined to avoid this embarrassment, he then tries to change the subject, but in describing talk about the weather as foolish, he offends the person he is most keen to impress. When Sybil tries to warn him off he tries for another change of subject, with even more disastrous results. The harder he tries to get out of an embarrassing blunder, the more he makes another.

COLONEL When I went out for my stroll this morning, I thought it was going to be rather warm [he twitches] but in the event it turned out quite cool and then it started to cloud over after lunch, contrary of course to what the forecast said [he twitches] and it won't surprise me if we get a little rain tonight.

SYBIL Still it's been a lovely summer hasn't it?

[Basil strides in.]

BASIL Ah, Colonel! How delightful to see you again.

[The Colonel turns round.]

COLONEL   … Sorry!

BASIL   How delightful to see you again. We met last year at the Golf Club dinner dance, you may remember?

[A pause.]

COLONEL   No, I don't.

BASIL   Fine, we didn't talk for long, just good evening really, a blink of the eye and you'd have missed it. As indeed you did, most understandably.

COLONEL   … Sorry!?

[The Colonel twitches. Basil stares, puzzled.]

BASIL   Sorry?

COLONEL   … What?

[Sybil nudges Basil.]

BASIL   Oh, I'd forgotten! Well, hasn't it been unremarkable.

COLONEL   … What?

BASIL   The weather. I was just thinking how unremarkable it's been really. Ha! Hardly worth talking about … in fact not worth talking about. Only a fool would, ha, ha, ha!

[Sybil nudges him. Basil looks at her and senses he should change the subject.]

BASIL   And how is that lovely daughter of yours?

SYBIL   (quietly) Dead.

A scene from Fawlty Towers.

WHAT MAKES THE GRADE?

For a Grade C, you need to sustain comments on character and situation by referring to more than one example. You also need to show understanding of implied meaning in dialogue.

For a Grade B, you need to develop your comments and opinions by showing where there is a significant change from an attitude or feeling you have identified. You should also explore different reactions to characters, behaviour and situations in the text

For a Grade A, you need to analyse a writer's methods of conveying meaning and evaluate alternative possible interpretations of meaning. You should be able to judge the likely effects of presentation on different kinds of audience.

Check yourself

Q1 Here's another extract from Harold Pinter's *The Caretaker*. What can you tell about the relationship between Mick and Davies in this scene? As there are very few stage directions, you will need to read the dialogue carefully in order to extract the information.

MICK   Uuh ... listen can I ask your advice? I mean, you're a man of the world. Can I ask your advice about something?

DAVIES   You go right ahead.

MICK   Well, what is it, you see, I'm, I'm a bit worried about my brother.

DAVIES   Your brother?

MICK   Yes ... you see, his trouble is ...

DAVIES   What?

MICK   Well, it's not a very nice thing to say ...

DAVIES   (rising, coming downstage) Go on now, you say it.

[MICK looks at him.]

MICK   He doesn't like work.

[Pause.]

DAVIES   Go on!

MICK   No, he just doesn't like work, that's his trouble.

DAVIES   Is that a fact?

MICK   It's a terrible thing to have to say about your own brother.

DAVIES   Ay.

MICK   He's just shy of it. Very shy of it.

DAVIES   I know that sort.

MICK   You know the type?

DAVIES   I've met them.

MICK   I mean, I want to get him going in the world.

DAVIES   Stands to reason, man.

MICK   If you got an older brother you want to push him on, you want to see him make his way. Can't have him idle, he's only doing himself harm. That's what I say.

DAVIES   Yes.

MICK   But he won't buckle down to the job.

DAVIES   He don't like work.

MICK   Work shy.

DAVIES   Sounds like it to me.

MICK   You've met the type, have you?

DAVIES   Me? I know that sort.

MICK   Yes.

DAVIES   I know that sort. I've met them.

MICK   Causing me great anxiety. You see, I'm a working man: I'm a tradesman. I've got my own van.

DAVIES   Is that a fact?

MICK   He's supposed to be doing a little job for me ... I keep him here to do a little job ... but I don't know. I'm coming to the conclusion he's a slow worker.

[Pause.]

     What would your advice be?

DAVIES   Well ... he's a funny bloke, your brother.

MICK   What?

DAVIES   I was saying, he's ... he's a bit of a funny bloke; your brother.

[MICK stares at him.]

MICK   Funny? Why?

DAVIES   Well ... he's funny...

MICK   What's funny about him?

[Pause.]

DAVIES   Not liking work.

MICK   What's funny about that?

DAVIES   Nothing.

[Pause.]

MICK   I don't call it funny.

DAVIES   Nor me.

MICK   You don't want to start getting hypercritical.

DAVIES   No, no, I wasn't that, I wasn't ... I was only saying ...

MICK   Don't get too glib .

DAVIES   Look, all I meant was—

MICK   Cut it!

This extract from *Fawlty Towers* follows the one you read on pages 50–51. From your reading of both extracts, explain what makes them successful as comic drama.

BASIL	Ah, Colonel! [He hastens ahead to make the introductions.] Colonel and Mrs Hall, may I introduce Mr and Mrs Tw … [A pause.] Have you met?
COLONEL	No we haven't.
BASIL	[to Mr Twitchen] Have you?
MR TWITCHEN	No.
BASIL	Oh, good. Well, what would you like to drink?
MRS HALL	What?
BASIL	To drink?
MRS HALL	I didn't catch the name.
BASIL	You didn't catch it? What a rotten bit of luck!
COLONEL	Well?
BASIL	Fine, thanks.
COLONEL	No, we still don't know the name.
BASIL	Fawlty. Basil Fawlty.
COLONEL	No, theirs.
BASIL	Oh, theirs! Oh I see, of course, I thought you meant mine. My, it's warm in here! I could do with a drink too. Another sherry?
COLONEL	Well, are you going to introduce us?
BASIL	Didn't I? Of course. [He looks at his watch.] Good Lord! Is that the time? I didn't realise. [in a businesslike manner] May I present Mr and Mrs? Now …
COLONEL	What?!!!
BASIL	[patiently] Mr and Mrs. [He lets out a little cry and faints backwards. He lies still for a couple of seconds, opens his eyes and looks up] Sorry! I fainted. Now, I'll get your tomato juices. [He rises.] Ah, I feel better for that. [He heads for the bar.]
MR TWITCHEN	[to the Halls] The name's Twitchen.
COLONEL	Hall. How do you do. Would you care to join us?

ANSWERS

A1

The writer uses dialogue which is naturalistic. The two characters speak like ordinary people and repeat themselves and say things that don't always follow on from the last thing. You can't tell what each of them thinks because Davies seems to be agreeing with Mick, but Mick eventually turns on Davies for saying what he's been saying himself. Perhaps this means he doesn't think Davies has the right to criticise his brother, but then he shouldn't have asked for his opinion in the first place if he was going to act like this. I think he's quite a sly bloke because he gets Davies to say something and then tells him off for it. Davies is not really sure what to say. He seems a bit nervous, but he gets a bit more confident when Mick seems to trust him. In the end Mick is sharp with him and he (Davies) probably wishes he hadn't said anything.

A2

What makes this funny is Basil. He is supposed to be the host but he doesn't behave like a host at all. He doesn't introduce the guests and he makes them more and more annoyed. If you are running a hotel, you shouldn't be rude like telling your guests 'rotten luck' when they ask for something. All the time they ask to be introduced he changes the subject to drinks or how warm it is and then he pretends to faint. They must think he's really stupid and never come to his hotel again. At the end, they introduce themselves

TUTORIALS

T1

This shows good grasp of Mick's cunning and Davies' uncertainty. These points could be made more convincing by quoting the lines where Davies 'seems a bit nervous' and 'gets more confident'. There is some willingness to explore meaning in 'Perhaps he …' and some personal response in 'but then he shouldn't have asked' and 'I think he's quite a sly bloke'.

For a Grade B, the comment on Davies' uncertainty could be sustained by looking at several moments where he pauses, asks a question or repeats what Mick has said. This would show more use of textual evidence. The comment on Mick's slyness could be developed by referring to moments where he seems to be leading Davies on. For example, he seems reluctant to say any more: 'you see … his trouble is …' and 'It's not a very nice thing to say …' His apparent trust in Davies at the start of the extract could be explored for its motives and its effects on Davies. This could involve analysis of his methods to trap Davies into an opinion about his brother.

There is a brief comment on the author and his use of naturalistic dialogue but not much. There needs to be some reference to the writer's dramatic purpose, referring to its likely effect on the audience. It is a passage which creates interest and tension by not revealing characters' motives, so that the audience is kept uncertain. This is writing in which the drama is in relationships rather than plot. For a Grade A, there could be exploration of the language as something evasive, ambiguous and misleading, rather than for honest communication.

T2

This is a very weak answer. It misses most of the point of the script because it doesn't identify Basil's motives. The answer looks at Basil's character but doesn't sustain comment on what is comic in character or situation. In the middle of the first sentence, Basil realises that the guests' name is Twitchen, which he thinks will embarrass the twitching Colonel. Desperate not to mention the name in case it adds to his previous blunders, he tries everything he can think of to avoid a disaster. In so doing, he causes far more outrageous blunders. The answer does comment on the fact that the guests introduce themselves, but this should be developed to show that in the end, Colonel Hall was not offended by the name, so all of Basil's attempts to spare his feelings were unnecessary. There could be analysis of his strategies to get off the subject of names, pretending to misunderstand, diverting them with an offer of a drink, feigning surprise at the time and the temperature. His final ruse of fainting and recovering is a desperate last attempt when he can think of nothing else. There could be some exploration of Basil's reluctance to mention the name 'Twitchen', connecting this situation with the earlier one, making him determined to avoid any further blunders.

- **In this chapter, you will develop your reading response to literary language and levels of meaning.**
- **If you can recognise that there is more to meaning than meets the eye, you will be able to appreciate subtleties of language and devices which create different levels of meaning.**

INTRODUCTION: LITERAL AND LITERARY LANGUAGE

Writing to convey necessary factual information – such as in a DIY manual or a first-aid handbook – must make meaning clear, and not cause doubts or uncertainty in the reader. If you have to read a manual twice, it is failing to be sufficiently clear. If you have to read a literary passage twice, it is succeeding in making you read for additional or alternative meaning.

Literal language avoids opinion and emotion. It excludes the writer's personality because its job is to transmit knowledge to the reader, not impressions or attitudes.

Literary language is different. It presents the subject loaded with the author's mood, attitude and values. Look at the examples of writing about places on pages 12–13 again.

SURFACE MEANING AND AMBIGUITY

Literal language has all its meaning on the surface. It calls a spade a spade and a pen a pen. Literary language, on the other hand, deliberately exploits varieties of meaning, through suggestiveness, ambiguity and metaphor. It may try to make the reader think of similarities between a spade and a pen by linking them, as in Seamus Heaney's poem D*igging*:

> Between my finger and my thumb
> The squat pen rests.
> I'll dig with it

Ambiguity can be unintentional, as in the statement 'He created a large impression when he sat down', or it can be intentional, making the reader react to a word in a way different from usual. Read the following description and try to identify what is ambiguous about it:

> His smooth hands waved persuasively and his plump features broke into a genial smile as he predicted the company's profits from the export of land-mines.

Usually, words like 'plump' and 'smooth' have a positive effect, suggesting comfort and cosiness, as they did when used to describe the landlady of the Green Dragon (see page 1), but a writer can use these words in a way which makes the reader react against comfort and cosiness. Because the character is

SURFACE FINISHES FOR CONCRETE

The surface finishes produced by tamping or striking off with a sawing action are perfectly adequate for a skid-proof, workmanlike surface for a pad, drive or pathway, but you can produce a range of other finishes using simple handtools once you have compacted and levelled the concrete.

Float finishes
Smooth the tamped concrete by sweeping a wooden float across the surface, or make an even finer texture by finishing with a trowel (steel float). Let the concrete dry out a little before using a float or you will bring water to the top and weaken it, eventually resulting in a dusty residue on the hardened concrete. Bridge the formwork with a stout plank so that you can reach the centre, or hire a skip float with a long handle for large pads.

Make a smooth finish with a wooden float

Brush finishes
Make a finely textured surface by drawing a yard broom across the setting concrete. Flatten the concrete initially with a wooden float, then make parallel passes with the broom held at a low angle to avoid 'tearing' the surface.

Texture the surface with a broom

Brush-finishing concrete

Exposed-aggregate finish
Embedding small stones or pebbles in the surface makes a very attractive and practical finish but it takes a little practice to be successful.
Scatter dampened pebbles onto the freshly laid concrete and tamp them firmly with a length of timber until they are flush with the surface (1). Place a plank across the formwork and apply your full weight to make sure the surface is even. Leave the concrete to harden for a while until all surface water has evaporated, then use a very fine spray and a brush to wash away the cement from around the pebbles until they protrude (2). Cover the concrete for about 24 hours, then lightly wash the actual pebbles. Cover the concrete again and leave it to harden thoroughly.

1 Tamp pebbles into the fresh concrete

2 Wash the cement from around the pebbles

Exposed-aggregate finish

Literary and literal language have very different purposes.

pleased with making money out of something that hurts people, the reader may see his smoothness and comfort as unattractive. The use of these words is no longer positive, but negative, provoking the reader into a moral judgement.

READING BENEATH THE STORY

Think back to the description of the marshes by Pip in *Great Expectations* (page 14), especially the passage where he begins to feel frightened by the vastness all around him:

> ... the dark flat wilderness beyond the churchyard, intersected with dykes and mounds and gates, with scattered cattle feeding on it, was the marshes; and that the low leaden line beyond was the river; and that the distant savage lair from which the wind was rushing was the sea; and that the small bundle of shivers growing afraid of it all and beginning to cry was Pip.

Dickens' purpose is to show how frightening an environment can be to an impressionable child. He uses 'wilderness' to make the area seem unlike home, and 'savage' to make the noise of the wind frightening; but the word that really creates a sense of menace is 'lair'. A lair is the den of a wild animal, so describing the wind coming from a 'lair' animates the wind as a predatory creature. It is not literally true that the wind lives in a cave, but the word 'lair' suggests that it does. Statement and metaphor work together to help you understand what lies beneath the surface of the story. Although this extract is literally about a boy and a landscape, the metaphorical meaning – the theme – *below* the story is about a child as the vulnerable prey of a predatory wider world.

UNDERCURRENTS OF MEANING – METAPHOR

Metaphorical language works in prose just as it does in poetry – and it can help us to comment on the author's ideas and attitudes which lie beneath the story.

Hardy, as we saw on page 13, believed that human beings, however educated or civilised, were as much influenced by natural impulses as the animals and plants. When, in *Tess of the D'Urbervilles*, he wanted to suggest that human beings were moved by Nature's force to grow, blossom and reproduce, he described Nature's energy and fertility as something powerful enough to touch and hear:

> Amid the oozing fatness and warm ferments of the Froom Vale, at a season when the rush of juices could almost be heard below the hiss of fertilisation, it was impossible that the most fanciful love should not grow passionate.

We know that plants grow in stem and leaf, and that sap rises, but Hardy magnifies the processes of growth, as if holding a microphone to amplify and record the 'rush' and 'hiss' of biological processes. Hardy does this to bring the reader up close to Nature, to see the urges and surges of living organisms reproducing and growing. By showing characters affected by these natural forces, he is implying something about human beings in general. His linking of plant and human life gives us a clue to his thinking. Hardy was influenced by Darwin's view that we have evolved like everything else, and are not so different from other products of nature. He is showing us what lies beneath the surface of human behaviour, and we read beneath the surface to glimpse something of his way of looking at the world, his philosophy.

UNDERCURRENTS OF MEANING – SYMBOLISM

Writers can exploit connections made by words. If they keep up a pattern of choosing words which remind the reader of something else, the result can be deliberately symbolic. In the following passage from *Lord of the Flies*, Golding describes the death of Simon, murdered by the other boys in a savage ritual. The description of a luminous gathering around his head suggests a halo, symbolising Simon's saintliness.

> Along the shoreward edge of the shallows the advancing clearness was full of strange, moonbeam-bodied creatures with fiery eyes. Here and there a larger pebble clung to its own air and was covered with a coat of pearls. The tide swelled in over the rain-pitted sand and smoothed everything with a layer of silver. Now it touched the first of the stains that seeped from the broken body, and the creatures made a moving patch of light as they gathered at the edge. The water rose further and dressed Simon's coarse hair with brightness. The line of his cheek silvered and the turn of his shoulder became sculptured marble. The strange, attendant creatures, with their fiery eyes and trailing vapours, busied themselves round his head. The body lifted a fraction of an inch from the sand and a bubble of air escaped from the mouth with a wet plop. Then it turned gently in the water. Somewhere over the darkened curve of the world the sun and moon were pulling; and the film of water on the earth planet was held, bulging slightly on one side while the solid core turned. The great wave of the tide moved further along the island and the water lifted. Softly, surrounded by a fringe of inquisitive bright creatures, itself a silver shape beneath the steadfast constellations, Simon's dead body moved out towards the open sea.

An author may use description of a setting to suggest things symbolically. Here, in another excerpt from Dickens' *Great Expectations*, the description of Mr Pumblechook's shop is through the eyes of young Pip, who feels oppressed and smothered, not allowed to develop and flourish: What he observes around him is affected by his feelings. The seeds in the enclosing drawers therefore suggest a lack of the conditions to develop into healthy plants.

> Mr Pumblechook's premises in the High Street of the market town, were of a peppercorny and farinaceous* character, as the premises of a corn-chandler and seedsman should be. It appeared to me that he must he a very happy man indeed, to have so many little drawers in his shop: and I wondered when I peeped into one or two on the lower tiers, and saw the tied-up brown paper packets inside, whether the flower-seeds and bulbs ever wanted of a fine day to break out of those jails, and bloom.

* floury

SYMBOLIC WRITING AND AUTHORS' IDEAS

An author's ideas can often be identified by reading beneath the events of a story. Hardy saw agricultural life in the nineteenth century changing as a result of technology. In *Tess of the D'Urbervilles*, he showed how farmworkers had to work harder to match the pace of new machinery, and describes a mechanical thresher and its operator as a harsh, unnatural influence on rural life. As you read through the passage, notice which words create these impressions.

Close under the eaves of the stack, and as yet barely visible, was the red tyrant that the women had come to serve – a timber-framed construction, with straps and wheels appertaining* – the threshing-machine which, whilst it was going, kept up a despotic demand upon the endurance of their muscles and nerves.

A little way off, there was another indistinct figure; this one black, with a sustained hiss that spoke of strength very much in reserve … By the engine stood a dark, motionless being, a sooty and grimy embodiment of tallness, in a sort of trance, with a heap of coals by his side: it was the engineman … He was in the agricultural world, but not of it. He served fire and smoke; these denizens of the field served vegetation, weather, frost and sun. He travelled with his engine from farm to farm, from county to county … He spoke in a strange northern accent: his thoughts being turned inward upon himself, his eye on his iron charge, hardly perceiving the scenes around him, and caring for them not at all: holding only strictly necessary inter-course with the natives, as if some ancient doom compelled him to wander here against his will in the service of his Plutonic master.

*relating to

The words 'tyrant' and 'despotic' in the first paragraph suggest ruthless dictatorship. The engineer is 'motionless' and does not communicate with the workers. He speaks like a foreigner and deals with fire and smoke, not Nature. The reference to Pluto could either suggest that he is only interested in money (as Pluto was the god of wealth) or that he is a servant of the Lord of Hell. The latter reference, together with the black and red colouring, suggest that the machinery is devil-like, a hellish intruder into the scene.

RECOGNISING IRONY

Irony comes from the Greek word *eironeia*, meaning 'pretended ignorance'. It is used to describe a statement that appears innocent on the surface, but has a different, and not innocent, meaning beneath. Recognising irony is a vital part of commenting on an author's purpose, because irony is usually an attempt to make us laugh at something foolish or to make a moral comment. Generally, it works by saying something that is the opposite of what the writer means.

IRONY IN ATTITUDE

Arthur Clough wanted to criticise the way people put too much value on wealth. In *The Latest Decalogue*, he wrote as if recommending the worship of money:

Thou shalt have one God only; who
Would be at the expense of two?
No graven images may be
Worshipped, except the currency.

What he meant was the opposite of what he literally said. He used irony to make the reader feel shocked by a frank statement of what may be true, but is not admitted.

IRONY IN SITUATION

In this extract from A *Kestrel for a Knave*, Barry Hines describes a school assembly. As you read through it, notice how the Headmaster's behaviour is made even more gross and unfair by being contrasted with the words of the hymn, and the supposedly religious purpose of an assembly.

Then a boy coughed – 'Who did that?'
Everybody looking round.
'I said WHO DID THAT?'
The teachers moved in closer, alert like a riot squad.
'Mr Crossley! Somewhere near you! Didn't you see the boy?'
Crossley flushed, and rushed amongst them, thrusting them aside in panic.
'There, Crossley? That's where it came from! Around there!'
Crossley grabbed a boy by the arm and began to yank him into the open.
'It wasn't me, Sir!'
'Of course it was you.'
'It wasn't, Sir, honest!'
'Don't argue lad, I saw you.'
Gryce thrust his jaw over the front of the lectern, the air whistling down his nostrils.
'MACDOWALL! I might have known it! Get to my room, lad!'
Crossley escorted MacDowall from the hall. Gryce waited for the doors to stop swinging, then replaced his stick and addressed the school.
'Right! We'll try again. Hymn one hundred and seventy five.'
The pianist struck the chord. Moderately slow, it said in the book, but this direction was ignored by the school, and the tempo they produced was dead slow, the words delivered in a grinding monotone.
'New ev-ry morn-ing is the love
Our waken-ing and uprising prove;
Through sleep and dark-ness safely brought,
Re-stored to life, and power, and thought.'
'STOP!'
The pianist stopped playing. The boys stopped singing.
'And what's that noise supposed to represent? I've heard sweeter sounds in a slaughter house! This is supposed to be a hymn of joy, not a dirge! So get your heads up, and your books up, and open your mouths, and SING.'
There was a mass bracing of backs and showing of faces as Gryce stepped round the lectern to the edge of the platform and leaned out over the well of the hall.
'Or I'll make you sing like you've never sung before.'

Hines' ironic treatment of the scene contrasts the joy and love and safety mentioned in the hymn with the atmosphere of brutal harshness in the school.

Louis Untermeyer, in *Portrait of a Machine* (which you looked at earlier – see page 35), describes a machine as a creature enjoying its revenge on its makers:

> It bears a deeper malice; lives to earn
> Its master's bread and laughs to see this great
> Lord of the earth, who rules but cannot learn,
> Become the slave of what his slaves create

The irony here is that human beings become slavishly dependent upon the technology they create to give themselves more freedom. The result of people's action is the opposite of what they intended.

IRONY IN SPEECH

Writers who want their readers to see something as ridiculous or unacceptable may avoid direct statement, and try to suggest a reaction by using language ironically. Irony is a powerful tool for making readers understand that there is more to what is being said than the literal meaning.

Siegfried Sassoon attacked the way some people treated casualties of the war by exaggerating a 'never mind' attitude. He does not mean what he says, but expresses ideas which he wants to criticise.

> Does it matter? Losing your sight?
> There's such splendid work for the blind:
> And people will always be kind.

Siegfried Sassoon.

In *Pride and Prejudice*, Jane Austen has Mr Bennett say, as he stops his daughter from her (unskilful) piano playing:

> That will do extremely well, child. You have delighted us long enough.

On the surface, this states praise and appreciation for her playing, and could be seen as a sign that he doesn't want her to go to any more trouble. However, it is more likely that he has heard enough and is finding a way of stopping her.

IRONY IN NARRATIVE

Irony does not always have to be conveyed in dialogue. Alexander Pope, describing a young woman's bedroom, lists what can be seen on her dressing-table:

> Puffs, powders, patches, bibles, billet-doux

By casually including 'bibles' (she has several!) in a list of cosmetics and personal trifles, it makes her attitude to religion appear trivial, no more important to her than any of the other things cluttering her table.

The following account of the last stages of a siege, taken from *The Siege of Krishnapur* by J. G. Farrell, may at first seem to be a straightforward description of some military action. However, the author's purpose is not to record heroic deeds.

> The Collector, in a remote and academic sort of way, was musing on this question of ammunition, considering whether there was anything left which still might be fired. But surely they had thought of everything. All the metal was gone, first the round objects, then the others. Now they were on to stones. Without a doubt the most effective missiles in this matter of improvised ammunition had been the heads of his electrometal figures, removed from their bodies with the help of Turtons' indispensable file. And of the heads, perhaps not surprisingly, the most effective of all had been Shakespeare's; it had scythed its way through a whole astonished platoon of sepoys advancing in single file through the jungle. The Collector suspected that the Bard's success in this respect might have a great deal to do with the ballistic advantages stemming from his baldness. The head of Keats, for example, wildly festooned with metal locks which it had proved impossible to file smooth had flown very erratically indeed, killing only a fat money-lender and a camel standing at some distance from the field of action.

The writer shows his sense of humour in the irony of this passage. The English official ruling this part of the Empire is faced with a horde of natives. Fortunately, he has the whole of his civilisation to make him superior. What this amounts to is that all the books and objects in the library are useless, except as things to fire from the cannon. The heads of the statues of great Englishmen, the symbols of English culture are used as cannon balls. Shakespeare makes a better cannon ball because he is bald. Keats is less good because of his long hair. Farrell is saying ironically that, for all the pride we may have in our civilisation, it may not amount to much in the end. He uses the episode to mock the idea that the English are a superior nation. Irony here is the key to the author's attitudes, concerns and ideas.

◀ WHAT MAKES THE GRADE?

> For a Grade C, you need to show a sustained response to writers' concerns, attitudes and purposes. This means showing, from a range of references, what the writer thinks and intends.
>
> For a Grade B, you need to develop comments on attitudes, feelings and ideas, comparing the time of writing and now. You also need to explore possible meanings, and ways in which language has influenced your understanding.
>
> For a Grade A, you need to analyse writers' techniques with close reference to language, and evaluate alternative interpretations.

Check yourself

Q1 In the extract from William Thackeray's *Vanity Fair*, Becky Sharp, a lady fallen on bad times, is visited by a former close friend. As you read through, think about her motives and how she treats Jos. Think particularly about the underlined words. What impression do you get of Becky Sharp in this passage?

Becky's little head peeped out full of archness and mischief. She lighted on Jos. 'It's you,' she said, coming out. 'How I have been waiting for you! Stop, not yet – in one minute you shall come in.' In that instant she put a rouge-pot, a brandy bottle, and a plate of broken meat into the bed, gave one smooth to her hair, and finally let in her visitor.

She had, by way of morning robe, a pink domino, a trifle faded and soiled, and marked here and there with pomatum*; but her arms shone out from the loose sleeves of the dress very white and fair, and it was tied round her little waist, so as not ill to set off the trim little figure of the wearer. She led Jos by the hand into her garret. 'Come in,' she said. 'Come, and talk to me. Sit yonder on the chair;' and she gave the Civilian's hand a little squeeze, and laughingly placed him upon it. As for herself, she placed herself on the bed – not on the bottle and plate, you may be sure – on which Jos might have reposed, had he chosen that seat; and so there she sat and talked with her old admirer.

'How little years have changed you,' she said, with a look of tender interest. 'I should have known you anywhere. What a comfort it is amongst strangers to see once more the frank honest face of an old friend!'... 'I should have known you anywhere,' she continued; 'a woman never forgets some things. And you were the first man I ever – I ever saw.'

'Was I, really?' said Jos. 'God bless my soul, you – you don't say so.'

'When I came with your sister from Chiswick, I was scarcely more than a child,' Becky said. 'How is that dear love? Oh, her husband was a sad wicked man, and of course it was of me that the poor dear was jealous. As if I cared about him, heigh-ho! when there was somebody – but no – don't let us talk of old times,' and she passed her handkerchief with the tattered lace J across her eyelids.

'Is not this a strange place,' she continued, 'for a woman, who has lived in a very different world too, to be found in? I have had so many griefs and wrongs, Joseph Sedley, I have been made to suffer so cruelly, that I am almost made mad sometimes. I can't stay still in any place, but wander about always restless and unhappy. All my friends have been false to me – all. There is no such thing as an honest man in the world. I was the truest wife that ever lived, though I married my husband out of pique, because somebody else - but never mind that. I was true, and he trampled upon me, and deserted me. I was the fondest mother. I had but one child, one darling, one hope, one joy, which I held to my heart with a mother's affection, which was my life, my prayer, my – my blessing; and they – they tore it from me – tore it from me,' and she put her hand to her heart with a passionate gesture of despair, burying her face for a moment on the bed.

The brandy bottle inside clinked up against the plate which held the cold sausage. Both were moved, no doubt, by the exhibition of so much grief.

* scented oil

ANSWER

A1 In this passage, some readers may take pity on Becky because she has suffered bad luck and cruelty. She seems to be an innocent victim. She pours out her suffering, her lack of love and family, her loneliness, and she finally breaks down, unable to go on because she is so upset. This impression is caused by words such as 'tender' and 'despair'. Thackeray seems to add to this sentimental and sympathetic view of her by narrative detail by making her seem weak and vulnerable – her littleness and frailty are frequently mentioned.

Although she seems a victim, she is not that helpless or innocent. At the beginning of the passage, the author refers to her 'archness and mischief', and this fits the way she overacts the part of innocent victim. Everything she does is designed to get sympathy – like referring to her lost husband and child. When she breaks down in tears, she just happens to use a handkerchief with a letter J on it, which is the first letter of the name of her visitor, who she describes as the first man she ever saw. This suggests she has kept it since their first relationship.

The writer makes us look below the surface of appearance. He reminds us that she has hidden some things in order to appear innocent and charming. She hides her real motives just as she hides the signs of her real life – her make-up, her alcohol and her cold snack. In reality, her looks are now in need of help from cosmetics, her happiness comes from a bottle and she's living on junk food. The fact that these are below the surface reminds us that she is putting on a show. When Thackeray mentions the clinking of the bottle or the 'sausage', the reader is reminded of the real nature of her life which she is trying to hide. In the last line, he uses the word 'moved' literally to mean that the objects were displaced, but also to suggest that her speech was so emotionally moving that it could affect a brandy bottle and a sausage. This is such a comical thought that it stops us being sentimental or sympathetic. At first glance, this could be a romantic scene, but I think it shows Becky Sharp as a cunning woman trying to trap a man. Her life may be a bit of a wreck, but her 'poor me' attitude is only a façade.

TUTORIAL

T1 *This is a very good answer. It is well structured, the first part dealing with what may be thought, and the second paragraph looking more closely at motivation and behaviour. The last paragraph looks at the writer's narrative methods. This structure is well suited to discussion of different interpretations.*

There is sustained comment on Becky's speech and actions and the writer's use of language. There is developed comment on the handkerchief and the connection between concealed objects and concealed motives. There is close attention to language, particularly to 'moved' and the reference to smallness. Discussing the passage as one which could be sentimental or not shows ability to evaluate different interpretations, and there is analysis of Thackeray's methods in the references to the objects in the bed. As well as showing these strengths, there is a personal judgement at the end which shows strong engagement and insight.

William Thackeray.

CHAPTER 8

MAKING EFFECTIVE COMPARISONS

- In this chapter, you will learn to compare features of language, theme and attitude.
- If you can compare and contrast effectively, you will be able to show skills of appreciation and evaluation.

INTRODUCTION

When reading a passage or a poem, ask yourself firstly if the writer makes the same point, or uses the same kind of language, throughout the text. If you find that there is a range of ideas, and a variety of language, you can compare attitudes or ideas or language *within* the text you are dealing with. Secondly, try to remember anything else you have read that is similar, or different, in ideas or in the way language is used. This will allow you to make comparisons *between* passages and poems.

COMPARISON WITHIN A PASSAGE

You may want to compare two parts of a story where a character behaves in a similar way (allowing you to sustain a statement about character) or two parts where a character behaves differently or is changed (allowing you to develop a point about complexity of development of character). An example of the latter might be:

You may want to compare two parts of a story where a character behaves differently or is changed.

> He goes from being shy and nervous to being more confident. In the first paragraph, he is surprised that everybody is so happy, and he is surprised that they welcome him. For example, he thought the staff were 'remarkably cheerful' and he was 'reassured' to find a desk to work with his name on it. But later, he had got used to this and began to expect more, when he said, 'I don't see why I should stay late because the place is in chaos'.

COMPARISONS BETWEEN TEXTS

Alternatively, you may want to show a similarity or a difference between two separate accounts:

> In both of these passages, you can see how parents influence their children, and how children react to problems by getting angry, but they have to learn that sometimes it's better to be calm and think before doing anything rash. The first one shows you how the mother has strong feelings but hides them, but the other one only gives you the child's feelings.

You may also want to compare two characters responding to a situation. Your comparison will be more effective if you deal with differences *and* similarities, as this shows that you can explore and evaluate.

They have different ideas about education and children. The Headmistress thinks kids need to be kept in order, and the teacher thinks they need freedom. She doesn't trust them, and he does. Anyway, you realise that he's too soft when they are rude behind his back and make up excuses for not doing their work and she's a bit hard when she won't listen to the kids. They're both a bit right and a bit wrong.

STRUCTURED COMPARISON

A structured comparison needs to make clear which things are alike and which are not. You should try to structure your comparison by pointing out things which are similar and things which are different; this will give your comments a sense of range and discrimination. It is also worth saying something about style as well as meaning. For example, it is more effective to write:

Although both of these poems are written in blank verse and modern language (and one is a sonnet and the other one is a double sonnet), they give a very different impression of war.

Than:

These two poems take a different view of the subject of war.

Commenting on style as well as subject matter shows that your study is not of the war itself, but of poetry written about the war.

EXTENDED COMPARISON

Sometimes you may be asked to compare two poems which are similar, and sometimes to contrast two poems which are different. The similarity or difference may be in one or a combination of the following:

- ideas;
- attitudes;
- feelings;
- purpose;
- use of language;
- verse form.

In linking your comments about similarity and difference, there are some simple but very powerful words and phrases that will help you to go from a sustained response to a developed one, and to evaluate different qualities and responses. Starting a sentence with one of the following linking phrases shows that you can handle conflicting evidence or interpretation, and draw conclusions from evidence.

Although …	On the other hand, …
Alternatively, …	Perhaps …
Also, …	So …
Because …	Some people may think …
Despite …	This could mean …
Even if …	This may be …
However, …	This suggests …

COMPARING IDEAS, ATTITUDES AND FEELINGS

Anything you read will contain feelings and attitudes, and will also produce feelings and attitudes in you. Try to deal with both of these aspects in your comparison, so that you show understanding of what the writer feels and thinks, and explore your response to those feelings and ideas. After all, you may share the writer's feelings and attitudes or you may not! Remember, too, that other people may respond differently. Anything you add to show how others may respond – or may have responded at the time of writing – will improve your comments, as shown in the following example:

> Rupert Brooke's poem (1914) makes war exciting and almost refreshing and fun when he writes about it like 'swimmers into cleanness leaping'. Wilfred Owen (in 'Dulce et Decorum Est') doesn't see it as sport, though, and he makes out that it's like falling into something which kills you, so you're 'drowning' and choking for breath. When you read Rupert Brooke's poem, you think 'Yes, I'll have a go' but then you read Wilfred's and you think, 'I'm not going to risk that happening to me,' so he's warned you off. When they were writing, young men were being encouraged to join up, and Brooke's poem would have made them feel good about it.

Comparing different images of war.

COMPARING PURPOSE, LANGUAGE AND FORM

As well as commenting on *what* a poet has to say, you need to comment on the *how* and *why*. The previous example does some of this, but it's worth making sure that you've said something about the author's intentions. You may not be certain about this – and there's usually no way of telling if you're right – but you should explore an author's reasons for choosing to write in the first place, and choosing form and words for the purpose.

> He's probably not as strong as his father, or he's no good at physical work like digging. You can tell he admires him when he writes as if he's proud of his Dad, almost boasting about him, 'By God the old man could handle a spade'. When he thinks that his pen is his spade, and he can still be good at something like his Dad, he writes a short sentence as if he's made his mind up and settled something, 'I'll dig with it'.

COMPARING YOUR OWN ATTITUDES

It is good to show that your own response to a character or situation can develop and change over the course of your reading. This shows that you are an active reader, not content with a quick opinion that you stick with for the rest of the book. Recording how your view changes can be a useful way of showing response to a poem's structure, or the way a writer has presented an idea.

> When I first read it, I thought she was safe from the lion because she wasn't afraid of it, and the poet's message was that you shouldn't be afraid of things, but it still eats her in the end, which I didn't expect. The poem is called 'A Cautionary Tale' so it's warning you that fear can be a useful thing, really.

Recording the way in which you have two or more attitudes to something shows that you can cope with complexity and ambiguity. If you can show two ways of responding then decide on one, you will have shown ability to evaluate alternative responses. Useful phrases in this context include:

This could mean …

Another meaning is that …

I think it's this because …

WHAT MAKES THE GRADE?

For a Grade C you need to give a personal response to the ideas and feelings conveyed by what you have read, and comment on aspects of language and structure.

For a Grade B you need to explain what is characteristic of a writer's style, or of the time it was written. You also need to comment on ideas and attitudes which are relevant to life today or to the time when the author was writing.

For a Grade A you need to make comparisons between different texts and different writers, commenting on similarities and differences in ideas or language. You should be able to make judgements about why one text is better than another, or explain why a text has become to be regarded as a major achievement.

Check yourself

Q1 Re-read Hughes' poem *Thistles* below and then read the following poem by Jon Stallworthy, also called *Thistles*. Compare the two, making a list of the similarities and differences between them.

Against the rubber tongues of cows and the hoeing hands of men
Thistles spike the summer air
Or crackle open under a blue-black pressure

Every one a revengeful burst
Of resurrection, a grasped fistful
Of splintered weapons and Icelandic frost thrust up

From the underground stain of a decayed Viking.
They are like pale hair and the gutturals of dialects.
Every one manages a plume of blood.

Then they grow grey like men.
Mown down, it is a feud. Their sons appear,
Stiff with weapons, fighting back over the same ground.

Ted Hughes

Half grown before half seen,
like urchins in armour
double their size they stand
their ground boldly, their keen
swords out. But the farmer
ignores them. Not a hand

will he lift to cut them down:
they are not worth his switch
he says. Uncertain whom
they challenge, having grown
into their armour, each
breaks out a purple plume.

Under this image
of their warrior blood
they make a good death,
meeting the farmer's blade
squarely in their old age.
White then as winter breath

from every white head
a soul springs up. The wind
is charged with spirits: no –
not spirits of the dead
for these are living, will land
at our backs and go

to ground. Farmer and scythe
sing to each other. He
cannot see how roots writhe
underfoot, how the sons
of this fallen infantry
will separate our bones.

Jon Stallworthy

ANSWER

A1 **Similarities**
Attitude and ideas
Respect for savagery and survival of a
natural species
Nature a battleground

Language suggesting warfare
Hughes: 'spike', 'weapons', 'feud', 'fighting',
'plume of blood'
Stallworthy: 'armour', 'swords', 'warrior',
'infantry', 'purple plume'

Animating language
Hughes: 'revengeful', 'fistful', 'hair', 'sons'
Stallworthy: 'boldly', 'challenge', 'head',
'meeting', 'writhe', 'sons'

Differences
Verse
Hughes: capitalised line-beginnings, blank
verse
Stallworthy: not capitalised at line
beginnings, so looks informal, but has firm
structure of rhyme, varied at the end

Attitude and ideas
Hughes: connection with warriors/invaders
of the past – Vikings
Stallworthy: present-day warriors without a
battle to fight

Hughes: resurrection/rebirth
Stallworthy: spirits live on

Hughes: thistles resist a farmer's chopping
Stallworthy: thistles accept being chopped
down in old age

Hughes: revengeful against man
Stallworthy: warrior-like but not sure who
their enemy is

Hughes: makes them carry on the battle
through their offspring
Stallworthy: makes them appear longer-
lasting than man, rather than in conflict
with man.

TUTORIAL

T1 *These two poems are similar in their use of metaphorical language to create a sense of warrior-like toughness. The attitudes of both writers are also similar, admiring this wild plant. They both make Nature seem a battleground, but Hughes makes the battle with man more obvious. The main differences are in Stallworthy's use of rhyme (though it is not immediately obvious) and his view of thistles as patiently outliving men, rather than confronting them.*

SELECTING AND USING TEXTUAL REFERENCES

- In this chapter, you will learn how to use textual references efficiently and appropriately.
- If you use textual references well, you can show knowledge, and ability to select, illustrate and comment.

INTRODUCTION

When you comment on texts you need to be very clear about the points you are making. You will not get high marks for rambling on about what you think if it is not closely related to what you have read. It's very important to support your comments with appropriate references, and it's also important to do something purposeful with them. Merely quoting chunks of text will not help you, as copying doesn't show any skill in understanding, explaining or analysing what you have read.

ILLUSTRATIVE REFERENCES (*TECHNIQUE*)

When you comment on the way something is written, you need to identify what the writer is doing, and give an example which illustrates it. You can use a technical term if you wish, but it is more important to show how the technique works. In the following examples, the students don't mention alliteration, but it is clear that they understand it and can comment on the way it is used:

> He uses words with sounds which are like the sound of water – like 's' and 'sh' sounds in the line 'the shingle scrambles under the sucking surf'.
>
> He doesn't say straight out that the machine is alive, but the words he uses to describe it are words that make you think of a living creature – 'hiss' and 'flank' and 'iron muscles'.

Listing literary devices is pointless unless you are able to comment further.

What is important is that you don't simply list features. Always pick out some detail and comment on it. There's no point in saying that the writer uses onomatopoeia or a simile and a metaphor without some detail and explanation of how these things create meaning and feeling.

SUPPORTIVE REFERENCES (ARGUMENT)

When you are stating an opinion as part of an argument or the answer to a question, you need to make a clear statement then follow it with some evidence which fits what you are saying.

> She is quite a fussy person. She doesn't like dirt and she has a dream about living in a perfect country cottage with a perfect country stream and a perfect family. You can tell this because she doesn't just walk down the path, she 'picks her way daintily' and her feet 'wince' on the cinders. She doesn't think much of the garden or the cottage because she doesn't want to live in a place 'like this'. Another thing that tells you about her is the way she thinks the boy is oily and dirty but he is only like this because he works with cars.

It's useful to include some details which *don't* support your argument, so that you can show that you have looked at two views before deciding on one:

> Although he offers to help and gives her some money, which could be kind, he's really doing it to keep her quiet and make her think that he's really generous and on her side.

RUNNING REFERENCE

This is a useful way of using quotation without spending time writing out full lines. Use just what you need to show your knowledge.

> The scene has violence in it from the start, because in the opening line the clouds are 'slashed' and the sunlight that peeps through 'leaks' like blood from a wound, and the gulls are 'flaked off' the sky by squalls which are 'abrasive', like a Brillo pad!

DISPLAY REFERENCE

This is where you may quote a few lines and display them with indentation to make them stand out. This is fine, but don't expect marks if this is all you do! Make sure that if you quote a few lines, something in each line has a comment. Examiners will expect you to use more lines in writing your comment than you use to write out your quotation. Look at this example of a commentary following a display:

> Slashed clouds leak gold. Along the slurping wharf
> The snugged boats creak and seesaw. Round the masts
> Abrasive squalls flake seagulls off the sky

> There is a lot of violence in this scene, with violent verbs ('slashed' and 'flaked') used to contrast with the cosiness of the harbour ('snugged'), and the gusts of wind are rough and 'abrasive', so that even seagulls can't stay in the sky.

In this case, the commentary offers no more than the example of running quotation above, so it is worth asking whether the displayed three lines are worth writing out at all. If it's not necessary to display quotations, don't. Use time and ink for detailed comment instead.

MAKING THE MOST OF REFERENCES: SECSI

If you are making a point about something you have read, it helps to have a purposeful paragraph structure, so that it is clear to your reader what you are doing. SECSI (an acronym of Statement, Evidence, Comment, Scheme of things, Interpretation) is one practical way of making the most of quotation:

Statement

You open with your opinion, attitude or idea, for example: Wilfred Owen wanted to shock his readers.

Evidence

Display your reference, for example:

> Blood comes gargling from the froth-corrupted lungs
> Obscene as cancer, vile as incurable sores on innocent tongues

Wilfred Owen.

Comment

You make sustained comments on your reference:

> He chooses images which are frightening and repulsive – not just 'froth-corrupted' lungs, which is something you can see, but 'gargling' blood, which is something you can hear. And then he compares it with diseased 'innocent' tongues which makes it seem unfair. All the time he chooses words with ugly harsh sounds 'g' and 'c (k) ' and lots of hissing 's' sounds.

Scheme of things

This is connected with the writer's purpose in ideas, style or attitude:

> He wanted to be realistic and make the reader see real physical details instead of images of flags and duty and heroic deeds. He was like a documentary poet not a propaganda poet and he thought people like Jessie Pope used pretty words to hide ugly facts, so he used ugly words for truth.

Interpretations

Show that ambiguity in the text, or different attitudes in different readers, can result in opposing responses.

> Some people may think this is horrible and disgusting because they don't want to read about people's lungs being frothy with gas when you read a poem, but I think he is saying we shouldn't expect poetry to be pretty and nice but about real things that are happening that matter. It is the truth and he said he was not concerned with Poetry (big P) but with pity.

The SECSI sequence allows you to show engagement with an issue, insight into textual detail, personal response and awareness of effects on different readers.

The SECSI sequence can be very valuable when you are analysing text.

STATEMENT
EVIDENCE
COMMENT
SCHEME OF THINGS
INTERPRETATIONS

▶ **WHAT MAKES THE GRADE?**

For a Grade C, you need to sustain references to aspects of language, structure and themes to support your views.

For a Grade B, you need to develop detailed references to language, theme, structure and contrast.

For a Grade A, you need to analyse language, structure and presentation, making apt and careful references to what you have read.

Check yourself

QUESTIONS

Q1 Here is a poem (*Last Lesson of the Afternoon* by D. H. Lawrence) and a student's response to it which makes general comments and general reference. What detailed references from the poem could you choose to lift the response to a higher grade? The numbered brackets in the response indicate where a reference could be included.

When will the bell ring, and end this weariness?
How long have they tugged the leash and strained apart,
My pack of unruly hounds! I cannot start
Them again on a quarry of knowledge they hate to hunt,
I can haul them and urge them no more.

No longer now can I endure the brunt
Of the books that lie out on the desks; a full threescore
Of several insults of blotted pages, and scrawl
Of slovenly work that they have offered me.
I am sick, and what on earth is the good of it all?
What good to them or me I cannot see!

So, shall I take
My last dear fuel of life to heap on my soul
And kindle my will to a flame that shall consume
Their dross of indifference; and take the toll
Of their insults in punishment? – I will not!
– I will not waste my soul and my strength for this.
What do I care for all they do amiss?
What is the point of all this learning of mine, and of this
Learning of theirs? It all goes down the same abyss.
What does it matter to me, if they can write
A description of a dog, or if they can't?
What is the point? To us both it is all my aunt!
And yet, I'm supposed to care, with all my might.

I do not and will not; they won't and they don't; and that's all!
I shall keep my strength for myself; they can keep theirs as well.
Why should we beat our heads against the wall
Of each other? I shall sit and wait for the bell.

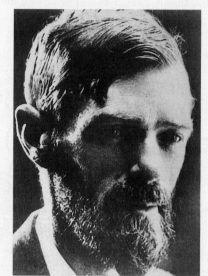

D.H. Lawrence.

This poem is about a teacher who doesn't like his job. He seems tired
[1] and he doesn't want to go on. Their work is really bad [2]. He
uses words for controlling them that make it seem like hard work
[3]. The class have been hard to handle and he can't control them
because they've been fighting against him [4]. I don't think he likes
them much because he thinks of them as animals and him a trainer
[5]. He uses a metaphor in lines 2–5 about him having to hunt
knowledge with them, but he can't anymore [6]. He uses metaphors
again when he talks about his energy like a fire burning, but he's
running out of fuel. There are lots of words to do with fire there [7].
His attitude is that his life is precious to him [8] and the kids don't
seem to care about him [9] so why should he bother. He thinks it's a
waste of time trying because he can't get through to them and they
can't get through to him so it's pointless and can only lead to getting
hurt [10]. I think he should get a grip because he's paid to teach
them and they need exams.

REMEMBER! Cover the answers if you want to.

ANSWER

A1

1 'weariness' or 'no longer ...' or 'I am sick'
2 'blotted' or 'scrawl' or 'slovenly'
3 'haul' or 'urge'
4 'tugged' or 'strained' or 'unruly'
5 'My ... unruly hounds' and 'hunt'
6 'I cannot start them again on a quarry of knowledge...'
7 'fuel', 'kindle', 'flame'
8 'my last dear fuel of life'
9 'insults', 'dross of indifference'
10 'beat our heads against the wall of each other'

TUTORIAL

T1

This response sustains comment on the teacher's feelings but doesn't develop comment on the stated or implied attitude of the children.

There could be comment on the implications of 'tugging the leash' as a metaphor for resisting control or a sign of enthusiasm for other things they find interesting. His view of their blotted and scrawled writing is that it is an insult to him, rather than a sign of their ability or needs.

There is a lively personal response at the end which relates to his attitude, but it is better to look at motivation from two angles rather than one. He may seem not to care about his job or the children's futures, but there could be exploration of what has caused his loss of interest.

It is worth analysing the poem for the frequency of words related to hunting, and exploring the appropriateness of this image and its effect on different readers. Lawrence's intention may have been to gain sympathy as a weary pack leader, but his view of children as a pack, and knowledge as something to hunt as if it is the prey, may tell us of Lawrence's attitude to children and to learning, as well as to teaching. The final comment could therefore be developed, pointing out its implications for real life.

CHAPTER 10

FACT AND OPINION

- In this chapter, you will learn to distinguish fact from opinion in non-fiction texts.
- If you can recognise what is fact and what is opinion, it will help you interpret writers' purposes and methods.

WHAT IS FACTUAL WRITING?

Very little writing – even if it is labelled 'non-fiction' – is purely factual. Writers find it very hard to keep their opinions and judgements out of what they write. Let's start with a fairly straightforward example. Look at this advertisement for a house.

SAUNTON

£249,000
- Magnificently situated individual detached house
- Superb south facing views over the golf course and out to sea • Central heating • 4 bedrooms
- 2 receptions • Bathroom • Shower room
- Cloaks • Detached garage • Approx 1 acre

How much of the description is factual and how much is opinion? Sometimes the two are mixed up within one statement, like the very first one where the facts are that the house is individual and detached, but the statement that it is magnificently situated must be a matter of opinion. If we were to set out the facts and opinions in columns, it would look like this:

Facts
- individual, detached house
- south-facing views over the golf course and out to sea
- central heating
- 4 bedrooms
- 2 reception rooms
- bathroom
- shower room
- cloakrooms

Opinions
- magnificently situated
- superb
- approx. 1 acre

Why is 'approx. 1 acre' in the Opinions column? Because what one person regards as close to one acre may be seen as considerably less than one acre by someone else! This illustrates the problem concerning fact and opinion: the more you think about some examples, the less clear cut they become. So should 'individual' be in the Facts column? Is it not possible that there is another house built to exactly the same design somewhere else? In the end, you have to use a combination of common sense and judgement in making such decisions.

BURIED OPINIONS

Just to complicate matters further, you may find opinions buried within facts!
Look at this passage from Paul Theroux's account of a journey around the
coast of Great Britain, *The Kingdom by the Sea*:

> In 1791, the Royal Sea-Bathing Infirmary was founded on the western
> cliffs of Margate. But nothing improved the tone of the place. In 1824, a
> traveller wrote, 'From an obscure fishing village, Margate, in the course of
> little more than half a century, has risen into a well-frequented, if not
> fashionable, watering-place.' A hundred years later, Baedeker's *Great
> Britain* described Margate as 'one of the most popular, though not one of
> the most fashionable watering-places in England.' So it had always been
> crummy and Cockneyfied, just like this, people down from London for the
> day shunting back and forth on the front in the cold rain, and walking
> their dogs and gloomily fishing and looking at each other.

Opinions within facts? Yes, because it is a fact that the 1824 traveller and the
Baedeker guidebook include the statements Theroux quotes, but those
statements are themselves only opinions. In this passage, there are some
obvious facts: the whole of the first sentence, and some of the last – we can
presume there were Londoners in Margate when Theroux visited, that it was
raining, that some people were walking dogs and some were fishing. But – to
stay with that last sentence – it is only Theroux's opinion that Margate was
'crummy and Cockneyfied'; and could a descriptive word like 'shunting' ever
be a fact, rather than an opinion, since no two people would probably agree
what it means? And would everyone have judged the rain to be cold, and were
all the people fishing 'gloomy'? Were any of them gloomy, or was it a case of
the writer transferring his own feelings about the place to other people?

*In Theroux's opinion Margate is
'crummy and Cockneyfied'.*

BURIED FACTS

The example from Theroux shows how careful you need to be when dealing with what may appear to be factual material. As stated earlier, you might think that categories of writing called 'non-fiction' really ought to be factual, but you cannot rely on that. Even autobiography may at times contain very few facts. Take this passage from Roald Dahl's *Going Solo*:

> It would seem that when the British live for years in a foul and sweaty climate among foreign people they maintain their sanity by allowing themselves to go slightly dotty. They cultivate bizarre habits that would never be tolerated back home, whereas in far-away Africa or in Ceylon or in India or in the Federated Malay States they could do as they liked. On the SS Mantola just about everybody had his or her own particular maggot in the brain, and for me it was like watching a kind of non-stop pantomime throughout the entire voyage.

I don't believe there is a single fact in the whole extract, but we can infer some – that is, read between the lines. 'Buried facts' of that kind would be:

- Roald Dahl had (possibly) visited Africa, Ceylon, and the Federated Malay States;
- he had been on a ship called the SS Mantola;
- there were men and women on the ship;
- he considered his fellow passengers to be 'slightly dotty'.

THE NEED FOR COMMON SENSE

If you are asked to identify facts and opinions in a passage, don't forget the 'buried' kind illustrated here. But equally, don't look for difficulties that aren't there: if a diary entry tells you that the author was 45 years old on that day, then believe it and don't wonder if (s)he had made an error! However distrustful you may be of advertising, you must accept that certain details of products or items (such as price, weight, country of manufacture, etc.) are more than likely to be factual, or the companies placing the advertisements would be in trouble with the Trade Descriptions Act.

WHAT MAKES THE GRADE? ▶

Distinguishing between fact and opinion is not assessed in isolation in the GCSE examination, but is likely to be part of broader questions asking you to comment on the effectiveness of non-fiction materials. One important aspect you should comment on is how the materials attempt to make you react in particular ways, and how this is done; the mix of fact and opinion may be one of the techniques used by writers to influence your feelings and reactions.

Check yourself

Q1 Look at the leaflet below about Granary Wharf in Leeds. On a piece of paper, head two columns 'Facts' and 'Opinions' and copy *all* the written information from the leaflet into the appropriate column.

Q2 a) How do you think the writer hopes readers will react to this leaflet?
b) How does the writer go about achieving this reaction?

G R A N A R Y   W H A R F

A unique place

Entertainments,

special events, music,

workshops, canal walks,

boat trips and eating

facilities for all

tastes...there's always plenty to see and do at

Granary Wharf.

It's friendly, it's fun

and it's free.

G R A N A R Y   W H A R F

FESTIVAL MARKET

30 shops, open 7 days a week

A fascinating selection of original goods and gifts, and a festival market (up to sixty additional stalls) every Saturday, Sunday and Bank Holiday Monday.

Shops open 10.00am to 5.30pm.

Right in the centre of Leeds

Granary Wharf is behind the Hilton Hotel in

Neville Street, just two

minutes walk from

Leeds Railway Station.

Access is via the

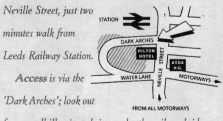

'Dark Arches'; look out

for a small illuminated sign under the railway bridge.

Ample parking. Special arrangements

for coaches.

GRANARY WHARF THE CANAL BASIN
LEEDS LS1 4BR TEL (0113) 2446570

Design: Ian Cave 0113 2740104

ANSWERS

A1 **Facts**
- entertainments, special events, music, workshops, canal walks, boat trips and eating facilities
- it's free
- 30 shops, open seven days a week
- a festival market (up to 60 additional stalls) every Saturday, Sunday and Bank Holiday Monday
- shops open 10 am to 5.30 pm
- Granary Wharf is behind the Hilton Hotel in Neville Street
- access is via the 'Dark Arches'
- illuminated sign under the railway bridge
- parking
- special arrangements for coaches
- address/telephone number

Opinions
- a unique place
- for all tastes
- there's always plenty to see and do
- it's friendly, it's fun
- a fascinating selection of original goods and gifts
- right in the centre of Leeds
- just two minutes' walk from Leeds Railway Station
- (look out for a) small (illuminated sign)
- ample (parking)

A2 a) The writer hopes readers will want to visit Granary Wharf because it will be a new experience for them. It will be enjoyable for the whole family because there are shops and entertainments and places to eat. The writer hopes that readers will think it is easy to get to Granary Wharf because it is 'right in the centre of Leeds'.

b) The writer uses colourful photographs to attract the reader, and large, eye-catching headlines. The language is easy to understand and makes Granary Wharf sound different and interesting. The name of Granary Wharf is printed at the top of both pages and is mentioned twice in the text. There is also a logo at the bottom of each page and details of the address, so the name and place becomes fixed in the reader's mind.

TUTORIALS

T1 *You should have found that task quite straightforward: words and phrases such as 'unique', 'for all tastes', 'always plenty to see and do', 'friendly', 'fun', 'fascinating' and 'original' are almost always going to reflect opinion rather than fact.*

There are some less obvious expressions of opinion, however. Not everyone would necessarily agree that Granary Wharf is 'right in the centre of Leeds', and since not everyone is able to walk at the same speed, it can't be 'just two minutes' walk from Leeds Railway Station' for everyone. The 'small' illuminated sign might appear to be anything but small if it shines into someone's bedroom window at night; and whether the parking is 'ample' or not will presumably depend on how many visitors turn up on particular days.

T2 a) *A better answer would quote 'unique'. A reference to the photos which show different attractions and people of all ages enjoying them would help. Add specific detail, e.g. Granary Wharf is close to the railway station and there is parking for cars/coaches.*

b) *You could point out that the headlines are in a larger-size print than the text, and the text on the left-hand page (which is the text mostly designed to attract) is larger than that on the right-hand page (which is mostly information). Comment on specific uses of language, e.g. the memorable effect of repetition and alliteration in 'it's friendly, it's fun and it's free'.*

Chapters 14 and 15 give more detail about the use of language and of structural and presentational devices in non-fiction texts.

CHAPTER 11

HOW INFORMATION IS PRESENTED

- In this chapter, you will learn how to recognise different ways in which information may be presented in non-fiction texts.

- If you can interpret information presented in a variety of ways, and comment on the effectiveness of the presentation, you will demonstrate high-level reading skills.

WHAT'S WRONG WITH WORDS?

When you think about reading, you probably think about words. In fact, many texts use other devices in addition to words, or even entirely in place of them. Where non-fiction texts are concerned, diagrams, charts, figures, pictures, maps or graphs may sometimes be a more efficient and effective way of conveying information than words alone.

In Chapters 1–9, you learned to interpret the language of literary texts, reading beyond the surface meaning of words to reach your own understanding and to establish the authors' intentions. That is a central purpose of reading literature, and as long as literary texts are read for pleasure, people will enjoy debating their meaning.

That debate would be highly inappropriate as far as most non-literary texts are concerned. These texts usually need to convey information precisely and unambiguously, and 'interpretation' is the last thing their writers want. In an effort to be precise, knowing that people often interpret words differently, writers of non-fiction frequently seek additional or different ways to convey their information.

In this chapter, we will look in turn at various categories of non-fiction writing, at some of the different presentational techniques they use and at how effective they are.

AUTOBIOGRAPHY AND BIOGRAPHY

In writing about their own or other peoples' lives, authors will often use pictures, especially photographs, both to make the text look more attractive and to allow the reader to visualise people, places and events more accurately. In *Going Solo*, Roald Dahl uses a variety of pictorial material; why do you think he includes the following copy of a flying assessment in one chapter?

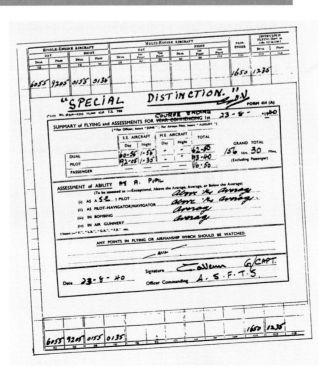

Roald Dahl might have used that photocopied sheet because:

- it would be quite complicated to describe in words;
- the detail would not interest everyone;
- anyone particularly interested can read it carefully for themselves;
- he might not have wished to seem vain by writing directly about his 'Special Distinction'.

JOURNALS, DIARIES AND LETTERS

Writers sometimes move away from straightforward text to convey a particular feeling or strong emotion. What sort of person do you think would start a letter to someone called Mr Fortescue in this way?

My dear 4oscue,

I came to 'leave a card' on you, as you axed me to the dinner yesterday – here it is –

The answer is Edward Lear, who you may have heard of as the nineteenth-century author of nonsense rhymes and other humorous texts such as *The Owl and the Pussycat*. Lear's personality would be hard to convey by conventional written means!

A quite different emotion is conveyed by George Bernard Shaw in a letter to his friend Stella Campbell. Shaw had heard of the death of Stella's son in the First World War; he sent a typed letter of sympathy to her which finishes in this way:

Oh damn, damn, damn, damn, damn, damn, damn, damn, DAMN

And oh, dear, dear, dear, dear, dear, dearest!

G.B.S.

The large hand-written 'DAMN!' gains huge effect by contrast with the neatly typed text around it.

TRAVEL WRITING

In Chapter 10 we discussed some examples of travel writing, which, although classed as non-fiction, often presents very personal opinions and views. In that way, it is similar to biography and autobiography, and tends to make similar use of pictures, maps and charts to add to the interest of the text and sometimes to hint at the author's ideas.

LEAFLETS

Many leaflets contain a great deal of potentially complicated information, and may therefore present it in various ways so that different people can understand it. For example, the Department of the Environment produced a leaflet in 1994 about saving energy. It contains ten pages of prose on the subject of how to save money and at the same time produce less carbon dioxide. On the back cover of the leaflet is this chart:

Ten Things *You* Can Do at Home (in cost order)	Typical cost (one-off payment) £	Typical annual saving £	Typical annual CO_2 saving kg
Only use the heat, lights and appliances you need	0	15–40	190–500
Lag your hot water tank	5–10*	10–15	125–190
Lag your hot water pipes	5–10*	5–10	60–125
Use energy-saving light bulbs**	5–15	10	85
Add to your heating system:			
– thermostat	10–15*	10–20	125–250
– thermostatic radiator valves	45–75*	10–20	125–250
– timer/programmer	35–45*	20–25	250–320
Fit draught-proofing to windows and doors	45–60*	10–20	125–250
Loft insulation should be 6 inches thick***			
– DIY	110–160*	60–70	750–880
– contractor	190–300	60–70	750–880
Install plastic secondary double glazing	120–600*	15–25	190–320
If you have cavity walls, seek advice on cavity wall insulation***	300–500	60–70	750–880
If you have an old central heating boiler, fit an energy efficient condensing boiler***	400–600# (extra cost compared with ordinary boiler)	100–130 (compared with old boiler)	1250–1700 (compared with old boiler)

*	DIY costs shown for these items
**	Annual savings figures relate to an average of four hours use per day, and include savings on the cost of replacement bulbs
***	Installing these items will lead to the most significant cuts in your fuel bills and in CO_2 emissions
#	Cost shown for gas condensing boiler, but oil-fired model also available

Some people prefer to read charts, while others prefer to read text if given the choice. The point is, that both groups of people would have been able to get the same information from this leaflet, but in their preferred style, because it uses both approaches.

NEWSPAPER ARTICLES

We shall look at aspects of newspapers in more detail in Chapter 17, but it is worth noting here that newspaper articles often use a range of graphic devices to present information. An article in *The Guardian* about the pop music industry contained the following graphs. Why do you think the information was presented in this way?

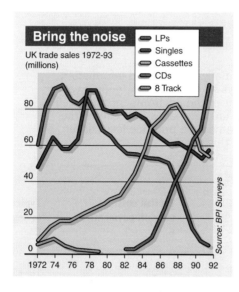

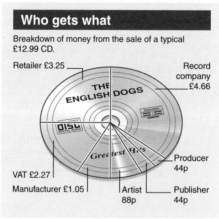

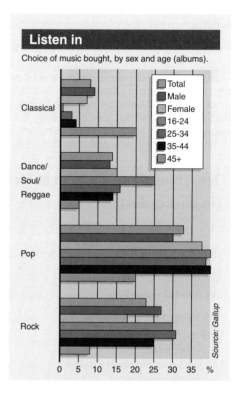

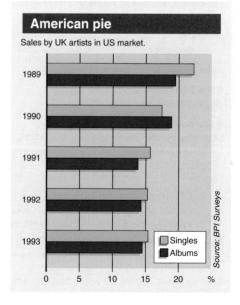

The most obvious reason for using graphs is that it saves the newspaper a vast amount of space. If you were asked to explain in words all the information given in these graphs, and all the possible interpretations of it, it would run to several pages of print. These last two examples, from the energy leaflet and the newspaper, underline the fact that to be a competent reader in this day and age you have to be able to read much more than words.

FACTUAL AND INFORMATIVE MATERIAL

All kinds of text come under this heading, including instructions for assembling or using items. As an example, look at this extract from the instructions for an answering machine:

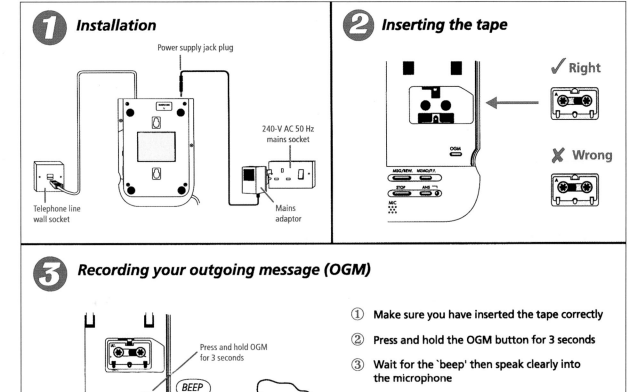

Do the pictures help? On the whole, yes, although you may have had to look very closely at the two pictures of tapes in Panel 2 before you could tell the difference between right and wrong. When words and pictures are used together in Panel 3, it is potentially confusing, as the talking head does not appear to be speaking into the microphone, as required in the instructions! So pictures, diagrams and charts can help, but they have as much potential for confusion as words.

WHAT MAKES THE GRADE?

When assessing your skills in reading non-fiction texts, examiners will be looking for you to comment on issues such as visual images and other aspects of presentation, as well as language. To move from a Grade D to Grade C, you need to show more than just understanding; you need to show some insight into the effect that the text might have on readers. To gain a Grade A, you need to analyse the kind of readers who might be influenced by such material, and why it might affect them in particular ways.

Check yourself

Look at the following extract from a booklet called 'Beach Safety Guidelines'.

Don't go alone

■ Swim with a friend – **Never go on your own**.

■ Make sure there are other people around - you never know when help might be needed.

Learn how to help

■ If you see someone in difficulty, tell somebody, preferably a Lifeguard if there is one nearby, **or**

■ Go to the nearest telephone, dial **999**, ask for the **Coastguard**

■ You can learn lifesaving and rescue skills.

Contact:

The Royal Life Saving Society UK on **01527 853943** or

The Surf Life Saving Association of Great Britain on **01392 254364**

THE WATER SAFETY CODE

FLAGS AND SIGNS TO LOOK OUT FOR

Learn what these flags mean

Red and yellow flags means Lifeguards are on patrol. You should only swim or boogie board in the area between the flags.

The red flag means it is dangerous to bathe or swim and you should not go into the water.

The quartered black and white flag indicates the area zoned for surf craft and malibu boards. It is not safe for swimmers and bathers.

Signs for your safety should look like these

FLAGS AND SIGNS

QUESTIONS

Q1 What is the purpose of this information?

Q2 In what different ways does it try to achieve its purpose?

Q3 What effect would the writer want it to have on its readers?

Q4 What different audiences might this booklet be aimed at?

ANSWERS

A1 To prevent accidents to swimmers at the seaside.

A2 By telling swimmers what to do and by showing information about seaside warnings.

A3 To make them think about being more careful when swimming.

A4 People who go swimming on the beach.

TUTORIALS

T1 This is a basic 'D-ish' answer. To move safely into Grade C and beyond, a more detailed answer would also suggest: to encourage more people to learn lifesaving and rescue skills, and to educate the public about the meaning of flags and other signs seen near beaches.

T2 Another basic answer. It could be improved by being more specific: swimmers (and potential rescuers) are given clear, bullet-pointed instructions; the flags and signs are shown in their exact shapes and colours. The cartoons should be mentioned: they attract attention because they make the page layout look more appealing, and some people will find them amusing.

T3 But also to be aware when others might be in difficulty, and to learn to avoid possible dangers by recognising warning signs.

T4 A good answer will recognise that information may have more than just the most obvious audience: this would also be of interest to parents, to people who might be attracted to train as lifesavers, to surfers who want to avoid causing problems to swimmers, and to members of the general public who want to know the meaning of warning flags and other signs at the seaside.

◀ *These pages are reproduced by kind permission of the RNLI's Sea Safety Initiative and a copy of the free booklet entitled 'Beach Safety Guidelines' is available by phoning 01202 663174.*

CHAPTER 12

FOLLOWING AN ARGUMENT

- In this chapter, you will learn to follow an argument in a piece of non-fiction text. You will also see how to identify what is implied rather than stated openly and recognise where arguments are not completely logical.

- If you are able to show insight when analysing the structure of non-fiction text, you will gain a high grade at GCSE.

WHAT'S IT ALL ABOUT?

Mastering this set of skills is crucial to show your ability in interpreting and analysing non-fiction text. To make clear what you need to achieve, this chapter will look in considerable detail at one complete text, a leaflet advertising Urathon bicycle tyres. It is a useful text for our purposes, since it is very clearly structured and quite simply laid out.

Have a good look at the whole leaflet (pages 89–90) before you read any further, so that you have a feel for the whole text before we look at parts of it in more detail.

THE PURPOSE OF THE LEAFLET

What would you say is the purpose of the leaflet? Clearly it is to sell Urathon cycle tyres. To achieve this purpose, the leaflet has to persuade you of several things: that you need the tyres, that they're suitable for your bicycle, that they're easily available, easily fitted, not too expensive, etc.

The structure of the argument is made very clear. Your attention is first captured by the headline on the cover: 100% PUNCTURE-PROOF TYRES! If you are a cyclist – and you probably wouldn't be reading this leaflet in real life unless you were – you would almost certainly be attracted by this promise.

THE STRUCTURE

Now that you have been drawn into the leaflet, you open it and see two columns of print either side of a large photograph (page 90). We'll return to the photograph later, but look for now at the print: see how it is divided into five sections, each with a bold headline.

These headlines take you through the argument and set out the reasons why you should buy these tyres. The first section reassures you that the tyres are available for all kinds of bicycles, and in a range of 'different' colours.

The next section sets out technical details of the tyres' construction, backed up by a diagram, then returns at the end to the reassurance that punctures are a problem of the past.

The third section moves on to the issue of safety, and links this to the coloured tyres, so these are no longer seen as just a fun idea, but a sensible choice.

Section four develops the safety theme, reminding you of what might happen if you suffer a puncture.

The last section tells you how simple it is to actually have your bicycle fitted with these tyres.

THE PRICE IS RIGHT

From £13.95 a tyre (with fitting FREE), URATHON Tyres are no more expensive than a conventional tyre. But they last longer and we guarantee that punctures will never stop you again!

Just call into your nearest ATS centre and say goodbye to punctures!

URATHON BIKE TYRES - The toughest tyres on the planet.

ATS.

YOUR LOCAL ATS CENTRE IS :

If you have difficulty finding URATHON PUNCTURE-PROOF TYRES call the TYRELINE on **01249 760 585.**

Urathon
BIKE TYRES -
guaranteed not to let you down!

GUARANTEED NOT TO LET YOU DOWN

Years of research and development have meant that we can now offer this revolutionary new tyre to fit all standard sizes of bike wheel. Virtually identical in ride and performance to normal tyres, URATHON Tyres are GUARANTEED NOT TO PUNCTURE and what is more they will outlast normal tyres!

Urathon
100% PUNCTURE PROOF TYRES!

Tyres actually reflect light in cars headlights, making the cyclist visible ...and safer. URATHON SAFETYBRITE Tyres are exactly the same as the black version, but the bright colours make them more fun and safer! Avoid winter road accidents and fit the URATHON

DON'T FORGET THE SAFETY ASPECT

Changing a tyre and fixing a puncture is a hassle, but consider the safety aspect. You may be out on a bike ride, or your kid's cycling around to the local shop when a puncture strikes. It's inconvenient, it's a nuisance and it's dangerous. With URATHON Bike tyres, there's no danger, you just keep on cycling !

FREE FITTING AND TECHNICAL ADVICE

ATS are already the country's leading Car Tyre sales and fitting company. Now you can get URATHON Bike Tyres at every ATS centre. Just visit your local centre - no appointment is necessary - and one of the skilled ATS technicians will advise you on the best Tyre for your requirements and fit it FREE, while you wait.

It couldn't be simpler !

AVAILABLE TO FIT YOUR BIKE

Whether you are fitting them to a Kid's BMX or an adults off-road bike URATHON tyres will be the perfect fit. With tread patterns to suit most aspects of cycling, all you have to do is tell the trained ATS technician which ones you want and leave it up to him ! URATHON Tyres come in Conventional Black, but if it's something different that you are looking for, check out Flouro Yellow...Hot Pink or Tornado Red! They're especially popular with the kid's !

HOW IT'S DONE

URATHON Tyres are made from the very latest technology which encapsulates an air-bubble foam core within a tough, resistant Urathane skin. Integral reinforcing bands ensure a firm grip on the wheel. Preset to tyre pressures recommended by professionals, the foam core consists of millions of minute air bubbles to ensure that the ride is virtually identical to a conventional tyre, while the tough outer skin deflects the toughest of objects. So, even if a nail or piece of glass should penetrate the tyre, NOTHING WILL HAPPEN! **Say goodbye to puncture kits, pumps and hassle !**

BRIGHT COLOURS ARE FUN...BUT THEY ARE SAFE TOO

When the short days are with us there is nothing more frightening than the dark roads. URATHON SAFETYBRITE

When you start to close the leaflet you see a further section of text which offers a guarantee and mentions an attractively low price, then on the back face of the leaflet there is a brief recapitulation of price, properties of the tyres, and advice about how to obtain more details (page 89).

IDENTIFYING IMPLICATIONS

You can now see that the leaflet is structured very sensibly with regard to what we earlier defined as its purpose. The language of the text is mostly straightforward, and the sequence of the sections is logical. Overall, the layout of the leaflet reinforces the structure and logic of the argument.

But what are the implications in the text? In other words, what is it suggesting to you when you read it; how does it set about really persuading you that these tyres are what you need?

For what appears to be a simple leaflet, it is actually quite sophisticated. Let's look at it again, section by section.

- The first section cunningly mentions both adults and children, and also the role of the ATS 'technician' to emphasise that these tyres are serious, not just a fun or fashion item. If they have to be fitted by a 'technician', the implication is that they are complicated technological items, and are not just bicycle tyres. However, so as not to risk becoming too serious, mention of the fluorescent colours is brought in.

- Section two follows a similar pattern. This is where the language of the leaflet is less straightforward – purposely so, because the manufacturer wants you to be impressed by the technology behind the tyres. Leaflets of this kind will risk almost losing readers in these circumstances, because they know that most of us would not admit to being confused by the technical information, but would pretend to understand and be impressed by it. However, the writer does not push this technical language too far, and returns to the good news of no punctures, making sure that your attention is fully restored by using upper-case letters and bold print.

- The third section uses one of the commonest tricks in advertising: fear. The implication here is that if you don't fit fluorescent tyres to your bicycle (or to your children's bicycles), you or they are more likely to have an accident. So while you may have thought the coloured tyres were a rather silly idea, you're made to think again.

- Having got you worried, section four continues to play on your fear of accidents. A puncture may not be just inconvenient or a nuisance – it may be dangerous. The implication is that if a child has a puncture, he or she may be at the mercy of – what? The leaflet doesn't spell it out, but the implication is clear: if you can 'just keep on cycling', you can escape any undefined threat.

- By the time you reach section five, you are probably pretty sure you need these tyres, so details of fitting are provided. Although the cost of the actual tyres has not yet been mentioned, you are told (in upper case again, to make sure you notice) that fitting is free (and simple, underlined) – so wouldn't it be silly not to get some?

- When you turn over the page, you see the price for the first time, and it probably seems very cheap. But note that it is 'from £13.95', the implication being that full-sized tyres for adult bicycles will be much dearer. One other point on this page: it says that the Urathon tyres are 'virtually identical in ride and performance to normal tyres': this repeats an implication first suggested in the second section, that they may not actually be as comfortable as conventional pneumatic tyres.

INCONSISTENCIES

Although this is a well-structured leaflet of its kind, you may by now have noticed a couple of inconsistencies in the message it gives.

For example, are the tyres really a fun item for children (especially the fluorescent ones) or a serious accessory for adults? The leaflet is at pains to emphasise that Urathon tyres are available in 'Conventional Black', but makes considerable play on the safety aspect of the coloured tyres. If the colour is so important, why make black ones at all? Presumably because most adults would not buy them, and the company wants to sell as many tyres as possible.

The large and dominating photograph is also of a youngish boy, which appears to reinforce the fun/child aspect of the tyres – and it is inconsistent with the safety message of the leaflet, as he is not wearing a helmet or protective elbow and knee pads. There is a real tension in the whole text between safety and fun, young people and adults.

WHAT MAKES THE GRADE? ▶

To gain a Grade C mark for your non-fiction Reading skills, you must be able to understand what a text is about, but also to see the implications in the text, in other words, to read beyond the obvious surface meaning. For higher grades you must also be able to identify any inconsistencies in the author's viewpoint, or in the subject-matter of the text.

Check yourself

QUESTIONS

Q1
a) Look at the page from the Oxfam appeal leaflet opposite. Analyse it in a similar way to the Urathon tyre leaflet and explain the argument.
b) Look at the leaflet again and explain the implications.
c) Finally, explain any inconsistencies in the leaflet.

How can your £2 a month help poor people to help themselves?

These days, £2 won't buy very much. But if you give £2 a month to Oxfam, your donation is stretched much further. We support people who are helping themselves, so they contribute their hard work, their time and energy to make every penny go further.

Photo: Nick Fogden/Oxfam

Support a health worker for over 6 months

In India, £2 a month would help train a voluntary health worker for over 6 months safeguarding HUNDREDS of people.

Plant 670 trees

Your £2 a month could supply 670 seedlings every year, which will be planted out by Ethiopian volunteers to help re-green their land.

Photo: Sarah Errington/Oxfam

Clean water for a whole community

In Sudan, £2 a month will help provide enough tools for villagers to dig a well and give their whole community a permanent supply of clean, safe water.

People in the Third World don't want to live on hand-outs. All they want is the opportunity to work themselves out of poverty – and the chance to live dignified and independent lives.

Photo: Jenny Matthews/Oxfam

OXFAM

274 Banbury Road, Oxford OX2 7DZ
Registered Charity No. 202918

Q2 a) Look at the extract from the obituary of Dame Violet Dickson, which appeared in *The Daily Telegraph* on 1 January 1991. Analyse it in a similar way to the Urathon tyre leaflet and the Oxfam appeal. What does the obituary tell us about Dame Violet (the argument)?

b) What does the writer suggest about her (the implications)?

c) Are there any apparent inconsistencies in the writer's attitude towards her?

Dame Violet Dickson

Dame Violet Dickson, who has died aged 94, was a celebrated, indeed an awesome, figure in Kuwait, where she lived for more than 60 years, and where she remained for several weeks after the Iraqi invasion in August 1990.

During her 60 years in Araby – half of them as a widow – Violet Dickson knew many of the chief actors in its history, among them King Abdul Aziz ibn Saud of Saudi Arabia, King Faisal of Iraq, four Kuwaiti rulers and many tribal sheikhs. She moved with equal ease among western diplomats and travellers such as Bertram Thomas, Gertrude Bell, Freya Stark, Wilfred Thesiger and Ian Fleming.

Dame Violet's knowledge of Kuwait, and in particular her unparalleled grasp of the feuds and rivalries festering among the kingdom's 600-strong royal family, made her an indispensable resource for incoming British ambassadors and visiting notables.

Her 80th birthday party, held in a tent in the embassy compound in the summer of 1976, was a major event in the life of the British community; and the heavens laid on an almighty thunderstorm for the occasion.

Yet, for all her prestige, Dame Violet continued to occupy the modest seafront house that had been her home since her arrival in 1929, when she had been carried ashore in a sedan chair with her husband, Col. Harold Dickson, the political agent and later the local representative of the Kuwait Oil Company.

Dame Violet was a mountainously large, sturdy-legged woman, who talked in a surprisingly small, sharp voice. She spoke Arabic in a Bedouin dialect, though she never learnt to read or write the language. She was an intensely practical person of simple tastes, never bored, and wholly without intellectual pretensions.

The same artlessness was evident in her appearance; the hair was scraped back into a bun, the feet were thrust into ankle socks and flat shoes, the torso enveloped in a huge, shapeless dress, and the whole surmounted by a little cotton sun hat.

During the Second World War, she donned a shabby coat and skirt made by a Kuwaiti tailor out of a piece of man's suiting.

Dame Violet was dismissive of women and made no secret of her preference for male company. This distaste for her own sex, she happily admitted, was often reciprocated, notably by certain Arab princesses, who hid in the cupboard during her visits to their palace.

Violet Penelope Lucas-Calcraft was born on Sept. 3 1896 at Gautby in Lincolnshire, where her father was a land agent in charge of the local estates belonging to the Vyners of Newby Hall in Yorkshire. As a child, her special delights were collecting butterflies and birds' eggs, pastimes interspersed with the trapping and skinning of moles.

Young Violet was educated at Miss Lunn's High School, Woodhall Spa, and at Les Charmettes at Vevey in Switzerland, from which she returned with some difficulty on the outbreak of the First World War.

ANSWERS

A1

a) The argument is that if you give £2 to Oxfam, it is put to good use because it funds projects which encourage people in the Third World to help themselves and so become less dependent on charity. It gives examples of projects, and ends by stating outright the main theme, that helping people to help themselves gives them dignity and independence.

b) The first implication is that you may be surprised at how much a £2 donation could achieve, when that amount won't buy much in our society. A second implication is therefore that anyone reading this leaflet would have to be very mean not to donate £2.

c) There are no obvious inconsistencies in this page, except the lack of clarity about the monthly £2 donation: the page makes three claims about what £2 a month will achieve, but does not say for how many months the £2 needs to be given to achieve these outcomes.

A2

a) Dame Violet was born in Lincolnshire and educated partly in Switzerland. She lived in the Middle East for most of her life, and died at the age of 94. She knew a great deal about Kuwait, its history and its royal family, and provided useful information to important British visitors. She was a very large woman, with a small voice, who did not care much about her appearance, and preferred the company of men to women.

b) The writer suggests that Dame Violet was an eccentric person. She was 'mountainously large' and 'sturdy-legged' yet had a 'surprisingly small, sharp voice'. Although she mixed with rich and famous people, she always lived in a 'modest' house. Although she was 'intensely practical' she was not very clever ('wholly without intellectual pretensions') and she took little pride in her appearance. She would wear 'ankle socks and flat shoes', or even items made out of men's clothing. She preferred men to women, and Arab princesses, 'who hid in the cupboard during her visits to their palace', clearly found her frightening. Even as a child she trapped and skinned moles alongside more normal pursuits.

TUTORIALS

T1

a) *This is a good, detailed answer of Grade C standard. To raise the grade further, you could mention that the photographs show people working on projects, rather than people suffering, and so emphasise the positive message of the leaflet.*

b) *Again, a sound Grade C answer. To achieve a Grade A, you need to spell out the deeper implication that, as it goes towards projects which encourage self-help and independence, anyone refusing to make a donation is not just harming the charity, but actually preventing people in the Third World from achieving dignity and independence which will make them less dependent on charity in the future.*

c) *You might additionally point out that the leaflet is in fact very consistent by sticking to the theme of the £2 donation and illustrating (through the three photographs as well as in the text) what this can achieve. Do not be afraid to 'reverse' a question in this way to show that you have appreciated the structure of a text.*

T2

a) *On an examination paper, you would probably be given an approximate number of words to write in answering this part of the question, so that your ability to summarise the main points of an argument is tested. You will usually be asked to summarise an argument in ten to twenty per cent of the length of the original. The suggested answer given here is about 75 words long (that is, about fifteen per cent of the original, which is about 500 words); if you have written much more, you need to practise selecting and presenting the main points from a passage.*

b) *Notice how, in answering this question, it is important to quote from the text to illustrate the points you make.*

ANSWERS

A2   c)   The writer appears to both admire Dame Violet and mock her. The first paragraph suggests she was a brave and respected person, and this tone continues until the mention of her 80th birthday party, when the writer says that 'the heavens laid on an almighty thunderstorm for the occasion'. This comment seems to mock Dame Violet, although in a gentle and affectionate way. When he describes her large size and her small voice, the writer's tone is a little more cruel, as is the comment that she was 'wholly without intellectual pretensions'. The description of her trapping and skinning moles, after the comment about young Arab princesses hiding from her, suggests that she was perhaps a rather bloodthirsty and frightening person; but the writer returns to gentle mockery when he starts the next paragraph 'Young Violet'. Overall, the writer seems to have some affection for Dame Violet, but also seems to find her a contradictory and sometimes bizarre character.

TUTORIALS

T2   c)   *An introductory comment which sets out your point of view is one feature of a very good answer.*

Quotation is particularly important here to make any inconsistencies absolutely clear.

A good answer will end with a statement which sums up the point of view you have presented and illustrated.

It is a quite different exercise to carry out an analysis of this kind on a piece of biographical writing. There is more text to read, and you need to have a good overview of it from several readings before you try to answer the questions. If you have answered question 2a with most of the detail mentioned here, then you would be performing at a good Grade D level; if you have managed most of question 2b, with actual quotations from the text, then your performance should be good enough for a sound Grade C. If you have done all that, and have explained the inconsistencies as well as the example here, your work is of Grade A standard.

CHAPTER 13

COLLATING MATERIAL AND MAKING CROSS-REFERENCES

- In this chapter, you will learn to:

  look at non-fiction texts which are similar in content or layout;

  describe the similarities and differences between them;

  refer to more than one text at a time by quotation and comparison.

- To gain a high grade in GCSE, you need to show an ability to cross-reference texts.

WHEN DO I USE THESE SKILLS?

The ability to collate and cross-reference texts may be particularly useful if you are:

- gathering material for a project;
- trying to compare descriptions of two similar items or objects you are thinking of buying;
- looking at a range of evidence about an event, so that you can try to decide what really happened.

As with all non-fiction material, it may not be only printed text which you need to collate or cross-reference: there may be pictorial, graphical or other material as well, and in this chapter we will look at some of the possibilities.

COLLATING

When reacting to texts, collating means comparing in detail. In other words, looking for similarities and differences, both obvious and more subtle (think back to the work you have done on following arguments and recognising implications and inconsistencies in Chapter 12).

CROSS-REFERENCING

Cross-referencing simply means referring to actual details in two or more texts, sometimes by direct quotation, to support your argument. High-level cross-referencing moves to and fro between texts, rather than looking first at one, and then separately at another.

COLLATING AND CROSS-REFERENCING PRINT

Look at the two following extracts. They are taken from a feature in *The Observer* in which two men talk about their work.

High-level cross-referencing moves to and fro between texts.

The lighthouse keeper

AT THE LIZARD lighthouse, my Saturday shift begins at 8pm and I'm on for eight hours until four o'clock in the morning. First, I go down to relieve the watchman, have a chat and check everything is OK. Then I'm up to the lantern to clean the lens before switching on the power. It's an 800,000-candle-power light with a range of 25 miles, and it flashes every second. We're the only legalised flashers in the country, so to speak.

Every half an hour or so, I check that the lamp's sequence and speed are correct; then, every two hours, I check the weather and send the details to the national weather centre at Bracknell. People don't realise how weather reports are done; it's little stations like us that provide the data. I also keep a sharp eye out for fog during the night. If I see it, I start the fog signal: two blasts every minute. It can be heard for eight miles. This is one of the busiest shipping lanes in the world, so if any lights come too close I warn them off with another blast. If anyone is in real trouble, I call out the coastguard.

The seafront attendant

WHEN THE WEATHER is good, Sunday is the busiest day of the week. It has been for the last 12 summers I've worked here. My job is to look after the bandstand and promenades during the summer season for Eastbourne Borough Council. I arrive at the bandstand between 7.30 and 8am. Turning up so early is my choice: it means I avoid the morning traffic and it gives me a chance to relax with a cup of tea in one of our deckchairs and enjoy the sight of the sun rising over the sea in front of me. Weather permitting, that is.

At this time of day, I see the occasional passer-by strolling along, who, without exception, says 'Good morning' with a smile. It's all so nice and civilised. The other seafront staff arrive at 9am, at the same time as a police search team, including a dog and his handler, to check the bandstand.

Sunday is the first day for the incoming military band, which plays every day for a week. For 12 weeks during the holiday season, different bands provide entertainment. After the search, which is purely a routine precautionary measure, I join the two full-time seasonal bandstand staff to tidy up, if needs be, and check out the microphones and see to any other of the band's requirements.

If you were asked to write about the similarities and differences in these men's working lives, how would you go about it? You could consider making a few notes in two columns headed 'similarities' and 'differences' under headings such as:

- their jobs;
- what they feel about these jobs;
- contact with other people;
- how attractive their lives sound.

You might then come up with a piece of writing like this:

The lighthouse keeper and the seafront attendant

Both men work in jobs which are close to the sea, but the seafront attendant seems to enjoy the sea more; the keeper is aware of the dangers of the sea, watching over 'one of the busiest shipping lanes in the world', especially for fog at night. Indeed, the weather is important to both men: the keeper has to send in regular reports, as well as warning shipping of fog, and the seafront attendant will be more or less busy depending on how good the weather is. Apart from the watchman he relieves, the keeper spends his shift alone, but the seafront attendant talks to passers-by and other staff. The seafront attendant's job sounds easier and more pleasant than the keeper's: the keeper has to watch hard and concentrate on the sea, the weather and shipping all the time. However, the attendant has to be present when police check for explosives under the bandstand. Both men sound proud of the work they do, and take their duties seriously.

This is a good, detailed answer; the introduction and conclusion both draw together similarities in the men's working lives and their attitudes, but the central part of the answer develops the differences. The only additional detail which could have been included to make this an even fuller answer is a reference to when the lighthouse keeper has to contact the coastguard; the words 'and unless he needs to call out the coastguard' could have been inserted after 'he relieves'. It is not necessary to quote from the text in an exercise of this kind, but one example is included here to show how a direct quotation can be worked into an answer.

WORKING WITH PICTURES

The next example shows how you might collate and cross-reference two sources which have some text but use pictures as well. If you were working on a science project concerned with pollution, you might want to draw together some information about summertime and wintertime smog. Take a good look at the smog diagrams on this page and on page 100.

Summertime Smog.

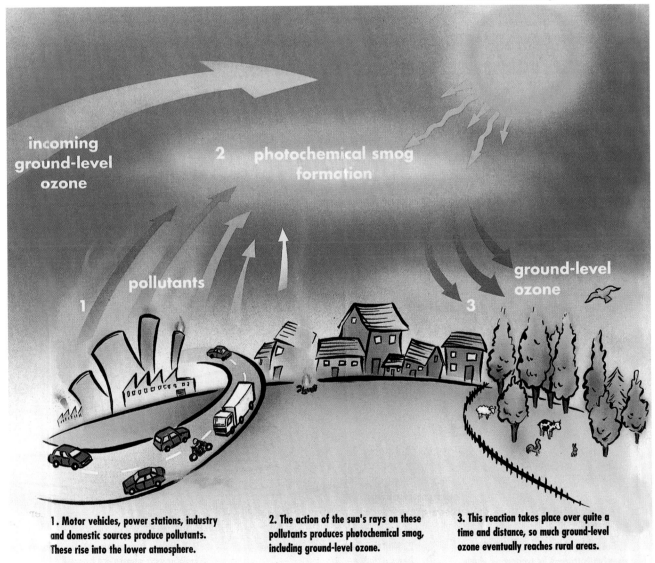

incoming ground-level ozone

2 photochemical smog formation

pollutants

ground-level ozone

1

3

1. Motor vehicles, power stations, industry and domestic sources produce pollutants. These rise into the lower atmosphere.

2. The action of the sun's rays on these pollutants produces photochemical smog, including ground-level ozone.

3. This reaction takes place over quite a time and distance, so much ground-level ozone eventually reaches rural areas.

99

How do you set about working with both text and pictures? First, you need to decide what each tells you: are the words concerned with one aspect of the subject and the pictures something else, or do they work together?

You may have noticed already that, although the two pieces of material come from a 'matching' pair of leaflets, the approach is slightly different. In 'Summertime Smog', the pieces of text at the bottom are numbered, and these numbers are placed on the picture to emphasise the sequence of events in the formation of smog, with a few key words and phrases repeated. In the 'Wintertime Smog' diagram, the numbers are not placed on the diagram, although key words and phrases are.

SUMMERTIME AND WINTERTIME SMOG

If you were using this information in a project, you might decide that it would be easier to keep the accounts of summertime and wintertime smog separate to avoid any confusion.

Wintertime Smog.

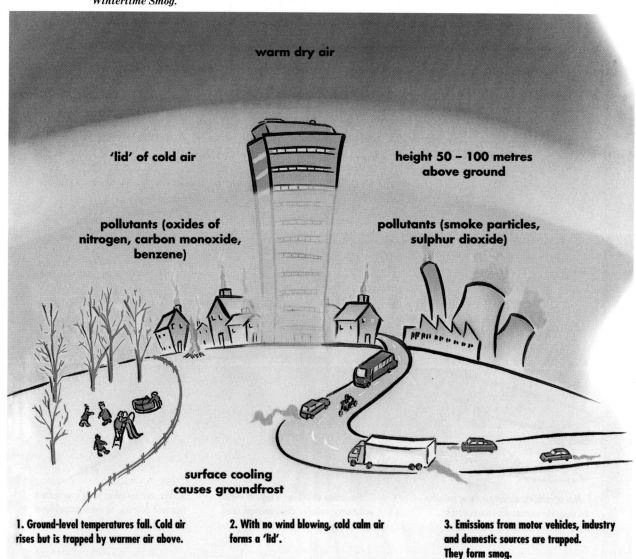

warm dry air

'lid' of cold air

height 50 – 100 metres above ground

pollutants (oxides of nitrogen, carbon monoxide, benzene)

pollutants (smoke particles, sulphur dioxide)

surface cooling causes groundfrost

1. Ground-level temperatures fall. Cold air rises but is trapped by warmer air above.

2. With no wind blowing, cold calm air forms a 'lid'.

3. Emissions from motor vehicles, industry and domestic sources are trapped. They form smog.

If you were trying to show a sophisticated grasp of the material, however, you would need to identify a common point – say pollutants produced by cars, industry and homes – and start from there. In this case you might begin your account something like this:

> Both summertime and wintertime smog are produced by pollutants from motor vehicles, industry and domestic sources. However, atmospheric conditions are very different in summer and winter, and so the nature of the smog is quite different in the two seasons. In summer, it is a substance produced by the effect of the sun's rays on the pollution rising from ground level, whereas in winter the actual pollutants do not change, but are trapped by a layer of cold air.

When collating and cross-referencing texts, other skills we have looked at in previous chapters are inevitably involved, skills such as distinguishing fact from opinion (Chapter 10), evaluating the different ways in which information is presented (Chapter 11) and following an argument, identifying implications and recognising inconsistencies (Chapter 12). If you are able to demonstrate these skills, as appropriate, while moving easily between two or more texts, you will be given a high grade for your reading skills, particularly if you are able to deal with texts simultaneously, rather than one at a time.

 **WHAT MAKES THE GRADE?**

Check yourself

Now that you have seen text and picture examples, have a look at the following holiday advertisements which appeared in a London evening newspaper.

EVENING STANDARD LEISURE BREAKS AND GLC OFFER

THE NILE IN STYLE

Eight days, full-board cruise with excursions £399 per person (GLC £389 pp).
Departures 10, 17 August and 7 September

JOIN the *Nile Pearl* for a wonderful journey through the ancient land of upper Egypt. The exclusive ship has 21 air-conditioned cabins, swimming pool, sun decks, restaurant and bar. There are 10 excursions included in the price, and all are accompanied by a qualified Egyptologist.

The price of just £399 per person (GLC: £389) includes return flights, transfers, excursions, all meals and on-board accommodation in a cabin with private facilities.

Why not extend your holiday in Egypt and take advantage of the sunshine, arrange some excellent resort diving or just simply relax? Readers (and GLC members) may choose to extend this holiday with an extra seven nights in Egypt, with a week at the Luxor Hilton with breakfasts each day for an additional £99 per person including transfers, or four nights at the Luxor Hilton and three nights at the Cairo Hilton including transfers and a pyramids and museum excursion for an additional £259 per person.

For full details of the *Nile Pearl* cruise holiday and optional extensions, call Goldenjoy Holidays on **0171 794 9818**, quoting Evening Standard Offer (and GLC members' last four digits of membership number).

SWITZERLAND IN SUMMER

Eight days half-board, departing Tuesdays or Wednesdays in August.
Just £299 per person (GLC £289)

SPEND a week in Lugano, where the flamboyant warmth of Italy combines with the cool efficiency of southern Switzerland. This region enjoys a lovely climate and unique cultural mix.

Accommodation is at a three-star hotel two minutes from the lakeside, with indoor and outdoor swimming pools, sauna, bar and sun terrace, in a room with private facilities. This exclusive offer price includes scheduled flights from Heathrow or Stansted to Zurich, half-board accommodation and rail transfers Zurich-Lugano.

For further details call Highlight Travel on **0990 143425**. (GLC members quote last four digits of membership number for additional £10 discount.)

QUESTION

Q1 Write a brief comparison of the two holidays in the form of an article (between 150 and 200 words long) which might appear on the travel page of the newspaper. Draw attention to any similarities or differences between what is offered for the price in each case, and suggest what kind of person each holiday might suit.

REMEMBER! Cover the answers if you want to.

ANSWER

A1 Holidays are offered to two different destinations: the Nile and Lake Lugano in Switzerland. The Nile holiday costs £100 per person more than the Swiss holiday, although both trips are for eight days. There are only three departure dates for the Nile cruise, but you can go on the Lugano trip any Tuesday or Wednesday in August.

The Nile trip is full board, and there is the opportunity to extend the stay by seven days in one hotel or by four days in one hotel and three in another. The Lugano holiday is half-board, and you cannot extend the stay. The trips are organised by different companies, but both are offered at a discount to GLC members if you quote a membership number.

The photograph of Lugano shows you the attractions of the area, while the Nile holiday offers excursions accompanied by a qualified Egyptologist. We recommend the Nile holiday to readers who are interested in a more active holiday looking at historical remains, while those in search of a relaxing holiday in a pleasant climate will prefer Lugano.

TUTORIAL

T1 *This answer meets the requirements of the task – it compares the holidays, suggests a suitable clientele for each and is the right length (just over 180 words). A mention of actual prices would be helpful in this context.*
Basic departure/return details are compared.

Useful comparison of what you actually get with each holiday.

Although the discount is important, you still haven't told the customer what the actual price is.

An appropriate summary of what the holidays offer.

The model answer here is of Grade C standard. To achieve higher, you would certainly need to remember to mention the actual price of the holidays, and you might have made the holidays sound more appealing by giving a little less dull, factual detail and by using some of the descriptive language from the advertisements themselves, e.g. words such as 'exclusive', 'wonderful', 'excellent' (the Nile) or 'flamboyant warmth', 'cool efficiency', 'lovely climate', 'unique cultural mix' (Lugano).

- In this chapter, you will investigate how writers use language to achieve particular effects in non-fiction texts.

- To improve your GCSE grade, you need to comment in detail on how writers achieve their effects through using a range of language techniques.

WHAT WRITERS TRY TO DO

All texts are written for a purpose, and skilful writers will try to influence how you respond to their texts through the techniques they use. In this chapter, we'll revisit some of the texts used in Chapters 10–13. Since you are already familiar with these texts, looking more closely at certain aspects of the language used in them will help to strengthen your understanding of how they achieve their effects.

SLY PERSUASION!

In Chapter 10, we saw how single words which convey the writer's opinion can masquerade as facts. If you are not on your guard, this device can often mislead you into believing that what you are told is the truth. Examples we noted were:

- the house advertisement which used words such as 'magnificent' and 'superb' (page 76);

- Paul Theroux describing Margate as 'crummy' (page 77);

- the leaflet about Granary Wharf which, amongst many examples, used words such as 'unique' and 'fascinating' (page 79).

This technique is, of course, the stock-in-trade of advertisers or people who are trying to sell you something. How often have you been persuaded to buy something simply because the advertiser told you that it was wonderful? If, as in the Theroux example quoted, the word is also slangy and casual, then you are even more likely to believe it, as it sounds convincingly friendly and trustworthy (see 'Dear Reader' page 106 for some other aspects of this technique).

FEELINGS

The Theroux piece on Margate also provides an example of how writers sometimes use physical descriptions to evoke feelings in readers. He writes about:

> people down from London for the day shunting back and forth on the front in the cold rain

Theroux is up to quite a lot in these apparently simple words! For a start, 'shunting' (rather than, say, 'walking' or 'strolling') suggests people going to and fro, like railway carriages in a siding. This already creates a miserable, aimless feel. When we are further told about 'the cold rain', this convinces us that Margate is really a pretty dreadful place, full of sad, wet people.

NOTHING BUT THE TRUTH?

Advertisers in particular are skilled at not telling the whole truth, while not exactly lying! Remember the leaflet for the bicycle tyres which would not puncture (Chapter 12, pages 89–90)?

You may recall that these tyres were advertised as costing '*from* £13.95', and that the ride they give is *virtually* identical to normal tyres. No lies are told here – but it's hardly the whole truth!

A similar technique is when a writer avoids saying exactly what he or she means. This may be because they are frightened of the consequences (if, for example, they are writing about someone still alive who might accuse them of libel) or because they are trying to sound clever or inventive. This is certainly the case in the obituary of Dame Violet Dickson (Chapter 12), where the writer says that she was:

> wholly without intellectual pretensions

when he really means she was probably not very clever.

APPEALING TO OUR WORST INSTINCTS

That last example has a touch of implied snobbery in it, and this is the next area for us to consider. Think back to the tyre leaflet and the mention of the 'technicians' who will fit the tyres. This is rather like calling dustmen 'refuse disposal operatives': it doesn't change the job they do, but makes it sound grander for a while and makes us feel that we are being provided with a much more important service than if it was described in plain language.

Snobbery is also present in the 'Nile in Style' holiday advertisement (Chapter 13, page 101), where words and phrases such as 'exclusive' and 'accompanied by a qualified Egyptologist' are designed to capture the interest of those easily persuaded that certain lifestyles can be bought for a few hundred pounds. Unsurprisingly, the other holiday advertisement offers the same kind of temptation, referring to:

> where the flamboyant warmth of Italy combines with the cool efficiency of southern Switzerland.

In fact, that is also an interesting example of the first technique we looked at – opinion masquerading as fact – but only very confident, well-travelled readers would dispute the descriptions of the flamboyant warmth of Italy or the cool efficiency of southern Switzerland: most would unthinkingly accept this as true.

A variation on the straightforward approach to snobbery is the use of what has been called 'technobabble' – language which you may not quite understand, but which sounds very impressive. The tyre leaflet shows an example of this when it says that the puncture-proof tyre

> encapsulates an air-bubble foam core within a tough resistant Urathane skin.

The product must be good, mustn't it, if it can be described in such terms? Or that is what the advertisers want us to believe.

COLOURFUL PHRASES AND OTHER DEVICES

Far more interesting are original, colourful phrases which genuine writers use in an effort to persuade you of an idea or to create a particular picture in your mind. Roald Dahl is capable of this, as for example in the extract from *Going Solo* in Chapter 10 (page 77), when he writes of the passengers on the boat:

> just about everybody had his or her own particular maggot in the brain...

In typical Dahl style, this is both amusing and, the more you think about the image, disturbing. It is certainly a more creative use of language than anything we have seen in tyre leaflets or holiday advertisements.

Writers use a number of devices to make us take notice of what we are reading. As well as the sort of images we have seen Roald Dahl use, you may encounter rhymes, puns, deliberate misspellings and so on. Sometimes the simplest of methods can stop you in your tracks and make you realise the intensity of feeling the writer is trying to convey. An example of this would be the repetition used by George Bernard Shaw in the letter to Stella Campbell which we looked at in Chapter 11 (page 82) or the repetition backed up by alliteration in the Granary Wharf leaflet (Chapter 10, page 79) when it says:

> It's friendly, it's fun and it's free.

DEAR READER

When you come across such simple yet powerful writing, you feel as though you are being taken into the confidence of the writer – there is no attempt to mislead or puzzle you. There are other techniques used in non-fiction writing to make it seem that the writer is talking directly to you, so that you feel sure of the sincerity of what you read. Sometimes you will be directly questioned, to draw you into a mental discussion and make you think for yourself about the subject matter of a text. We saw this technique used in the Oxfam leaflet in Chapter 12:

How can your £2 a month help poor people to help themselves?

A similar, but more direct approach is to address you in the tones of a command. This can make you feel that you are being wilfully awkward if you don't then obey it. This is illustrated in the heading to the Department of the Environment energy-saving chart we looked at in Chapter 11:

Ten Things *You* Can Do at Home

Note how the use of upper-case initial letters and the highlighting of 'You' add to the commanding tone of this statement.

Another aspect of this technique is to adopt a very friendly, conversational style (sometimes called a 'colloquial' style) to make it sound as though you are being spoken to directly by someone who then begins to sound like a personal friend and so who becomes very hard to ignore. Good examples of this occur in the accounts of the daily routines of the seafront attendant ('Weather permitting, that is') and the lighthouse keeper we encountered in Chapter 13. When the keeper comments:

We're the only legalised flashers in the country, so to speak.

you may groan at the feeble pun, but it probably makes you feel friendly towards him and, indeed, remember what he has said.

HUMOUR

Mention of the lighthouse keeper's pun brings us finally to humour, a frequent weapon in the armoury of writers who are trying to engage the interest of their readers. Jokes may be both linguistic and visual – remember Edward Lear starting his letter to Mr Fortescue (Chapter 11, page 82)? And here is the early twentieth-century comic writer, P.G. Wodehouse, writing to his adopted daughter, Leonora (whom he calls Snorky) where the comedy is partly in the situation but partly also in the language, which uses the 'smart' talk of the 1930s:

Darling Snorky,
You may well imagine the excitement your letter caused in the home. Mummie was having a bath when she got it and rushed out with a towel round her shrieking for me. Winks barked, I shouted, and a scene of indescribable confusion eventuated.

Humour which depends on words alone often achieves its effect through exaggeration. The writer of Dame Violet Dickson's obituary (Chapter 12, page 94) gives us a vivid mental image of her physical size by describing her as:

> mountainously large

and later in the same extract uses the technique of grotesque or inappropriate contrast, when he describes her dress-sense:

> the torso enveloped in a huge shapeless dress, and the whole surmounted by a little cotton sun hat.

The writer's use of the word 'torso' is interesting here. The word is most often used of bodies, and dismembered bodies at that! The result is that it exaggerates still further the contrast between the huge bulk of Dame Violet's body and the little sun hat perched on her head. This may be rather cruel writing, but it is undeniably effective in creating a vivid picture of its subject.

WHAT MAKES THE GRADE?

To achieve a Grade C for your reading skills, whether you are reading literary or non-literary texts, you must be able to show by quotation and discussion that you understand how writers use language to affect the response of readers. To achieve higher grades, your analysis of the effects of vocabulary, figures of speech and other devices such as humour or irony needs to be detailed and thorough, and may involve comparing texts.

Check yourself

QUESTIONS

Q1 Read the following extract from Bill Bryson's account of a journey around Great Britain, *Notes From a Small Island*. He is in a small hotel in Bournemouth.

Write down one example in this passage of each of the following writing techniques described in this chapter:

- opinion made to sound like fact;
- humour;
- addressing the reader;
- effective descriptive language.

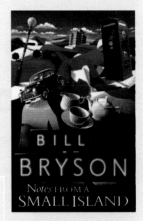

> Among the many hundreds of things that have come a long way in Britain since 1973, and if you stop to think about it for even a moment, you'll see that the list is impressively long, few have come further than the average English hostelry. Nowadays you get a colour TV, coffee-making tray with a little packet of modestly tasty biscuits, a private bath with

fluffy towels, a little basket of cotton-wool balls in rainbow colours, and an array of sachets, little plastic bottles of shampoo, bath gel and moisturizing lotion. My room even had an adequate bedside light and two soft pillows. I was very happy. I ran a deep bath, emptied into it all the gels and moisturizing creams (don't be alarmed; I've studied this closely and can assure you that they are all the same substance), and, as a fiesta of airy bubbles began their slow ascent towards a position some three feet above the top of the bath, returned to the room and slipped easily into the self-absorbed habits of the lone traveller, unpacking my rucksack with deliberative care, draping wet clothes over the radiator, laying out clean ones on the bed with as much fastidiousness as if I were about to go to my first high-school prom, arranging a travel clock and reading material with exacting precision on the bedside table, adjusting the lighting to a level of considered cosiness, and finally retiring, in perky spirits and with a good book, for a long wallow in the sort of luxuriant foam seldom seen outside of Joan Collins movies.

Q2 Read the following extract from a letter written to his mother by Wilfred Owen, the war poet, from France in 1918. What could you say has recently happened to him, and what is his state of mind? Examine closely the language of the letter to help you in this.

You will guess what has happened when I say I am now Commanding the Company, and in the line had a boy lance-corporal as my Sergeant-Major. With this corporal who stuck to me and shadowed me like your prayers I captured a German Machine Gun and scores of prisoners.

I'll tell you exactly how another time. I only shot one man with my revolver (at about 30 yards!); the rest I took with a smile. The same thing happened with other parties all along the line we entered.

I have been recommended for the Military Cross; and have recommended every single NCO who was with me!

My nerves are in perfect order.

I came out in order to help these boys — directly by leading them as well as an officer can; indirectly, by watching their sufferings that I may speak of them as well as a pleader can. I have done the first.

Of whose blood lies yet crimson on my shoulder where his head was — and where so lately yours was — I must not now write.

It is all over for a long time. We are marching steadily back.

Moreover

The War is nearing an end.

Still,

Wilfred and more than Wilfred

REMEMBER! Cover the answers if you want to.

ANSWERS

A1 **Opinion made to sound like fact**
- few have come further than the average English hostelry
- can assure you that they are all the same substance

TUTORIALS

T1 *This is a 'recognition' exercise. If you were asked to spot similar features in an examination, you would be asked to explain them as well to gain a Grade C or higher. Here are some suitable explanatory comments:*

Opinion made to sound like fact
Either of these examples would do: Bryson states these opinions very firmly, as though there is no possible argument with them – but they are opinions and not facts.

A1 Humour
- hostelry
- emptied into it all the gels and moisturising creams

Addressing the reader
- if you stop to think about it for even a moment you'll see that . . .
- don't be alarmed

Effective descriptive language
- a fiesta of airy bubbles
- laying out . . . prom
- a long wallow . . . Joan Collins movies

T1 Humour
You could have chosen either of these. The first example is of humorous language, using a consciously old-fashioned word. The second example is of visual or 'situational' humour. If you noticed that the whole passage is written in a mockingly humorous way, so that picking out individual examples of humour is difficult, then you are achieving a level of response and analysis worthy of a Grade A.

Addressing the reader
Again, either example will do. What Bryson achieves here is to make it seem as though he is talking directly to you and this means that (a) you believe him, and (b) you feel honoured.

Effective descriptive language
The word 'fiesta' sounds lively, fun, exotic and fits in with the general air of self-indulgence which Bryson is describing. In the second example, Bryson makes himself sound like an eager, handsome young teenager rather than a weary middle-aged traveller. The third example conjures up visions of expensive and far-fetched lifestyles such as those seen in American TV mini-series.

A2

What has happened is that many British officers have been killed, and Owen has had to lead an attack with a company of very young soldiers. Owen's state of mind seems to be at first a sort of confident, patriotic enthusiasm, shown in the section from the start of the second paragraph to the end of the fourth paragraph.

Then comes an unexpected comment about his nerves: 'My nerves are in perfect order.'

The reason for Owen's sudden lack of confidence is shown by his use again of the word 'boys' to describe the soldiers. To his mind, they are too young and innocent to be caught up in this terrible war. When he writes, 'I have done the first' we realise that Owen feels guilty for not having spoken out sufficiently about the sufferings of the soldiers.

Someone, presumably a close companion of Owen, has been killed in the latest raid, and his 'blood lies yet crimson' (in other words, still fresh – not yet dry) on Owen's shoulder. This brings back to him the memory that his mother's head was on his shoulder not long ago.

The last four lines of the letter may mean that the troops are withdrawing from the front line, or the words may be a metaphor, suggesting that Owen is in despair at how the world he knows has sunk to this condition. Certainly the language of these closing lines, and the way he signs off, suggest mental turmoil and anguish.

T2

This is in the first paragraph: 'I am now Commanding the Company, and in the line had a boy lance-corporal as my Sergeant-Major'. It would be helpful to make this direct reference.

For example, 'I captured . . . I shot . . . The rest I took with a smile . . . I have been recommended' etc. Always use quotation to support points.

We can deduce that the reality is exactly the opposite of what Owen says, or he wouldn't feel the need to say it. You would need to make this comment to obtain a high grade.

Explain what 'I have done the first' means – Owen has led the men well as an officer.

You might comment here that the words show a disturbed mind, unable to separate present from past, mixing the memory of a dead comrade with thoughts of his mother.

An insight such as this would gain high marks.

Evidence of personal response to the extract – a good way to end.

CHAPTER 15

STRUCTURAL AND PRESENTATIONAL DEVICES IN TEXTS

- In this chapter, you will learn to evaluate ways in which writers structure and present non-fiction texts to achieve specific effects.
- If you are able to analyse these techniques and effects in detail, you will improve your GCSE grade for Reading.

WHAT ARE STRUCTURES AND DEVICES?

You will have noticed already from the range of non-fiction texts we have studied in Chapters 10–14 that they do not rely just on the power of words to achieve effects. Let's recap the structural and presentational devices we've already seen in use.

STRUCTURES

Breaking up the text

Writers of non-fiction usually try to present easily digested text. There are some exceptions to this – private letters and diaries, for example, may be quite difficult for outsiders to interpret – but the point of most non-fiction is to convey information to the reader. It is therefore important for this information to be presented clearly. Do you know the riddle about how to eat an elephant? The answer, of course, is 'in bite-size chunks'. Many examples of non-fiction we have already seen are structured in what we might call 'bite-size chunks'.

What this means is that writers may use some or all of the following techniques:

- short sections of text with headings, e.g. the Granary Wharf leaflet in Chapter 10 (page 79);
- small amounts of text spread about a page, often arranged around one or more illustrations, e.g. the inside of the Urathon tyres leaflet in Chapter 12 (page 89);
- key words or phrases in a list (often 'bullet-pointed') rather than continuous prose, e.g. the house advertisement in Chapter 10 (page 76);
- charts, graphs or maps, which, if well presented, can take the place of many words, e.g. the information about music sales in Chapter 11 (page 84).

These techniques are also used in this study/revision guide: they are one way of trying to ensure that you understand what is important even if only glancing quickly at the information.

Headings

The function of headings changes depending on the nature of the material. The heading of the house advertisement (page 76) is the name of the village where the house is situated: that is what prospective buyers will first be interested in. The headings in the extract from the Granary Wharf leaflet (page 79) first of all try to attract your attention ('A unique place'), then reassure you that it's convenient ('30 shops, open seven days a week') and easy to reach ('Right in the centre of Leeds'). Some people might not even read the rest of the print: those three headlines alone would be enough to persuade them to visit Granary Wharf.

The headings in the Urathon tyre leaflet (pages 89–90) are similar – there is hardly any need to read the rest of the words, except in one important place: one section is headed 'HOW IT'S DONE', and the manufacturers would clearly quite like the reader to be dazzled by details of the technology. The heading therefore invites you to read that section, whereas the others tell you the main points about availability, colours, safety, fitting, price and so on without the reader feeling the need to know more.

Headings can be used to make the reader think, or even to feel guilty in the hope that the writer's message will make its point. For example, the energy-saving chart (page 83) is headed 'Ten Things *You* Can Do at Home' – it would take a strong-minded reader to ignore that, especially with the italicised 'You'! Similarly, the Oxfam leaflet (page 93) has a main heading which attracts your attention by asking a question (and assuming that you would want to know the answer) and then three sub-headings which answer this question in different ways. This technique ensures that even the quickest glance at the page will get the message across to a reader.

PRESENTATIONAL DEVICES

Structural devices are those which affect how the text is written; presentational devices are to do with the appearance of the text on the page. There is some overlap here in terms of how the reader responds to the material, but we will keep the structure and presentation separate here to make the explanation clearer.

Among the most common presentational devices are:

- frames;
- illustrations;
- colour;
- different print styles and sizes;
- logos, symbols, etc.

Frames

A presentational device sometimes used with headings, or on its own, is to put a frame around text to make it stand out on the page. At its most simple, this can be seen in the house advertisement (page 76) and the holiday advertisements (page 101), while a fancier example is the energy-saving chart (page 83).

Illustrations

Illustrations serve a number of purposes. Above all, they make text look more attractive and interesting, and at the same time present an image of the information, product or idea in which the writer is trying to interest you. So, for example, the photograph of the house in the advertisement (page 76) is intended to attract you; the photograph of the boy riding his bike in the Urathon leaflet (page 90) is intended to suggest that the tyres are fashionable and appealing to a certain group of people; and the photographs of the people in the Oxfam leaflet (page 93) are intended to make the reader feel that he or she could contribute to this sense of well-being by contributing to the charity. The Oxfam leaflet is a particularly interesting case, as appeals often use pictures of people in poverty, or who are diseased, starving or threatened by cruel regimes. In this instance, the writer of the Oxfam leaflet has decided to present a very positive aspect of charity work, and the photographs are an important feature of this image.

Advertisements, or publicity of any kind which has selling something as its main purpose, will often employ illustrations, for obvious reasons. More informal drawings may be used to make a book look more attractive, or to help

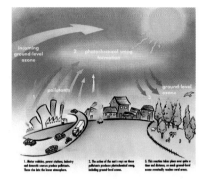

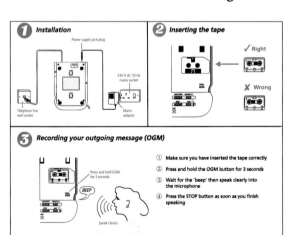

explain aspects of the text. The diagrams about summertime and wintertime smog (pages 99–100) are much simpler for a general reader to follow than words, even if words might convey a more detailed and accurate scientific picture. This brings us to the notion of audience, which we will explore more fully with regard to the media in Chapter 17.

Colour

Most of the texts used in Chapters 10–14 employ colour to some extent. It is obvious that colour can add to (or sometimes detract from) the effect of a text. Full-colour printing is expensive, and so the colour range used in some non-fiction materials may be limited, but it can still be eye-catching. The use of just black, white and yellow in the Urathon leaflet is a case in point. The Oxfam leaflet may look a little dowdy and cheap, but even that fact is used to its advantage, as people who are thinking of giving to the charity wouldn't want to see their money being spent on colourful leaflets. The smog illustrations in Chapter 13 use colours in an almost childlike way. This subtly reinforces the message that they are simple to understand, and not off-putting to people who think scientific issues are complicated.

Print

If you look back through Chapters 10–14, you will see many different styles and sizes of print used in non-fiction writing. When responding to this aspect of texts, you need to consider:

- the use of different font sizes, for example, larger print in a heading and smaller print for information which the writer may not feel is so important (e.g. the Granary Wharf information on page 79);

- the use of different font styles to create particular effects or images, for example, a 'clean', modern font in the Urathon tyres leaflet and in the smog illustrations. This reinforces the modern scientific/technological aspects of both leaflets. With a huge range of fonts available on modern word-processing systems, writers often use them to create particular effects, such as 'old English' or 'medieval' fonts to suggest something tried, tested and traditional;

- the use of devices such as upper case, or bold and/or italicised writing to draw the reader's attention; for examples of this, see the Granary Wharf (page 79) and Urathon tyres (pages 89–90) leaflets, together with the italicised 'You' in the energy-saving leaflet mentioned above (page 83).

Logos and symbols

Just as illustrations may take the place of words, or help to explain words, writers of non-fiction may use logos and symbols to strengthen their message. Logos are mostly used to try and fix the image of a company or an organisation in the reader's mind, so that he or she instantly identifies it when seen again. Examples we have seen here are the ATS logo in the Urathon tyres leaflet and the Oxfam logo at the bottom of the appeal sheet.

Symbols are an economical way of either explaining or instructing. In the answerphone instructions (page 85), arrows, ticks and crosses help to explain the written instructions, while on the Oxfam appeal (page 93), a small pair of scissors in the bottom right-hand corner shows that, on the original leaflet, there was a page to complete, cut off and send away if you wished to contribute to the appeal.

SHAPE, SIZE AND PAPER QUALITY

Finally, let's think about the physical size and shape of some examples of non-fiction writing, and the importance of paper quality. This is an issue to which we'll return in connection with the media in Chapter 17 (page 123), but for now it is important to note that:

SAUNTON

NEW INSTRUCTION

£249,000
- Magnificently situated individual detached house
- Superb south facing views over the golf course and out to sea ● Central heating ● 4 bedrooms
- 2 receptions ● Bathroom ● Shower room
- Cloaks ● Detached garage ● Approx 1 acre

- the shape and size of some material is determined by the cost of where it is published, so the house advertisement in Chapter 10 might have been larger or smaller (or in colour), but the advertiser will have decided that this size and style was the best compromise between cost and attractiveness;

- advertising for tourist attractions in particular is often an A4 sheet folded into three (or sometimes one-and-a-third times A4 folded into four), so that it fits easily into a pocket. In such cases, a map of how to get there is usually on the back face when folded, so that it can easily be consulted while on a journey (the Granary Wharf leaflet on page 79, is an example of this);

- if there is a lot of information to convey, A4 paper folded and stapled into an A5 booklet is a common format (e.g. the energy-saving booklet referred to on page 83). This size is easily handled, and is convenient for posting.

Paper quality can give an important first impression to readers, so much writing of the kind we have discussed (except, of course, diaries, letters or conventional books such as biography and travel-writing) is published on glossy paper, which both looks attractive (e.g. in the case of an advertisement for a product such as the Urathon tyres, page 89) and is hard wearing. An example of this is the Granary Wharf leaflet (page 79), which might need to stand up to being carried around by a visitor. Non-glossy paper may also be used for a purpose: it could be cheaper for a large document, or it may underline the message of the words written on it: for example, the smog leaflets (pages 99–100) and the energy-saving leaflet (page 83) are both printed on recycled paper, which enhances the environmentally friendly messages they are trying to give. Similarly, the Oxfam appeal is printed on cheap, thin paper, because charity donors would not want to see their money apparently being spent on expensive paper.

WHAT MAKES THE GRADE?

You need to be able to comment explicitly on the *effects*, rather than just point out the uses, of structural and presentational devices in non-fiction texts to achieve a Grade C in your GCSE assessment. To achieve a Grade A, you need to analyse the effects in some detail, showing for example how particular emotional or persuasive effects are achieved and how they relate to a particular audience.

Check yourself

QUESTIONS

Q1 Look back at page 111 where we noted that the heading for the 'technical' section in the Urathon tyres leaflet is the only one which does not summarise the content of the section for readers. Refer to the leaflet itself on pages 89–90 and then rewrite the section heading so that it wouldn't be necessary to read in more detail to know how the tyres are made.

Q2 Look at the Lodge Inns leaflet which is reproduced below. Write a brief paragraph which comments on its effectiveness, mentioning aspects of the structure and presentation such as:

- use of headings;
- fonts and sizes of typeface;
- use of colour;
- use of photographs;
- overall layout;
- audience.

ANSWERS

A1   TYRES WILL NOT PUNCTURE

A2   The leaflet is aimed primarily at business people, but also families who are travelling. The text is in short sections, so it is easily understood, and the main features of the rooms in the Lodge Inn are bullet-pointed to make them stand out. Some headings are used, with frames around them, so that the reader's attention is drawn to the name of the company, the price of the rooms and the convenience of the facilities. The photographs make the reception area and the restaurant look very welcoming, and emphasise that the rooms are for men and women, although children are not shown. The photographs are of smart, smiling people, giving the idea that the Lodge is somewhere for successful, happy people.

The map gives clear instructions for reaching the Lodge, and shows that the expected audience for the leaflet will be travelling by car, as the instructions only work if coming off the motorway. The leaflet is effective: it is colourful and gives all the information someone would need to decide if they wanted to stay there, and what to do and how to get there if they did want to stay.

TUTORIALS

T1   *This answer would not show a Grade C awareness of the purpose of headings. The task here was to write a heading which summarised the technical content of the section, so a better answer would be:*

AIR-BUBBLE FOAM CORE IN TOUGH PLASTIC SKIN

This uses everyday words like the other section headings, but suggests the special qualities of the tyres.

T2   *This is correct, but a more analytic answer would have commented on the colour of the bullet-pointed text: it mirrors the colours of the company logo and so links the listed features with the company name. An A-Grade answer would comment on the font used for the 'Lodge Inns' name: it is slightly ornate, to give the impression of somewhere smart, but is not 'over the top'.*

An additional point about children would be that their accommodation is only detailed in a small-print footnote, so presumably families with children are not the main audience.

A more analytic answer would comment that there is too much small print on the map for a driver to read.

A more critical answer would say that the leaflet is quite cluttered, and would question why some information about eating is in the section headed 'The Best Pubs & Restaurants' and why some is in the white panel after the map. A top-class answer would go on to suggest that this may be to try and capture trade in food and drink, even if the person reading the leaflet decided not to stay there.

The answer given would merit a Grade C; the additional comments suggested in this Tutorial would raise the level of performance to that of Grade A.

CHAPTER 16

DIFFERENT FORMS OF NON-FICTION

- In this chapter, you will learn to recognise the particular qualities of different categories of non-fiction texts.
- If you are able to analyse and evaluate the effects that these qualities have on readers, you will gain a high GCSE grade.

AUTOBIOGRAPHY/BIOGRAPHY

Biography: fact or opinion?

Some would argue that autobiographies and biographies are often fictional, at least in part. This may be so, but for the purpose of GCSE English they are treated as non-fiction texts. However, they are books about people's lives, and as such are bound to contain judgements or opinions alongside facts. Sometimes fact and opinion will be mixed: an author may give a factual account of an event, but then claim to know what was going through the minds of the people involved, or what it tells us about their personalities. If you are responding to such texts, it is important for you to have thought about issues concerning fact and opinion, which were raised in Chapter 10 (pages 76–78).

An additional feature of autobiography and biography is that the author may put forward a particular point of view or argument, for example, that he or she was treated badly by relatives or that a well-known person was dishonest. For this reason, you should also remember Following an Argument (Chapter 12, pages 88–95) when responding to such texts, and be on guard for implications and inconsistencies in what the author says.

Autobiographies and biographies are the category of non-fiction which is closest to fiction in terms of structure, style and imagination, so your ability to respond to the author's use of language is particularly important. Chapter 14, Uses of Language in Non-Fiction texts is therefore relevant.

JOURNALS/DIARIES/LETTERS

These texts have obvious similarities to autobiography, but may present even more problems when judging the balance between fact, opinion or downright untruths. If you are responding to journals, diaries or letters which were written without publication in mind, they will probably be mostly truthful, but may still contain a good deal of opinion. If they were written with a view to publication, they will probably be as carefully crafted as an autobiography or a novel, and so you need to be aware of the issues raised in Chapters 10, 12 and 14 mentioned above. Remember also that in texts which were intended to be private, writers may use a number of techniques or presentational devices (e.g. jokes, sketches) which they might not have used in a more formal situation, and that these may give you particular insights into the attitudes and intentions of the writer. A close look at Chapters 11 (pages 81–82) and 14 (pages 106–109) is a good idea to help you respond to this category of non-fiction text.

TRAVEL WRITING

Travel writing frequently has an autobiographical element to it, or aspects of biography if a modern writer is retracing the footsteps of someone from an previous era. It can also have the intimacy of a journal, and may even be written in the form of letters or a diary, so all the points made previously in this chapter have some relevance to your response to travel writing.

In looking at travel writing in Chapter 11, we saw how fact and opinion (Chapter 10, pages 76–78) and the author's use of language (Chapter 14, pages 103–7) are particularly important when analysing text. Travel writers often set out on a journey in order to pursue an idea, or to prove a point. For example, in this book we have used extracts from Paul Theroux's *The Kingdom by the Sea* and Bill Bryson's *Notes From a Small Island*. The latter is a recreation of the first journey some twenty years later, as Bill Bryson wanted to see whether Paul Theroux's experiences of Britain and the British still rang true. Many places have been visited and described by more than one writer, and examination boards may decide that one way of testing your powers of collating and cross-referencing non-fiction text is to use two or more pieces of travel writing describing the same place, or with a common theme.

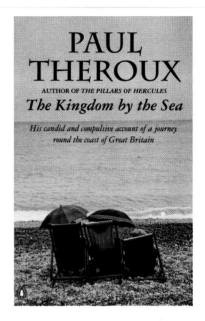

LEAFLETS

This term covers a variety of texts, ranging from pure information which might be published by a government department (e.g. about an aspect of safety in the home), through a mixture of information and advertising (e.g. about a historic building open to the public) to pure advertising (e.g. about a commercial product or a business service).

Whatever the purpose of the leaflet – and that should be your starting-point when responding to one – it will always be trying to convey information to you as powerfully as possible. The information may contain fact, opinion, arguments, inconsistencies, striking language and a whole range of structural and presentational devices. In other words, all the previous chapters in this section of the Study and Revision Guide are relevant.

NEWSPAPER ARTICLES/ OTHER FACTUAL AND INFORMATIVE MATERIALS

More will be said about newspapers in Chapter 17, but at this point you should remember that newspaper articles, or any other form of non-fiction which claims to be setting out facts or giving information, will almost certainly be using some of the techniques discussed in previous chapters. When responding to texts of this kind, go through a mental checklist, such as:

- who's it for?
- what's it for?
- what's the balance of fact and opinion?
- how is it presented?
- what's it all about?
- how is it written?
- what do I feel about it?
- is it successful?

If you are able to discuss and analyse a piece of text along those lines, with reference to appropriate detail, you will convince the examiner that you are a skilled reader of non-fiction.

WHAT MAKES THE GRADE?

In Chapters 10–15, you've been given some guidelines on what you need to do to obtain good grades when responding to particular aspects of non-fiction texts. There are two additional general points to make here.

You are likely to gain a Grade C if you are able to identify aspects of texts, such as the use of fact and opinion, the presentation of an argument, the use of appropriate language and presentational features, etc. What distinguishes a Grade A performance is the analysis you are able to make of these aspects: why has the writer done this? In other words, what effect does it have on the audience, and who is that audience?

Secondly, to gain a high grade you need to develop your ideas in detail, supporting what you say by referring to a number of examples within the text (or in other texts if that is relevant). Do not be afraid to risk your own interpretations and explanations. Personal response is highly rewarded in GCSE English when well supported by example and analysis.

Check yourself

QUESTION

Q1 The following extract is taken from Blake Morrison's 'memoir' (a brief, informal biography) of his father, *And when did you last see your father?* It describes an incident in Blake Morrison's childhood; he, his sister, his mother and his father have gone to watch a car race, and have become stuck in a traffic jam. Read the passage, and then write a brief paragraph on what it tells you about (a) Blake Morrison's father and (b) Blake Morrison himself, and give examples to show how you know this.

My father does not like waiting in queues. He is used to patients waiting in queues to see him, but he is not used to waiting in queues himself. A queue, to him, means a man being denied the right to be where he wants to be at a time of his own choosing, which is at the front, now. Ten minutes have passed. What is happening up ahead? What fathead has caused this snarl-up? Why are no cars coming the other way? Has there been an accident? Why are there no police to sort it out? Every two minutes or so my father gets out of the car, crosses to the opposite verge and tries to see if there is movement up ahead. There isn't. He gets back in and steams some more. The roof of our Alvis is down, the sun beating on to the leather upholstery, the chrome, the picnic basket. The hood is folded and pleated into the mysterious crevice between the boot and the narrow back seat where my sister and I are scrunched together as usual. The roof is nearly always down, whatever the weather: my father loves fresh air, and every car he has owned has been a convertible, so that he can have fresh air. But the air today is not fresh. There is a pall of high-rev exhaust, dust, petrol, boiling-over engines.

118

ANSWERS

TUTORIAL

A1 (a) Blake Morrison's father is impatient ('does not like waiting in queues') and rather self-important ('used to patients waiting in queues to see him, but . . . not used to waiting in queues himself'). He is used to getting his own way (he wants to be 'at the front, now'). His impatience shows again, as he wonders why there aren't any police to sort out the 'snarl-up' and 'every two minutes or so' he gets out of the car to see if anything is moving then 'steams some more.' The passage describing the car also suggests that he likes getting his own way: every car the family has owned has been a convertible so that father 'can have fresh air' which he likes, but it means that Blake and his sister are 'scrunched' into the back seat because of the folded hood. It seems as though the father does not think much at all about other people, because even today the hood is down, although the air is not fresh but 'a pall of high-rev exhaust, dust, petrol, boiling-over engines.'

(b) We learn that Blake remembers his father as an impatient, aggressive and self-centred man, as the details given in (a) above show. However, all this is seen through Blake's eyes: we have only his word for it. Blake was uncomfortable in the heat ('the sun beating onto the leather upholstery, the chrome, the picnic basket') and is squashed (or 'scrunched') in the back seat. We are reminded that Blake is only a child during this episode by the way he refers to 'the mysterious crevice between the boot and the narrow back seat' – children are often fascinated by dark nooks and crannies.

T1 A *fuller answer* would make the point that Mr Morrison is probably a doctor (the word 'patients'; 'queues' suggest this).

You could also say that he tends to be dismissive of others, or to be rude to them: he assumes that a 'fathead' has caused the 'snarl-up'; and if 'snarl-up' is the word he prefers to 'jam', it reinforces the impression that he is aggressive.

A *Grade A answer* would comment that the word 'steams' makes the father sound like an overheating car, so it is an effective word in itself but is relevant to the situation in a gently humorous way.

A *good answer* would point to the irony between the attitudes the father shows in this extract, and the fact that he is a doctor and therefore (presumably) is dedicated to helping people.

A *fuller answer* would make this point more strongly by saying that the aggressive-sounding words (like 'fathead' and 'snarl-up') are put into his father's thoughts by Blake – there is no other evidence that this is what his father was thinking (although you could argue, of course, that Blake might simply be quoting things that his father actually did say).

A *Grade-A answer* would point out the power of 'scrunched': it is an onomatopoeic word and also a slangy word which a child might use.

This is a good example of personal response on which to end the answer.

CHAPTER 17

DIFFERENT FORMS OF MEDIA TEXTS

- In this chapter, you will learn to recognise the particular qualities of different forms of media texts.
- If you are able to analyse and evaluate the effects that these qualities have on readers, you will gain a high GCSE grade.

WHAT ARE MEDIA TEXTS?

In the context of GCSE English, media texts are radio, film, television, magazines and newspapers. There is some overlap between non-fiction texts and media texts, particularly where print-based media (such as newspapers and magazines) are concerned. For GCSE English assessment, television, radio and film will be analysed differently than in a media-studies course, where technologies, working practices, ownership and control rather than language and presentation may be the main focus.

As with non-fiction texts, your response to media is all about how particular effects are achieved and the success of a text in relation to its target audience and intended purpose.

Assessing your ability to respond to media texts poses some problems for examination boards if they do not include this aspect of reading within coursework. Because it is not practical to show film or video clips or play radio recordings to large numbers of candidates, any examination of media response is likely to use print-based materials.

AUDIENCES

A great deal of non-fiction writing is addressed to particular audiences: those who like travel, those who are interested in charities, those who want to read about the lives of other people, etc. Audiences in media terms tend to be broader groups, categorised by income and/or occupation in addition to, or rather than by, interest. You should be aware that some media texts are aimed very much at broad groups which might be labelled low-, middle- or high-income. Until recently, the media were often known as 'the mass media', and this usefully conveys the idea that writers working in the media need to identify carefully which members of a potentially huge audience they intend to target: for example, are they trying to interest all car enthusiasts from all income groups, or just anyone within one income group? One of the tips at the end of Chapter 16 (page 118) was to start thinking about non-fiction texts in terms of the audience they're aimed at, and this is also a good starting-point when analysing media texts and their effectiveness.

As an example, look at the following lead article from a magazine called *Countryside*, which is distributed to members of the National Farmers Union. It is unlikely that the nature of the audience would be in doubt, given the content of the article.

NFU

COUNTRYSIDE

The Journal for NFU Countryside Members   June 1997

British food is clearly the best, and how to prove it beyond doubt to supermarkets, caterers and the general public, is the aim of a new industry-wide farm standards initiative being promoted by NFU. Alison Pratt reports.

Our livestock industry, and the whole of agriculture, learned some salutary lessons in 1996. The BSE crisis so alarmed our customers that they now want to know, more than ever, that the animals and crops which provide their food have been grown, reared and produced to the highest possible standards.

NFU has undertaken to support and promote high quality food production and husbandry standards in conjunction with industry bodies such as the Meat and Livestock Commission (MLC), the Milk Development Council and representatives from the arable and horticulture sectors. The NFU has also held discussions with the multiple retailers many of which run their own assurance schemes.

NFU is currently looking at a single "baseline" standard which would ensure that farmers and growers comply with all relevant food hygiene, health and safety, animal welfare and agrochemical usage regulations. NFU President, Sir David Naish said, "Such a baseline standard would ensure that, in a few years time, the bulk of food and raw materials leaving British farms would have been produced under independently-audited farm assurance schemes."

Inspection, enforcement and auditing are the key aspects of a standardised farm assurance scheme. How else are consumers to know that they are certain to be served the quality they expect from British food? The extra layers of the scheme could, of course, impact upon producers' costs when measures such as registration, inspection and self-assessment are introduced. But the possibility of expanding into new markets and ensuring customer loyalty to British produce can only benefit the industry.

NFU and indeed, the whole of the food production industry, is at the beginning of a long process, consulting and formulating the new standards and structures to ensure the new scheme will be acceptable to producers, processors, retailers and, especially, the consumer.

"It is not enough any more to blithely say that we produce food of the highest quality to some of the toughest standards in the world," said Sir David Naish. "BSE has shown us that such a claim counts for nothing if we cannot prove it. We must show to the satisfaction of all that the very highest standards are being pursued at all times."

British food is the best by far

EXPECTATION AND INTERPRETATION – AN EXAMPLE

AUDIENCE

Look at the article again, but this time just the map and the headline underneath. If you had seen only these, you could have expected the article to be about restaurants or traditional dishes rather than farming. Knowing where the article was published and reading the actual content is necessary if you are to make proper sense of it. Because the particular audience for this article will have certain expectations, it does not need to be balanced in its views. Many people not involved in food production would feel that the article puts forward a very biased view, offering opinions as facts.

LANGUAGE AND PRESENTATION

It appeals to the patriotism of readers both in the frequent references to Britain and in the eye-catching map with parts of the Union Jack overlaid onto it. In case readers do not want to study the whole text, the argument is summed up in the brief, bold paragraph at the start. For those who do wish to read the whole article, their eyes are led to the start by the large green initial capital. Although it is an article which is fighting the corner for farmers, the very subtle background to the page is an idyllic rural scene, again mostly in restful, calm shades of green. In media terms, this apparently straightforward article is very skilfully presented to appeal to its target audience and to appear both strong-minded but reasonable in its argument.

MEDIA LANGUAGE

When analysing and responding to the language used in media texts, you will need to adopt an approach like that described in Chapter 14 (pages 103–7). Media texts will use:

- single words or phrases which try to influence how you feel, often dressing opinion as fact: for example, the opening of the above article: 'British food is *clearly* the *best* . . .';

- evocative phrases which influence your feelings but which do not stand up to close analysis: for example, 'A Mars a day helps you work, rest and play';

- claims which are truthful up to a point: for example, a disinfectant which 'kills all *known* germs' is not in fact claiming to kill *all* germs, though the advertisers hope that is what you will think;

- snobbery and its opposite, fear: for example, frequent uses of terms like 'exclusive' or 'executive', and all those television advertisements which try to make you worry about how white your washing is;

- direct appeals to the reader/listener/viewer: for example, eye contact in television advertisements or documentaries can draw you into the action and make it difficult for you to ignore or disagree with the speaker (you will learn more about using these techniques in your own speaking in Chapter 34);

- humour, such as punning newspaper headlines: the example on the left taken from a sports page, shows an Italian footballer who plays for Chelsea.

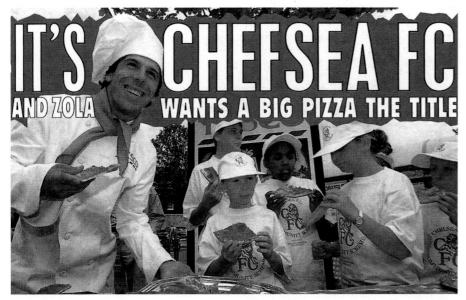

CONTENT AND PURPOSE

Media texts angle their content as well as their language and their presentation at target audiences. The NFU magazine (page 121) is an obvious example, and the tabloid press, particularly papers such as *The Sun*, the *Daily Mirror* and the *Star* base their content around what might be called 'human interest stories' rather than British politics or international news. Headlines are often jokey, as in the above example, and not always 'politically correct' especially if dealing with political matters. For example, one tabloid headline famously attacked a French politician Jacques Delors with the headline 'Up Yours, Delors', and when the Argentinian ship the *Belgrano* was sunk during the Falklands War, one tabloid headline crowed, 'Gotcha!'.

The media often display a stereotypical view of their audience and its interests: men's and women's magazines have very different contents, and even some broadsheet papers run special pages or articles for women readers which assume they, and not men, are interested in matters such as fashion, health and emotional well-being. Men's magazines tend to deal with sport, cars and travel.

If you think about the content of media texts in relation to their target audience, you will be able to judge how effective they are likely to be in achieving their purpose, whether that purpose is reinforcing strongly held views (as in the extract from the NFU magazine) or capturing the interest of an educated audience through the use of a headline such as this from the *Independent*:

> **French say non to le business speak Anglais**

STRUCTURAL AND PRESENTATIONAL DEVICES

As with language, many of the techniques we have noted in Chapter 15 (pages 110–13) as typical of non-fiction texts will also be evident in media texts. However, in a magazine, the use of headings, lists, frames, illustrations, different font styles and sizes will often be more extreme than in an information leaflet. The magazine, as a commercial publication, is out to catch the interest (and the money) of an audience and so will set out for maximum visual effect (and maximum linguistic effect through highly emotional – or intriguing – headlines). A similar contrast can be seen between tabloid newspapers, which more and more exhibit magazine-like qualities to the almost total exclusion of 'serious' news, and the broadsheet papers which use fewer illustrations, a more consistent typeface, longer stories, analytical features, and less contrived headlines.

PHYSICAL QUALITIES

In Chapter 15 we noted that the way in which leaflets can be folded, or the texture of the paper on which a text is printed, can affect its appropriateness to purpose and audience (page 113). The same is true of media texts. Tabloid newspapers are smaller and easier to handle than broadsheets, many of which now also produce daily or weekly supplements in tabloid size. You might consider whether this relates to the audiences: are tabloids read more by busy working people in crowded places, whereas broadsheets are read by people with more space and leisure in their own homes? Are tabloids easy to fold into a large pocket, while broadsheets need a briefcase? Do broadsheets cling to their size partly out of snobbery, and acknowledge their awkwardness by now issuing tabloid supplements? These are the kinds of questions you should ask about the physical qualities of media texts.

WHAT MAKES THE GRADE?

> To obtain Grade C for your responses to media texts, you need to show a personal and critical awareness of the nature of the material, that is, how the contents, style, structure and presentation relate to its intended audience and purpose. A Grade A candidate will discuss points of language in detail, cross-referring within and between texts where appropriate, and showing some awareness of the social and cultural backgrounds of different media audiences.

Check yourself

QUESTIONS

Q1 Look closely at the following two magazine covers. Write down:

a) what the covers have in common;
b) what makes them different;
c) what the cover of each magazine suggests about its contents;
d) what the intended audience is for each magazine.

Give as many details and as much evidence for your answers as you can. Write paragraphs of 60–80 words in answer to questions (a) and (b) and of about 100–120 words in answer to questions (c) and (d).

A1

a) Both covers are in colour and the titles stand out in white on a coloured background. Both magazines have pictures on the cover and both have several headlines in a range of bright colours which 'trail' stories inside so as to capture the interest of browsers in a shop, and both use some frames around these pieces of text. Both covers include date, price and barcode information.

b) The main illustration on the cover of *Woman* is a photograph of two well-known soap-opera characters, looking straight at camera and so catching your eye. Two smaller photographs are also of smiling people looking at the camera. The illustration on the cover of *The Lady* is a line drawing of part of a stately home in subdued pastel shades, and it is the only picture on the cover. The whole of the cover of *Woman* is in bright colours.

c) The cover of *Woman* suggests the contents are mainly about homes ('kitchen and bathroom makeovers') and relationships, both real ('Happily married. . .' and 'After 28 years . . .') and in the world of soap-opera ('It's Payback Time!'). Health matters are also included ('9 years . . .' and 'Phew!'), and two competitions are mentioned, one for a holiday and one for car, cash and a holiday. The cover of *The Lady* suggests that articles about cultural pursuits (such as literature, landscapes, architecture) and finance are the main contents, although a holiday is also trailed. An important aspect of the contents is information about jobs, holiday and retirement homes.

d) *Woman* is for an audience of young to middle-aged women who are interested in the make-believe world of television, their own health and relationships, and who aspire to 'dream' holidays, better cars and more money. *The Lady* is for two quite different audiences: one of well-off women who pursue a cultured lifestyle, and the other of those looking for employment with the first group. A third audience, really a subset of the first, is those elderly women who are seeking retirement homes. These audiences are suggested by the content and layout of the covers; *Woman* is bright and breezy and puts a soap-opera scandal centre-page, while *The Lady* is dignified and subdued; the use of a traditional font for the title and main headline reinforces this quality.

T1

You should make the point that the overall colourful effect is intended to be eye-catching and cheerful; explain as well as describe in answers to questions like this.

A good explanatory comment.

Don't overlook obvious features such as this.

You might have added that both covers refer to holiday offers/competitions.

You could also have commented on the facts that:

- all the typefaces on the Woman cover are modern, but The Lady uses traditional typefaces for the title and main headline;
- text and illustration are mostly separate on The Lady, but on Woman they run across and into each other, to give a much busier effect.

An analytical answer would comment that the size and positioning of the main photograph on Woman suggests that the imaginary relationship is likely to be of more interest to readers than real-life stories, and therefore that gossip or stories about film/TV characters (and the actors who play them) may be a significant aspect of the contents.

You might have commented that in this case it is a holiday offer, not a competition.

You could take this analysis further and say that the audience for Woman is probably not rich, but comfortable (i.e. middle income), and may have aspirations to 'improve' socially, e.g. through home improvements.

A sophisticated answer would raise the issue of whether the first audience of The Lady is quite as comfortable and secure as it might seem: the words 'The very special weekly magazine' on the cover are perhaps an attempt to reassure the readers that they are still special, and the prominence given to the classified advertisements box suggests that a number of fairly desperate people will be among the readership. Another audience might be of women who don't belong to any of these groups, but aspire to the kind of lifestyle which the illustration on the cover suggests.

SECTION II
Writing

CHAPTER 18

USING ACCURATE SPELLING

- In this chapter, you will learn to improve your spelling by understanding some basic rules.
- If you can spell accurately across a wide range of vocabulary, it will improve your chances of gaining a good GCSE grade for your writing.

WHY IS SPELLING IMPORTANT?

Most of us make occasional spelling mistakes. However, if you are constantly misspelling words, particularly common, everyday ones, you are likely to have two problems, one 'personal' and one 'public'. The 'personal' problem is that poor spelling will make you less confident about your writing. When you are trying to express your thoughts, ideas or feelings, you may be slowed down by worries about your spelling, and so your writing may lack fluency. You may be so concerned about your spelling that you are reluctant to write much at all. The 'public' problem is that good spelling is seen as an important social skill, an aspect of good manners as well as good communication. People may unfairly dismiss or ignore what you have written if they see bad spelling.

Good spelling is seen as an important social skill.

CAN YOU IMPROVE SPELLING?

Many students believe that they are poor spellers, and that there is nothing much they can do about it. Others believe that the most you can do is to read as many texts as possible in the hope that they will somehow 'catch' good spelling from the authors. Neither of these beliefs is true: you can improve your spelling, but you do need to go about it in a systematic way.

In this chapter, we will look at some of the regular patterns of English spelling which can be learnt. But there are other approaches which you need to adopt as well. You should:

- think about families of words: for example, once you can spell 'disappear' correctly, you should have no problems with other forms such as 'disappeared', 'disappearing', etc.;
- think about the origins of words: for example, you are unlikely to make the common mistake of leaving the 'n' out of 'government' if you remember that its job is to 'govern' us;
- learn technical words from other school or college subjects, for example scientific or technological terms;
- be aware of common words which have unusual spellings and do not appear to follow the patterns explained below, such as 'neither' and 'leisure';
- always proof-read your work, using dictionaries and computer spell-checkers where appropriate (see below).

DICTIONARIES AND SPELL-CHECKERS

You should make it a habit to use these facilities whenever they are available. They do different jobs, and each provides both benefits and potential problems.

SPELL-CHECKERS

If you are using a word-processing programme, spell-checkers are very useful for picking up mistakes and alerting you to the need for corrections. Remember, however, that spell-checkers:

- will not pick up every mistake, especially if the mistake you have made is itself a word. For example, if you have typed 'if' when you meant to use 'of', the spell-checker will not alert you to it;

- will not always suggest the correct alternative, especially if there are different spellings of words with the same sound. For example, you may have typed 'thete' and the computer suggests 'there', which is what you intended to type. However, unless you also have a sophisticated grammar check on your system, it will not be able to tell you that you really should have used 'their';

- are sometimes set for American rather than English spellings.

For these reasons, it is always a good idea to proof-read your work yourself, so that you pick up the first kind of problem mentioned above, and it is often a good idea to use a dictionary alongside a spell-checker, so that if you are given some alternative spellings by the computer, or if you have a nagging doubt that it may not be suggesting the correct word, as in the second case above, you can look and think further.

Even if you have access to a spell-checker, don't desert your dictionary!

DICTIONARIES

Spell-checkers may sometimes give you a clue if you have no idea how to spell a word. However, using a dictionary is important for these reasons:

- it can alert you to the meanings and usage of words, and so make you realise that the spell-checker has suggested an inappropriate word;

- if you read the dictionary entries in detail, these can teach you about the meanings and spellings of related words, and help you build up your knowledge of word families and word origins.

WAYS OF LEARNING SPELLINGS

There are different ways of learning all kinds of things. Some of us learn by doing, some by reading and thinking, some by watching or listening to others, and so on. Often we use a mix of methods. Learning spelling is no different, and you must decide for yourself how you are likely to learn most effectively. There are four main approaches:

- **sight-based approach:** looking at different written versions of a word to decide which looks right, or trying to see the word in your mind's eye;

- **sound-based approach:** trying to work from the sounds of words, maybe saying the whole word out slowly aloud, or breaking up words into shorter sections which you say to yourself;
- **rule-based approach:** trying to remember spelling rules, or thinking about the spelling of similar words, or going straight to a dictionary for help;
- **manual approach:** writing out the word with different spellings and seeing which one feels right.

None of these rules is the best or correct way to learn spelling – if you favour one, stick to it and develop it all you can. If you can try to use two or even all four of the approaches – say by using your favourite approach first and then one of the others as a further check – that will probably help you learn more correct spellings more quickly.

LEARNING NEW SPELLINGS

When you meet a new word it is important to impress it on your memory in as many ways as possible. To do this you can use the LOOK, COVER, WRITE, CHECK method:

LOOK at the word
COVER it up
WRITE it down
CHECK that you have written it correctly.

This is better than looking at each letter and writing them down one by one, as it gives you a 'feel' for the word and you are more likely to rely on patterns you already know in the writing phase.

SPELLING RULES

Many people believe that the spelling of English is so irregular that it is impossible to learn rules. This is not true. While some other languages have a higher proportion of predictable spellings, English does obey rules and patterns for much of the time. If you learn just a few of these, your spelling will improve dramatically.

Note that there are often a few exceptions to these rules, and it is of course important that you learn the exceptions. However, don't overdo that: exceptions are exceptions, and it is the general rule which you most need to remember!

- The letter 'q' is always followed by 'u' except in the name of the country 'Iraq'.
- 'i' comes before 'e', except when it follows 'c': e.g. 'priest', 'friend', 'brief' but 'ceiling', 'deceive', 'receive'.

Note exceptions: when the vowel sound is 'a', as in 'neighbour' and 'weigh'; also 'neither', 'foreign', 'seize', 'sovereign', 'counterfeit', 'forfeit', 'leisure'.

DOUBLING RULES

- 'l', 'f' and 's' are doubled after a single vowel at the end of a one-syllable word: e.g. 'call', 'miss', 'stuff', 'tell', 'toss'.

  Note a number of exceptions in very common words: 'bus', 'gas', 'if', 'of', 'plus', 'this', 'us', 'yes'.

- Words ending with a single vowel + single consonant double the consonant if adding an ending which begins with a vowel: e.g. 'shop–shopped–shopping'; 'flat–flatter–flattest'; 'swim–swimmer–swimming'.

SINGLING RULES

- 'All' followed by another syllable drops one 'l': e.g. 'also', 'already', 'always', 'although'.

  Note an exception: 'all right' should be written as two words. If you make it 'alright', you are showing understanding of this spelling rule, but are misapplying it.

- 'Full' and 'till' drop one 'l' when added to another syllable: e.g. 'hopeful', 'useful', 'cheerful', 'until'.

END GAMES

- An 'i' or 'ee' sound at the end of a word is nearly always spelled 'y': e.g. 'hungry', 'county', 'rugby'.

  Note exceptions such as 'coffee', 'committee' and 'taxi', and some words which are borrowings from other languages (mainly Italian, e.g. 'spaghetti', 'macaroni').

- *Drop* the final 'e' from a word before adding an ending which begins with a vowel, but *keep* it before an ending which begins with a consonant: e.g. 'love–loving–lovely'; 'drive–driving–driver'; 'rattle–rattled–rattling'.

  Note there are some exceptions: e.g. as 'dye' and 'singe', which keep the final 'e' before 'ing' ('dyeing', 'singeing') to avoid confusion with 'die' ('dying') and 'sing' ('singing').

- If a word ends with a consonant followed by 'y', change the 'y' to 'i' before all endings except 'ing': e.g. 'heavy–heaviness'; 'fun–funnily'; 'marry–married–marrying'; 'hurry–hurriedly–hurrying'.

PLURALS

- Regular plurals are made by adding 's': e.g. 'dog–dogs'; 'horse–horses'; 'committee–committees'.
- Words ending 'y' after a consonant make the plural by changing the 'y' to 'ies': e.g. 'lady–ladies'; 'baby–babies'.
- Add 'es' to words ending with 's', 'x', 'z', 'sh', 'ch', 'ss': e.g. 'bus–buses'; 'fox–foxes'; 'buzz–buzzes'; 'wish–wishes'; 'church–churches'; 'miss–misses'.
- Most words ending with a single 'f' or 'fe' change the 'f' or 'fe' to 'ves' to form the plural: e.g. 'leaf–leaves'; 'wolf–wolves'; 'knife–knives'; 'wife–wives'.

'Dwarfs' doesn't follow the usual pattern.

Note exceptions: 'dwarf–dwarfs'; 'roof–roofs'; 'chief–chiefs'; 'safe–safes'.

Note also some words can take either 's' or 'ves' in the plural: 'hoof', 'scarf', 'wharf'.

HOMONYMS

These are words which have different spellings for different meanings but sound similar, e.g. 'their', 'there' , 'they're'; 'its', 'it's'; 'birth', 'berth'; 'were', 'where', 'wear', 'we're', 'weir'.

Generally speaking, you need to learn the meanings and/or the different grammatical functions of these words: there is advice on some of these in Chapter 19 (pages 135–37).

WHAT MAKES THE GRADE? ▶

Spelling is marked as part of your Writing skills in GCSE English. Although it is not given a separate mark (as it is in other GCSE subjects, including English Literature), it does make an important contribution to your overall performance.

To achieve a Grade C for your writing, you must be able to spell a wide range of words accurately. This means that you would be expected to spell common, everyday words correctly most of the time, although the occasional slip under the pressure of examination timing will not be heavily punished. You would also be expected to have a reasonably accurate attempt at less common words.

Some common words which are often misspelt include:

argument	conscience	favourite	persuade
beautiful	deceive	friend	prejudice
beginning	develop	hoping	rhyme
behaviour	dining	immediately	rhythm
believe	disappear	jealous	suspense
business	embarrassed	language	unnatural
character	fascinate	necessary	
conscious	father	occasionally	

To achieve a Grade A, you would be expected to use a wider and more ambitious range of vocabulary, and to spell most of the words correctly most of the time. You would be unlikely to achieve a high grade if you made many mistakes in common spelling patterns such as those explained in this chapter.

Some more ambitious words which are often misspelt include:

antagonise	economically	onomatopoeia	terrain
atmosphere	environment	oppression	turbulent
channelled	facial	professional	turquoise
committed	hygienic	psychologically	tyrannical
competence	hypocrisy	rumour	villain
condemned	independent	stereotypical	viscious
connive	metaphorically	strikingly	
eccentric	naive	symbolise	

Check yourself

QUESTIONS

Q1 Which spelling patterns do the following words illustrate?

a) chiefs
b) deceive
c) shopping
d) hopeful
e) weigh
f) although
g) driving
h) funnily
i) leaves
j) question

Q2 Rewrite the passage on the right, correcting the spelling mistakes and noting which of the above rules are involved.

My nieghbour is hopefull of returning to the land of her berth one day, and she is driveing me mad with her constant chater about how much lovelyer than England most other countreys are. She has been all over the far and middle east, including Iraqu, were her best freind lives. I would happyly take a leaf out of her book – several leafs, to tell the truth – and visit foriegn places, but I'm always kept very busy at my job. I mend rooves, and after this winter's storms I've been busyer than ever. I'm hopeing to get a holiday soon, but it won't be until the better whether comes. I'm dying for a brake, but I'm a bit short of money at the moment – I hardly have enough to keep the wolfs from the door, never mind exciting holidays.

REMEMBER! Cover the answers if you want to.

ANSWERS

A1

a) 'chiefs': exception to the pattern that words ending with a single 'f' or 'fe' change the 'f' or 'fe' to 'ves' to form the plural

b) 'deceive': 'e' before 'i' after 'c'

c) 'shopping': words ending with a single vowel followed by a single consonant double the last consonant if adding an ending which begins with a vowel

d) 'hopeful': 'full' and 'till' drop one 'l' when added to another syllable

e) 'weigh': 'i' before 'e' does not apply when the sound is 'a'

f) 'although': 'all' followed by another syllable drops one 'l'

g) 'driving': drop the final 'e' from a word before adding an ending which begins with a vowel

h) 'funnily': if a word ends with a consonant followed by 'y', change the 'y' to 'i' before endings

i) 'leaves': words ending with a single 'f' change the 'f' to 'ves' to form the plural

j) 'question': 'q' is always followed by 'u'

TUTORIALS

T1

a) *It is a good idea to learn the exceptions carefully.*

b) *The 'i' before 'e' except after 'c' is a fairly reliable pattern.*

c) *Another regular and reliable pattern.*

d) *Putting double 'l' on the ends of words like this is a very common spelling mistake.*

e) *Not therefore an exception to the pattern: look carefully at the explanation in the chapter.*

f) *A regular, reliable pattern.*

g) *Remember, however, to keep the final 'e' if the ending begins with a consonant.*

h) *True of all endings except 'ing'.*

i) *There are exceptions – remember 'chief' and the others.*

j) *The only exception is the name of the country, Iraq.*

ANSWERS

A2 My neighbour[1] is hopeful[2] of returning to the land of her birth[3] one day, and she is driving[4] me mad with her constant chatter[5] about how much lovelier[6] than England most other countries[7] are. She has been all over the far and middle east, including Iraq[8], where[9] her best friend[10] lives. I would happily[11] take a leaf out of her book – several leaves[12], to tell the truth – and visit foreign[13] places, but I'm always[14] kept very busy at my job. I mend roofs[15], and after this winter's storms I've been busier[16] than ever. I'm hoping[17] to get a holiday soon, but it won't be until the better weather[18] comes. I'm dying for a break[19], but I'm a bit short of money at the moment – I hardly have enough to keep the wolves[20] from the door, never mind exciting holidays.

TUTORIALS

T2

1 *Exception to 'i' before 'e' as it's pronounced 'a'.*
2 *'Full' loses one 'l' at the end of words.*
3 *Homonym: think of 'birthday' for the correct spelling here.*
4 *Drop the final 'e' from a word ('drive') before adding an ending which begins with a vowel ('ing').*
5 *Words ending with a single vowel + single consonant ('chat') double the last consonant if adding an ending ('er') which begins with a vowel.*
6 *If a word ends with a consonant followed by 'y' ('lovely'), change the 'y' to 'i' before all endings.*
7 *Words ending 'y' after a consonant make the plural by changing the 'y' to 'ies'*
8 *The only word in English where 'q' is not followed by 'u'.*
9 *Homonym: 'where' refers to a place, 'were' is the past tense of the verb 'to be'.*
10 *'i' before 'e' except after 'c'.*
11 *See point 6 above.*
12 *Words ending with a single 'f' change the 'f' to 'ves' to form the plural.*
13 *An exception to the 'i' before 'e' pattern.*
14 *'all' followed by another syllable drops one 'l'.*
15 *An exception to the pattern mentioned in point 12 above.*
16 *See point 6 above.*
17 *See point 4 above, and beware of doubling instead of removing the 'e': that would give 'hopping', which has a totally different meaning.*
18 and 19 *Homonyms.*
20 *See point 12 above.*

See the Check Yourself section in Chapter 19 (page 138) for some more practice in correcting spelling mistakes.

USING APPROPRIATE PUNCTUATION

- In this chapter, you will learn about uses of the comma, the semi-colon and colon, dashes, brackets, question marks and exclamation marks, apostrophes and punctuating speech.

- If you learn how punctuation is used, you will understand subtle shades of meaning in what you read, and if you learn to use a range of punctuation accurately, you will be able to express meanings more clearly and precisely in your own writing.

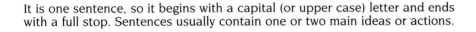

PUNCTUATING SENTENCES

FULL STOPS

Lord of the Flies.

Look at this extract from William Golding's *Lord of the Flies*:

> He was old enough, twelve years and a few months, to have lost the prominent tummy of childhood; and not yet old enough for adolescence to have made him awkward.

It is one sentence, so it begins with a capital (or upper case) letter and ends with a full stop. Sentences usually contain one or two main ideas or actions.

SEMI-COLONS

Because the sentence contains two definite ideas – a contrast between childhood and adolescence – Golding has separated them with a semi-colon; he could have chosen to write two separate sentences, but, as the two ideas are closely linked, he decided that the less complete break shown by the semi-colon was more suitable. Note how the same thing has been done in the previous sentence, where the words following the semi-colon develop and explain the first half of the sentence.

It is a good idea to use semi-colons yourself. Not only does it show your understanding of punctuation, but it helps you to develop and vary the style of your writing (see Chapters 20 and 21, for more on this).

COMMAS

Golding also uses the comma. In the example from *Lord of the Flies*, the comma is used to separate off from the main part of the sentence a group of words (known as a phrase) which add a description. If you read the sentence again, but miss out the words between the commas, you will see that it still makes perfect sense. However, the words 'twelve years and a few months' add useful information for the reader and so, although they are included, are marked off with commas to show that they are additional to the main idea of the sentence.

The comma has other uses as well. Sometimes its main purpose is to help the reader by indicating places in a long sentence where a slight pause will clarify the meaning. Look at this sentence from George Orwell's *Animal Farm*:

Animal Farm.

She knew that, even as things were, they were far better off than they had been in the days of Jones, and that before all else it was needful to prevent the return of the human beings.

That sentence is more easily understood if you pause at the commas when reading it. Now look at this extract from Harper Lee's *To Kill a Mockingbird*:

Of all days Sunday was the day for formal afternoon visiting: ladies wore corsets, men wore coats, children wore shoes.

In this sentence, the commas separate items in a list, one of the comma's most frequent functions.

COLONS

Note that Harper Lee has also used a colon. This piece of punctuation is particularly useful for introducing a list, as in the above example.

OTHER PUNCTUATION

So far in this chapter, two other types of punctuation have been used. One of these is the dash (–), which is best used only occasionally, to emphasise an idea or statement. Look again at how two dashes have been used near the start of this chapter to make a point about the idea in Golding's sentence. Using dashes too frequently gives writing a rather frantic, breathless appearance and annoys the reader, but used sparingly they can direct the reader's attention to important points.

The other device used is brackets (or parentheses). These are most often used to add an explanation, an example or (as in the previous sentence) an alternative. Brackets are less striking (and less annoying to the reader if used frequently) than dashes.

There are three other pieces of punctuation you should be able to use. Two of them are quite straightforward. A question mark goes at the end of any direct question, as in this passage from Mildred C. Taylor's *Roll of Thunder, Hear My Cry*:

Mama stared into Mr Morrison's deep eyes. 'Whose fault was it?'
Mr Morrison stared back. 'I'd say theirs.'
'Did the other men get fired?'
'No, ma'am,' answered Mr Morrison. 'They was white.'

Note that the questions are directly quoted in this passage. If, however, a question is merely reported during an account or narrative, a question mark is not used. An example of this (from the same book) is:

When I asked him if he wanted to come work here as a hired hand, he said he would.

The exclamation mark, like dashes, must be used sparingly. It is used to indicate anger, surprise, humour or any strong or unexpected feeling, as in this extract from Rukshana Smith's *Salt on the Snow*:

Before she could be questioned Julie shouted, 'I know because I was there! That's how my head got bruised. Because he threw a brick at the window.' 'It wasn't me, prove it!' yelled Jim.

Note how the words 'shouted' and 'yelled' give a clue that exclamation marks might be appropriate; but remember that punctuation alone cannot convey feelings – it can only strengthen the impact of well-chosen language.

APOSTROPHES

The item of punctuation which causes most trouble these days is without doubt the apostrophe. Many writers panic, particularly when they see the letter 's', and start putting apostrophes everywhere. In fact, the rules are quite simple.

Missing Letters

First of all, the apostrophe shows where one or more letters have been missed out, so in the above passage from *Salt on the Snow*, the apostrophe in the word 'That's' shows that an 'i' has been left out (in a more formal situation, the speaker would have said 'That is'), and the apostrophe in the word 'wasn't' shows that an 'o' has been left out (if the speaker had used more formal English, he would have said 'was not'). Note that the apostrophe is placed where the missing letter would have been.

If more than one letter is left out, you still only put one apostrophe into the word. Here is another example from *Salt on the Snow*:

'I've been too busy at work to keep an eye on things here, but I'll be watching you from now on.'

In both instances where apostrophes are used here, two letters have been left out. The spoken version of 'I have' has become 'I've', and the spoken version of 'I will' has become 'I'll'. Notice that this last example shows how important it is to use apostrophes correctly, or the word 'I'll' might be confused with 'Ill' (meaning unwell), just as 'we'll' (that is, 'we will') might be confused with 'well' (not ill!) unless an apostrophe is correctly inserted. Watch out for certain instances where the apostrophe might stand for different letters; for example, 'he's' could be a spoken version of 'he is' or 'he has'.

Possession

The other main use of apostrophes is to show possession. Look at this passage from Barry Hines' A *Kestrel for a Knave*:

One lap of MacDowell's shirt curved out from beneath his sweater, and covered one thigh, like half an apron. Billy's shirt buttons had burst open all down the front. One button was missing, the corresponding button-hole ripped open. Their hair looked as though they had been scratching their scalps solidly for a week, and their faces were the colour of colliers'.

BARRY HINES

In a raw, mean town a boy turns to the one thing he can trust. Her name was Kes.

A KESTREL FOR A KNAVE

The three apostrophes used here all show possession: we are told about the shirt which belongs to MacDowell, and then the shirt which belongs to Billy; the final word in the extract is comparing the colour of their faces to the colour of colliers' (or coal-miners') faces. Note that if the writer had not put an apostrophe at the end of the word 'colliers', the meaning would have been quite different – he would have been suggesting that MacDowell's and Billy's faces were the colour of coal miners, whatever that is! The apostrophe, however, makes it clear that the boys' faces are the colour of colliers' faces, as the apostrophe makes the reader mentally refer back to an earlier word in the sentence which could be linked with 'colliers''.

A similar function of the possessive apostrophe will have become obvious to you throughout this book. It is used when a book is ascribed to an author, as in William Golding's *Lord of the Flies* or Rukshana Smith's *Salt on the Snow*. The same is true of pictures (Leonardo da Vinci's Mona Lisa), music (Beethoven's ninth symphony), films (Hitchcock's *Psycho*) and so on.

Princess's last words

The apostrophe used to show possession.

When using an apostrophe to show possession, an 's' is put after the apostrophe if the word does not already end with one. However, if the word already ends with 's' but is not a plural (for example, 'bus' or the name 'Chris'), it is usual to add another 's' after the apostrophe, so you would have 'The bus's seats were very comfortable' or 'It was Chris's birthday last week'.

If the word is a plural – like 'colliers' in the example from A *Kestrel for a Knave* – you only need to put the apostrophe: do not add another 's'. Some words have a plural form which does not end in 's', for example 'women', 'children', 'geese'. In these cases, an 's' should be added after the apostrophe, so we would have 'The women's votes were crucial to the candidate's success' or 'The children's clothes were stolen from the changing rooms'.

The only real difficulty with this use of the apostrophe is making sure that you put it in the right place. If you look again at the last sentence of the paragraph about the extract from A *Kestrel for a Knave*, you will see that it says *the boys' faces*. That means 'the faces belonging to the two boys, MacDowell and Billy'. If it had said *the boy's faces*, it would not have made much sense, as it would have meant the two or more faces belonging to one boy!

I think it's lost its way

CONFUSING APOSTROPHES

There are two potentially confusing uses of the apostrophe in words which are pronounced similarly but which have different meanings. If you remember that apostrophes generally replace missing letters, you should not have any problems, but it may be worth making a special effort to learn these examples:

It's/Its

The first spelling, which is the shortened version of 'it is', would be found in sentences such as 'It's a long way from here'. The second spelling, without the apostrophe, means 'belonging to it', for example: 'The dog lost its ball.'

Who's/Whose

In the first of these, 'who's' = 'who is'and might be found in sentences such as 'Who's going to carry this for me?' The other form, without the apostrophe and with an 'e' on the end, means 'belonging to whom', for example 'Whose house is that?'

These examples may appear to contradict what has been said above about using apostrophes to show possession, but in this case there is no apostrophe because the words themselves contain the notion of possession. The same is true of 'hers', 'his', 'ours', 'yours', 'theirs'.

PUNCTUATING SPEECH

The final aspect of punctuation we need to cover is speech marks, which are sometimes known as inverted commas or quotation marks. The most common use of speech marks is, of course, to punctuate direct speech. Look at this passage from *Lord of the Flies*:

> "I don't care what they call me," he said confidentially, "so long as they don't call me what they used to call me at school."
> Ralph was faintly interested.
> "What was that?"
> The fat boy glanced over his shoulder, then leaned towards Ralph.
> He whispered.
> "They used to call me 'Piggy'."

This extract illustrates the main rules of punctuating speech. These are:

- put all spoken words inside the speech marks (the speech marks themselves can be double commas, as in the above example, or single commas, as in the previous examples from *Roll of Thunder, Hear My Cry* and *Salt on the Snow*);
- each new piece of speech must begin with a capital letter, but one piece of speech can be broken up by other words as in Piggy's first sentence above, in which case the speech continues with a small (or lower case) letter;
- any punctuation of the speech goes inside the speech marks, for example the comma after 'me' in the first sentence and the question mark at the end of Ralph's reply;
- if another set of quotation marks is needed within the speech marks, for example when Piggy mentions his nickname, then use single commas if you are already using double commas, or double commas if you are already using single commas;
- if you start a passage of direct speech with words such as 'she said', 'he asked', then you need to put a comma after these words and before the speech marks, as in this example from *Salt on the Snow*:

> Rashmi pointed to the ceiling and Julie said, 'Not where, how?'

Speech marks are also used in handwritten text for the titles of books, films and works of art.

WHAT MAKES THE GRADE?

Punctuation is assessed as one aspect of your Writing skills in the GCSE examination. To achieve a Grade C, your punctuation is expected to make meanings clear and coherent. In other words, you should at least be using commas, full stops, exclamation and question marks accurately, and should make few mistakes in punctuating speech. You would also be expected to use apostrophes correctly, and not to confuse forms such as 'its' and 'it's'. To achieve a Grade A, your punctuation should be more ambitious, and usually accurate – that is, you should be using the full range of punctuation explained here, including semi-colons and colons.

Check yourself

QUESTIONS

Q1 What are the different uses of the comma?

Q2 Punctuate this extract from *Lord of the Flies*:

> piggys specs shouted ralph if the fires right out well need them

Q3 Look again at this example of apostrophes:

> The women's votes were crucial to the candidate's success.

How would the meaning change if the second apostrophe were placed *after* the 's' (candidates')?

Q4 Punctuate this passage from *Animal Farm*:

> but the men did not go unscathed either three of them had their heads broken by blows from boxers hoofs another was gored in the belly by a cows horn another had his trousers nearly torn off by jessie and bluebell and when the nine dogs of napoleons own bodyguard whom he had instructed to make a detour under cover of the hedge suddenly appeared on the mens flank baying ferociously panic overtook them

Q5 Explain the different ways in which colons and semi-colons are used.

Q6 The following is 'A tall story' written by Billy Casper, a character in A *Kestrel for a Knave*. Billy cannot spell or punctuate very well, as you will see. Rewrite his story, using it as an opportunity to test yourself again on spelling (remind yourself of common spelling patterns in Chapter 18, pages 128–9) and on punctuation which you have learned about in this chapter. You may need to add an occasional word to improve the flow of Billy's writing.

One day I wolke up and my muther said to me heer Billy theres your brecfst in bed for you there was backen and egg and bred and butter and a big pot of tea when I had my brekfast the sun was shining out side and I got drest and whent down stairs we lived in a big hous up moor edge and we add carpits on the stairs and in the all and sentrall eeting. When I got down I said wers are Jud his goind the ary my muther saide and hees not coming back. but your dades coming back i sted. there was a big fire in the room and my dad came in caring his cas that he tulke a way with him I havent seen him for a long time but he was just the sam as he went away I was glad he hed come back and are Jud had gon away when I got to school all the teacherr were good to me they said allow Billy awo you gowing on and they all pated me on the head and smiled and we did interesting thing all day when I got home my muther saide I not gowing to work eny more and we all had chips beans for awur tea then we got redy and we all went to the picturs we went up stairs and had Ice cream at the intervells and then we all went home and had fish and chips for awur super and then we went to bed.

ANSWERS

A1
- separating items in a list
- separating phrases
- marking pauses for sense
- in direct speech after 'he said', etc.

A2
"Piggy's specs!" shouted Ralph, "if the fire's right out, we'll need them –"

A3
It would then mean that the success of more than one candidate had depended on the votes of the women.

A4
But the men did not go unscathed either. Three of them had their heads broken by blows from Boxer's hoofs; another was gored in the belly by a cow's horn; another had his trousers nearly torn off by Jessie and Bluebell. And when the nine dogs of Napoleon's own bodyguard, whom he had instructed to make a detour under cover of the hedge, suddenly appeared on the men's flank, baying ferociously, panic overtook them.

A5
Semi-colons (;) are used to separate long sentences into complete units of sense which are closely linked to each by meaning. Colons (:) are used to introduce a list.

TUTORIALS

T1
The comma is a particularly useful device for helping readers make sense of written text. Take care, however, that you use full stops to indicate the end of sentences. Note a special use of the comma in the previous sentence: the word however should always be followed by a comma, and have a comma before it if it is not the first word in a sentence.

T2
This is how William Golding punctuated the passage. You too should have placed the speech marks (single or double commas) around the actual speech, put in the two capital letters (always used for names), the two apostrophes ('Piggy's' to show possession and 'fire's' as a shortened form of 'fire is'), the exclamation mark ('shouted' is a clue to the need for it). If you put a full stop after 'Ralph' followed by a capital 'I' for 'If', that would be an acceptable alternative. Golding has used a dash at the end to suggest Ralph was going to say more, but if you have put a full stop (or even another exclamation mark), that would be perfectly acceptable.

T3
Remember that the position of the apostrophe is crucial, particularly in words which could be plural or singular, as in this case.

T4
Orwell's own version is shown here. It would be possible to punctuate this as two sentences only, the second starting at 'Three of them' and continuing right to the end, with commas rather than semi-colons after 'hoofs', 'horn' and 'Bluebell'. However, it would then be a long and very complicated sentence, and this is a good example of how semi-colons and commas can be used together to make meaning clear. Note that Orwell begins his last sentence with 'And'; this is often supposed to be an error, but used carefully, it can be a striking stylistic feature – here, it draws your attention to how the men were eventually driven away in panic.

T5
Semi-colons are stronger in their effect than a comma, but not so strong as a full stop. The above example from Orwell's Animal Farm shows how they can help to build towards a climax more effectively than several totally separate sentences would have done. Colons are less commonly used, although you may come across some writers who also use colons (rather than a comma) to introduce direct speech (e.g. 'He said: "When will you be home?"') or to give an example which follows on from the first part of a sentence (e.g. in To Kill a Mockingbird, Harper Lee writes 'Miss Maudie's benevolence extended to Jem, and Dill, whenever they paused in their pursuits: we reaped the benefits of a talent Miss Maudie had hitherto kept hidden from us.'). You are advised to keep to the main use of colons, and certainly to use commas in direct speech.

ANSWERS

A6 One day I woke up, and my mother said to me, 'Here, Billy, there's your breakfast in bed for you.' There was bacon and egg, and [1] bread and butter, and a big pot of tea. When I had my breakfast the sun was shining outsIde and I got dressed and went downstairs. We lived in a big house up Moor [2] Edge, and we had carpets on the stairs and in the hall, and central heating. When I got down I said, 'Where's our Jud?' [3]
'He's gone in the army,' my mother said, [4] 'and he's not coming back, but your dad's [5] coming back instead.' There was a big fire in the room, and my dad came in carrying his case that he took away with him. I [6] haven't seen him for a long time, but he was just the same as he went away. I was glad he'd come back and our Jud had gone away. When I got to school, all the teachers were good to me. They said, 'Hello, Billy, how are you going on?' and they all patted [7] me on the head and smiled, and we did [8] interesting things all day. When I got home [9] my mother said, 'I'm not going to work any more,' and we all had chips [and] beans for our tea. Then we got ready and we all went to the pictures. We went upstairs and had ice-cream at the intervals, and then we all [10] went home and had fish and chips for our supper and then we went to bed.

TUTORIALS

T6 *This is not the only way to punctuate the piece, but is acceptable. Spellings have been corrected, but grammar has not, except for inserting one 'and' near the end. Note that Billy's misspellings are sometimes very strange - they do not neatly illustrate the patterns explained in Chapter 18.*

1 *It is sometimes said that you should not use commas after 'and', but 'bacon and egg' and 'bread and butter' are combinations of words which are best treated as units and separated in a list.*

2 *Note capital letters for people's names, for the word 'I', and for the name of a place (Moor Edge).*

3 *Note need for a question mark.*

4 *Note starting a new line for a new person speaking.*

5 *Note apostrophes for missing letters.*

6 *It would be possible to use a semi-colon between 'him' and 'I'.*

7 *Note need for question mark*

8 *A semi-colon after 'smiled' would be possible: it would make the following words even more dramatic.*

9 *It would be possible (but not necessary) to put a comma after 'home' (similarly, the comma after 'school' five lines above is optional).*

10 *The comma after 'intervals' is not essential, but it does help divide the sentence into one part about the pictures and one part about going home.*

CHAPTER 20

USING DIFFERENT SENTENCE STRUCTURES

- In this chapter, you will learn to use informal and formal written English appropriately and to vary the ways in which you write according to the purpose of your writing.
- This will enable you to demonstrate the range of sentence structures needed to gain a high GCSE grade.

APPROPRIATE USE OF INFORMAL/ FORMAL WRITTEN ENGLISH

FICTION

When you start to plan a piece of writing, your first consideration should be whether the context of the writing is formal or informal. In Chapter 29, we shall be seeing how this affects spoken English, but it is an equally important decision in planning writing. If you were given the following titles for imaginative writing, which do you think would make use of an informal style, and which might suit a more formal style?

- The argument
- Spring
- First Love
- My most embarrassing moment

You would probably agree that the first and last titles suggest a style of writing which involves a lot of dialogue and informal language, including slang, to give the effect of addressing the reader directly in a 'chatty', engaging way. The other two titles would probably suggest reflective, descriptive writing in a more formal style, much less like the informality of spoken language. Look at this extract from a GCSE student's story called 'Viva España':

> "'ere, Trace, what's the time?"
> "Will you stop asking that, for God's sake? It's just gone two."
> "Don't you think we ought to cover up? We've been out here since half ten this morning." Sharon squinted up at the midday sun and reached for her lipstick, which melted as soon as she applied it to her lips.
> "Hell's bells, Sharon, don't you want to get brown or something?"
> "Yeah, but . . ."
> "But what?"
> "Well, I'm going dead red and I feel sort of sick."

Informal English is used to good effect to create the two characters. Sharon drops the 'h' in 'here', uses abbreviations (e.g. 'what's', 'don't', 'we've'), misses out words ('half [past] ten') and uses slang ('Yeah', 'dead [red]'), giving the impression of a casual, and perhaps not too bright, young lady. Tracey's impatience with her friend is shown by her use of phrases such as 'for God's sake', 'hell's bells' and the incomplete sentence, 'But what?'.

Informal or non-standard English is fine when used for particular, planned effects such as this. In your fiction writing, however, you need to be conscious that different degrees of formality will be necessary, depending on the precise purpose and the audience you are writing for. Even in the above example the

The powerful description of Meg conjures up a vivid image.

writer uses a more formal style in the sentence which describes Sharon putting on her lipstick: the use of the words 'squinted' and 'midday' set the scene precisely, and the use of the word 'applied' shows the writer's ability to use language precisely and to create effective contrasts.

Formal English can be particularly effective in conveying an appropriate atmosphere through description. This is the beginning of a student's story called 'The Outsider':

> Wait. It was all she could do. Time was rushing past and there was nothing her old and bony hands could do to hold it back. She did not know the time but knew that this was probably her last night on earth. Meg was to spend her last night alone, as she had spent most of her life.

This passage is formal in spite of the fact it uses simple words and phrases. All words are given their full forms and sentences are carefully constructed. The first sentence contains one word only which helps it to stand out. Note the phrase 'old and bony'. It could have been written as 'old, bony' but the use of 'and' gives it a more formal and considered sound. Good fictional writing may often use an informal style for particular effects, but you will need to show your awareness of when this is appropriate, and also that you can use language formally and precisely to create character and mood, as in the above example.

NON-FICTION

Non-fiction writing can be informal, for example, if you are writing a personal memory, when you may include realistic dialogue or your own casually expressed thoughts. More often, it is expressed formally, since you are usually trying to explain or persuade in this kind of writing. For example, here is the start of a GCSE student's account of work experience:

> The words 'work experience' have always conjured up a host of emotions, from when I first heard them and slotted them somewhere far off in the haze of the future. A mixture of excitement, curiosity, interest and hope mingled with a slight apprehension as the two-week period drew nearer.

You can see that the language and the structure of the sentences is formal – the author is writing for an unknown audience, so a degree of formality is courteous; the purpose is to explain a feeling clearly and without risk of misunderstanding.

The structure of the sentences is more complex than in Sharon and Tracey's dialogue. You would not write or speak to a friend like this – you'd be more likely to start, 'The thought of work experience really freaked me out, you know!' These examples show that it is not just the choice of individual words which makes writing formal or informal, but also how those words are structured into sentences.

VARYING YOUR SENTENCE STRUCTURE APPROPRIATELY

Achieving the right degree of formality and informality in your writing is therefore not just a matter of avoiding slang or abbreviations. It goes deeper than that. You need to be able to vary how you structure sentences too.

Simple Sentences

A simple sentence contains just one basic thought or idea, and normally includes a subject and a verb:

> I laughed.

Here, 'I' is the subject, and 'laughed' is the verb.
Simple sentences are not necessarily so short; they can be much longer:

> No escaped prisoners of war were found hiding anywhere in the extensive network of underground passages.

The above sentence is defined as 'simple' because it contains only one main verb.

Compound Sentences

A compound sentence joins one or more simple sentences together. For example, you might write in a story

> She had been gone for only a month. He felt lonely without her.

Alternatively, you could join these simple sentences into a compound sentence:

> She had been gone for only a month, but he felt lonely without her.

Neither arrangement is better than the other. It depends on the needs of the writing. Sometimes, a series of short, simple sentences will convey an atmosphere of excitement or an agitated state of mind. At other times, longer, more complicated sentences will be necessary to explain a difficult idea, to suggest a character's confusion, or give the writing a continuous flow.

Complex Sentences

Complex sentences are different from compound sentences. Without getting too technical, they join together several ideas without just using words such as 'and', 'but', 'or'; instead, the basic grammatical structure of the sentence changes. For example, here are two more simple sentences:

> He had lost his interest in fishing. He decided to take up golf.

These could be made into a compound sentence:

> He had lost his interest in fishing and decided to take up golf.

To show your ability to use different grammatical structures, however, the two simple sentences could be formed into a complex sentence such as the one shown in the cartoon caption on the right. The word 'because' makes the connection between the two parts of the sentence clearer.

Because he had lost his interest in fishing, he decided to take up golf.

143

Short sentences can be used for action, longer ones for description.

FICTION

Let's see how varying sentence structures can add to the interest of fiction writing by returning to the student's work we looked at earlier. 'Viva España' ends like this:

> They stop and sit down on the cool, soft sand. She hugs her knees and looks up at him, the breeze now blustery and blowing her fine hair about. He sits with his legs folded under him, picking up handfuls of sand and letting it trickle slowly back through his fingers. While the waves lap quietly on the sand, distant music can still be heard. He whispers something in her ear and they laugh. He gently pushes back her hair so that he can see her face clearly; when he moves his hand, the hair falls back into her face. And he kisses her.

The sentences here are varied effectively. Every time something important happens – when the couple stop and sit down, when he whispers to her, and when they kiss – the sentences are simple and short. In between, when the surroundings or the actions of the couple leading up to the kiss are being described, the sentences are longer, and compound or complex. This is a technique you can use: it will help the action in your stories move quickly when necessary, but will also encourage you to add descriptions and reflections which improve the overall effect and create more interest for the reader.

NON-FICTION

In non-fiction writing, varying sentence structures can be an important way of conveying information clearly. Rather like using short sentences to move on a story, you can use short sentences to make a point as simply and straightforwardly as possible. You can then use longer compound or complex sentences to elaborate or add detail, rather as you would use them for the descriptions or reflections in a narrative.

Look at a further extract from the work experience essay, which shows this technique in factual writing:

> I learned many useful things. One of these was how to use a sewing machine. I was pleased to discover how easy it was. Perhaps, though, I shouldn't have been so blasé! On a number of occasions I forgot to put the foot down, and had to spend the next few minutes surreptitiously (without much success) trying to free the machine from the acres of blue or red or white cotton which had become entangled in its depths.

Here the three short, simple opening sentences set the scene. The two sentences which follow, both complex and one quite long, add detail and sustain the reader's interest.

INCOMPLETE SENTENCES

Sometimes we speak or write in 'sentences' which do not appear to obey any rules or conventions of the kind described above. This can be an effective device, but it needs to be used sparingly. We have already seen examples above:

- in 'Viva España', where Tracey says to Sharon, 'But what?' In speech, we often use incomplete sentences that do not contain a main verb, and this adds to the reality of the situation. Sometimes incomplete sentences are a normal part of how we speak. Sometimes they are incomplete because the speaker did not finish his or her thoughts, because of interruption or distraction.

- in 'The Outsider', where the first sentence consists of just the one word 'Wait'. This makes the reader stop and think, and emphasises the atmosphere of quiet and stillness which the writer is trying to create.

WHAT MAKES THE GRADE?

The appropriate use of formal and informal English, and the use of varied sentence structures is one of the most significant aspects of Writing assessed in GCSE. For a Grade C, you are expected to be able to adapt your style of writing to different purposes and audiences, and to use a range of sentence structures. You may make occasional errors or misjudgements, but you are at least aware of the need for variety, and are prepared to have a go.

To achieve a Grade A, you need to show control of range – in other words, your judgement about when to use formal or informal English is sound – and you must maintain accuracy throughout your different sentence structures, as well as varying them appropriately in different types of writing.

Check yourself

QUESTIONS

Q1 Link the following groups of sentences into compound or complex sentences. You may miss some of the words out in your sentences.

a) In Folkestone I met old Walter Dudlow.
I was crossing the Leas.
I was heading west.

b) I came upon the diary.
It was lying at the bottom of a rather battered red cardboard collar-box.
I kept my Eton collars in it as a small boy.

Q2 Rewrite the following passage from a letter to a friend describing part of a week at an outdoor activities centre in a style appropriate for inclusion in your school or college Record of Achievement (tip: think about appropriate language and sentence structures):

I really got over being frightened of heights too! We climbed and abseiled a lot, and then guess what! The instructor said we were going potholing. I'm dead scared of the dark anyway, never mind being stuck in it! But I even got to lead a group through one tunnel. When we got out he said I'd done well, 'cos some of the others were even more scared than me.

ANSWERS

A1

a) In Folkestone I met old Walter Dudlow as I was crossing the Leas, heading west.

b) When I came upon the diary it was lying at the bottom of a rather battered red cardboard collar-box, in which as a small boy I kept my Eton collars.

A2

I was able to overcome my fear of heights through climbing and abseiling. Through taking part in a potholing expedition, I tackled my fears of darkness and claustrophobia, and demonstrated leadership qualities when I had to guide a group, some of whom were more scared than I was, through one tunnel.

TUTORIALS

T1

a) *This is how the sentence actually appears in Paul Theroux's The Kingdom by the Sea. There are other ways of joining these sentences, for example: a straightforward compound sentence could be 'I was heading west and crossing the Leas in Folkestone and met old Walter Dudlow'; alternative complex sentences could be: 'Heading west and crossing the Leas in Folkestone, I met old Walter Dudlow' or 'I was crossing the Leas in Folkestone, heading west, when I met old Walter Dudlow'. All are equally acceptable, and much more fluent than the three separate sentences. Look at some examples of your own writing, and if you tend to write in short, separate sentences, practise ways of joining them.*

b) *This is how the sentence actually appears in L. P. Hartley's The Go-Between. Again, you could have done it differently; for example, 'I came upon the diary lying at the bottom of a rather battered red cardboard collar-box, where I had kept my Eton collars when I was a small boy'.*

T2

You will not have written exactly this, but you should have used some complex sentence structures. Notice how the complex second sentence links the activity, the writer's fears and achievements, and other people's fears. The choice of language (e.g. 'overcome', 'claustrophobia') supports the formal style of the sentence structure: see Chapter 23 (pages 157–58) for more on this.

- In this chapter, you will learn how to structure your writing, using paragraphs, so that it achieves its intended purpose.

- If you use appropriate opening and closing paragraphs you can help your reader to understand your meaning and identify with your concerns.

WHAT ARE PARAGRAPHS?

You should think of paragraphs as part of the overall structure of your writing, something which organises meaning and makes your text more accessible to readers. A paragraph might therefore be a number of sentences which are connected by:

- topic or subject, e.g. describing a character in a story, or your feelings about one aspect of a controversial topic;
- narrative sequence, e.g. a train journey made by the central character in a story;
- an argument, e.g. reasons why you do or don't believe that the Loch Ness monster exists in an essay on world mysteries.

HOW LONG IS A PARAGRAPH?

You may have been taught to use paragraphs almost like a piece of punctuation: for example, 'Start a new paragraph every eight or ten lines.' Paragraphs are more flexible than that, and can be used not only to help you organise your writing so that its meaning is clear to readers, but also to contribute to the tone or atmosphere you are trying to create.

The question 'How long should a paragraph be?' is no different from 'How long is a piece of string?' The answer to both is 'As long as it needs to be'. Look at the following piece of journalism which appeared in the *Daily Express* in February 1958. It is a description of a public execution in Jedda:

Instinctively the man started, and in so doing raised his head. On the instant, with a swift and expert blow, the executioner decapitated him.

A long, slow sigh came from the onlookers.

Now a woman was dragged forward. She and the man had together murdered her former husband. She, too, was under thirty and slender.

Disturbing scenes are often reported in short paragraphs. Breaking up text in this way encourages the reader to pause and take in the full horror of the situation before reading on.

Most of the account is written like this, in short paragraphs. It is designed to shock and involve the reader by making each aspect of the event stand out. We tend to pause at the end of each paragraph when reading, and in this case that pause allows the horror of the situation, the reaction of the crowd, and the nature of the crime, to sink in. If all this had been written as one paragraph, there would have been a risk of readers hurrying through it without thinking so much about what they had read.

BEGINNINGS AND ENDINGS

OPENING PARAGRAPHS

When planning a piece of writing, you need to work hard at creating an opening paragraph which grabs your reader's attention. It may be a strong statement of opinion, a description of a mysterious character, or the expression of an original or unusual thought, depending on the type of writing. But whatever it is, it must appeal to the reader. Let's look at some examples from fiction and non-fiction.

L. P. Hartley's *The Go-Between* starts with a very short paragraph:

> The past is a foreign country; they do things differently there.

This is a successful opening because it expresses an idea which intrigues the reader and, being a single sentence paragraph at the very start of the novel, stands out and invites you to think about its meaning and to wonder what the story will be about. Although the language is plain, the idea is not.

As an example from non-fiction, consider the opening of Laurie Lee's autobiography, *As I Walked Out One Midsummer Morning*:

> The stooping figure of my mother, waist-deep in the grass and caught there like a piece of sheep's wool, was the last I saw of my country home as I left it to discover the world. She stood old and bent at the top of the bank, silently watching me go, one gnarled red hand raised in farewell and blessing, not questioning why I went. At the bend of the road I looked back again and saw the gold light die behind her; then I turned the corner, passed the village school, and closed that part of my life for ever.

A carefully built paragraph can evoke a memorable description.

Laurie Lee's purpose here is quite different: he is evoking a mood of sadness, parting with his family and the world of his childhood. He therefore builds a paragraph which contains a personal reference, the description of his ageing mother, references to the natural world which has so delighted him, and to the impersonal reminder of his childhood, the village school.

When you start a piece of writing, you therefore need to think about how you will interest the reader and at the same time set the scene for what is to come. Here are some openings written by GCSE students. The first is from a story called 'Journey to my Father', in which a girl is invited to spend some time with her father. Her parents have divorced recently and she lives with her mother.

> 'Visit him? Why should you want to do that? Don't I give you enough? Haven't we . . .'
>
>   Her voice droned on in the background. He was my father. Why shouldn't I see him?

This is a successful opening as it:

- uses direct speech, which always tends to involve the reader;
- conveys the mother's edginess through the repeated questioning;
- suggests the daughter's lack of patience as she lets her mind wander off what her mother is saying;
- sets up a conflict of loyalties in the story to come.

The second example is from a piece of non-fiction writing about advertising. It begins:

> I want to write about the way women are treated by the makers of car advertisements. For some reason they think that they can use women to sell their cars. It makes me furious, the way they treat women.

In its way, that is also a successful opening, as it:

- makes a clear statement about the subject of the writing;
- states the writer's views strongly and boldly.

On the other hand, it:

- is repetitive ('women' used three times in as many sentences);
- is very informal in tone, which might not be appropriate for the intended audience (see Chapter 20, pages 141–42).

CLOSING PARAGRAPHS

The ending of Laurie Lee's As I Walked Out One Midsummer Morning shows one very common technique in closing paragraphs:

> I was back in Spain, with a winter of war before me.

Here we see the one-sentence approach, like the opening of The Go-Between, but also the technique of using the ending to leave the reader wanting more. There is a sequel to Laurie Lee's book, and the odds are that anyone who had enjoyed As I Walked Out One Midsummer Morning would have their appetite to read the sequel whetted by that final paragraph. In a way, a final paragraph like that is not really final – it's more of a link to what comes next. It is a technique you can use if you wish to leave your readers wondering about what might have happened. That is what this student has done at the end of a piece of narrative writing called 'The Dare':

> I knew deep inside me that when I opened the door, something terrible would be waiting for me. But I wasn't prepared for this.

Here the reader is left to use the power of her or his own imagination to complete the story – not a technique you can use too often, and not because your own imagination has failed! To be successful, an ending like that has to follow powerful and detailed writing, which will have got the reader's mind working the way you want it to so that the ending they mentally supply is appropriate to what you have written before.

Genuinely final paragraphs tend to sum up what a book has been about. The theme of George Orwell's *Animal Farm* is how power corrupts and changes those who wield it. The final paragraph runs:

> Twelve voices were shouting in anger, and they were all alike. No question, now, what had happened to the faces of the pigs. The creatures outside looked from pig to man, and from man to pig, and from pig to man again; but already it was impossible to say which was which.

While finishing off the story on one level, on a deeper level this paragraph emphasises the central theme and leaves the reader thinking about it as he or she finishes the book.

You will often use a summing-up paragraph at the end of a piece of non-fiction writing. For example, the student who wrote about the use of women in car advertising finished with this paragraph:

> So I think that advertisers are wrong to use women the way they do. Buying a car is nothing to do with sex, and advertising like this is degrading to everyone involved.

Atticus in the film of To Kill a Mockingbird.

Another common style of ending is to use a paragraph which brings events to a tidy conclusion, leaving the reader with a satisfied feeling and a strong image of a central character. This is the technique used by Harper Lee at the ending of *To Kill a Mockingbird*:

> He turned out the light and went into Jem's room. He would be there all night, and he would be there when Jem waked up in the morning.

Here the reader feels the story is closed (note the symbolism of turning out the light on all that has happened, and the new start which the morning will bring) and the impression of Atticus as the caring, protective father is a reassuring and comforting note on which to end.

The story 'Journey to My Father' ends

> He was my father. However difficult it would make living with mum in the future, I couldn't ignore this kind and thoughtful man. Whatever had gone wrong between my parents was not my fault, and they were not going to punish me for it. To me, they were both good people, both part of me, now and for ever. Never mind the past, I thought, just let me get on with my life, and with both of them.

This is a satisfying ending, as it draws together the themes and the characters in the story and also has just a touch of the wonder-what-will-happen feel about it, so you are fairly certain that the reader will continue thinking about the story after he or she has actually finished it.

You must use paragraphs to achieve a Grade C for your Writing. At that level, you must at least be able to use paragraphs to structure stories or non-fiction writing in ways that help readers follow a narrative or an argument, which means that beginnings and endings must be at least clear and helpful.

In Grade A writing, examiners will expect you to show some of the more sophisticated techniques looked at here, especially beginnings and endings, but they will also expect you to link paragraphs coherently, so that the organisation of your writing is enhanced by them.

Check yourself

QUESTIONS

Q1 The following extract from *The Diary of Anne Frank* was originally in six paragraphs. Where would you put in the paragraph breaks, and why?

My longing to talk to someone became so intense that somehow or other I took it in my head to choose Peter. Sometimes if I've been upstairs into Peter's room during the day, it always struck me as very snug, but because Peter is so retiring and would never turn anyone out who became a nuisance, I never dared stay long, because I was afraid he might think me a bore. I tried to think of an excuse to stay in his room and get him talking, without it being too noticeable, and my chance came yesterday. Peter has a mania for crossword puzzles at the moment and hardly does anything else. I helped him with them and we soon sat opposite each other at his little table, he on the chair and me on the divan. It gave me a queer feeling each time I looked into his deep blue eyes, and he sat there with that mysterious laugh playing round the lips. I was able to read his inward thoughts. I could see on his face that look of helplessness and uncertainty as to how to behave, and, at the same time, a trace of his sense of manhood. I noticed his shy manner and it made me feel very gentle; I couldn't refrain from meeting those dark eyes again and again, and with my whole heart I almost beseeched him: oh, tell me, what is going on inside you, oh, can't you look beyond this ridiculous chatter? But the evening passed and nothing happened, except that I told him about blushing – naturally not what I have written, but just so that he would become more sure of himself as he grew older. When I lay in bed and thought over the whole situation, I found it far from encouraging, and the idea that I should beg for Peter's patronage was simply repellent. One can do a lot to satisfy one's longings, which certainly sticks out in my case, for I have made up my mind to go and sit with Peter more often and to get him talking somehow or other. Whatever you do, don't think I'm in love with Peter – not a bit of it! If the Van Daans had a daughter instead of a son, I should have tried to make friends with her too.

ANSWERS

A1

My longing to talk to someone became so intense that somehow or other I took it in my head to choose Peter.

Sometimes if I've been upstairs into Peter's room during the day, it always struck me as very snug, but because Peter is so retiring and would never turn anyone out who became a nuisance, I never dared stay long, because I was afraid he might think me a bore. I tried to think of an excuse to stay in his room and get him talking, without it being too noticeable, and my chance came yesterday. Peter has a mania for crossword puzzles at the moment and hardly does anything else. I helped him with them and we soon sat opposite each other at his little table, he on the chair and me on the divan.

It gave me a queer feeling each time I looked into his deep blue eyes, and he sat there with that mysterious laugh playing round the lips. I was able to read his inward thoughts. I could see on his face that look of helplessness and uncertainty as to how to behave, and, at the same time, a trace of his sense of manhood. I noticed his shy manner and it made me feel very gentle; I couldn't refrain from meeting those dark eyes again and again, and with my whole heart I almost beseeched him: oh, tell me, what is going on inside you, oh, can't you look beyond this ridiculous chatter?

But the evening passed and nothing happened, except that I told him about blushing – naturally not what I have written, but just so that he would become more sure of himself as he grew older.

When I lay in bed and thought over the whole situation, I found it far from encouraging, and the idea that I should beg for Peter's patronage was simply repellent. One can do a lot to satisfy one's longings, which certainly sticks out in my case, for I have made up my mind to go and sit with Peter more often and to get him talking somehow or other.

Whatever you do, don't think I'm in love with Peter – not a bit of it! If the Van Daans had a daughter instead of a son, I should have tried to make friends with her too.

TUTORIALS

T1

This is a statement of the theme of the diary entry, and so the end of this opening sentence is a logical first break.

All this section belongs together as it is about Peter and his 'mania for crosswords'.

This section is all about Anne and her thoughts about Peter. You may have inserted this paragraph break one sentence earlier, on the grounds that 'I helped him... on the divan' is about Anne and not Peter. However, that sentence describes something that actually happened, while this paragraph is about inner feelings. A better alternative would be to put the sentence about Anne sitting opposite Peter into a paragraph by itself.

This sentence belongs by itself as it describes what actually happened during the rest of the evening.

Another section on Anne's feelings – these two sentences clearly belong together.

You might argue that these sentences could go into the above paragraph, but while there is a logical connection between the subject matter, they form a neat, separate conclusion to the passage.

- In this chapter, you will learn the importance of presenting work neatly and clearly.

- You will also learn to use a range of presentational techniques which will help to clarify your meaning for the reader in different types of writing.

- Neatness and presentational skills are especially important when writing in timed examination conditions.

HANDWRITING

Fluent, legible handwriting is important, even in the computer age, as you have to use handwriting in the examination. If you can write quickly, but still neatly and legibly, you will have an advantage over candidates who struggle to finish in the time allowed, and those whose handwriting is untidy or illegible. Friends, teachers, examiners, employers: all react favourably to neat handwriting.

Your handwriting can be characterful, but it should not be so unusual that it distracts the reader from the content of your work. Try to develop handwriting which:

- is a sensible size – not too large, too small, too cramped or too spread out;

- keeps the spaces between words to the same size;

- shapes and joins letters consistently;

- makes clear distinctions between lower and upper case letters;

- leans one way, if it leans at all.

The pen you use is significant: it is easier to write neatly with fountain pens or roller balls than with biros, and different shapes and sizes of pens suit different hands. It is worth experimenting with styles of writing and pens to settle on a combination which you feel allows you to work comfortably, quickly and neatly.

Experiment with different types of pen.

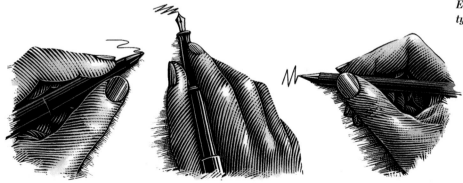

BREAKING UP THE TEXT

FICTION

One challenge in presenting written work in a way that is helpful to readers is to break up the text. When writing prose fiction, you will certainly need to use paragraphs effectively (see Chapter 21), and a lengthy narrative might have chapter headings. A newspaper or magazine story might have a headline and sub-headings as well as paragraphs. When writing poetry, you certainly need to think about structuring the text into lines and verses, and when writing drama scripts for the stage, you need to obey layout conventions which make it easy to follow the dialogue and any stage directions. Radio and TV scripts need additional directions for cameras, microphones and effects of various kinds, and you need to study examples of these if you are to write and present your own scripts in an easily-understood format.

NON-FICTION

It is when you are writing non-fiction that you need to think most carefully about using devices such as:

- titles;
- underlinings;
- margins;
- headings and sub-headings;
- frames;
- bullet points and numbers.

You can remind yourself about how these effects, and others mentioned below, work, by looking back at Chapter 11 (pages 82–5) and Chapters 15–17 (pages 110–17). The page from an Income Support claim shown here also reminds you how a few simple techniques can lift the appearance of a page.

Of course, the colour is also significant here, but if you are preparing a piece of writing for coursework, you may be able to use IT to help you produce similar techniques. Even in a handwritten examination answer, you can use most of the devices mentioned in this section to break up your text and make it both more attractive and more accessible to readers.

ILLUSTRATIONS AND GRAPHICS

FICTION

These techniques are again less relevant to fiction writing. Even if you choose to illustrate your own stories or poems, remember that it is the quality of writing on which you will be judged, and not your artistic skills. Presentational devices seldom add to the reader's understanding of fiction in the way that they can with non-fiction. However, illustration may be crucial to a narrative: in one of his Sherlock Holmes stories, *The Adventure of the Dancing Men*, Arthur Conan Doyle uses a series of drawings such as this to help explain the mystery (which involves breaking a code) and to challenge readers' powers of interpretation.

However, opportunities like that are unusual, and you should not spend much time trying to think them up: concentrate on the quality of the writing instead.

---

if you're on a YT but you're a special case

If you're a YT trainee, you'll get a weekly training allowance of at least £29.50 if aged 16 or £35 if aged 17 or over. This is more than the Income Support payment for most young people.

But some young people on YT may be able to get Income Support as well as the training allowance. For example, you could qualify if you are –

- A single parent and your child lives with you
- Living with a partner and with a child
- Living with a partner who is 18 or over and who is not working
- Living independently and your YT allowance is less than £36.15.

HOW TO CLAIM

1 Go to your local Social Security office and say you want to claim Income Support.

2 Fill in the form they give you and send it or take it back.

If in doubt about claiming, ask for advice at a Social Security office. See page 16 to find out how to find local offices.

NOTE: If you're on YT but employed full-time by the employer you're placed with, you'll not be able to claim Income Support. But if you have a child, you might be able to claim money from Family Credit. Look for a leaflet in post offices or Social Security offices.

I want to sift the matter to the bottom."

Holmes held up the paper so that the sunlight shone full upon it. It was a page torn from a note-book. The markings were done in pencil, and ran in this way :—

Holmes examined it for some time, and then, folding it carefully up, he placed it in his pocket-book.

"This promises to be a most interesting and unusual case," said he. "You gave me a few particulars in your letter, Mr. Hilton

NON-FICTION

Using illustrations and graphics in non-fiction writing can be extremely useful, and you will be rewarded for showing an awareness of readers' needs in understanding complex material. For example, the following is an extract from a government leaflet about smoke alarms in the home. There is a lengthy piece of text which goes into considerable detail, but then the reader is given these drawings and the checklist:

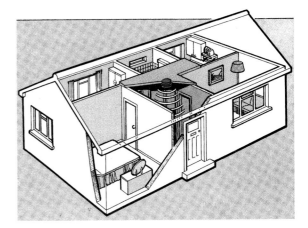

 Do make sure your smoke alarm is fixed on the ceiling at least 30 cm (12 inches) from the wall or light fitting. A central position is best. If it's designed for wall mounting, put it between 15 and 30 cm (6 and 12 inches) below the ceiling.

 Do put your smoke alarm where you will be able to reach it fairly easily – and safely – for regular testing and maintenance; not above stairwells, for example.

 Don't put your smoke alarm in any room which tends to get very hot (a boiler room for example) or very cold (an unheated outhouse).

 Don't put your smoke alarm in bathrooms, shower rooms or in cooking areas or garages where the smoke alarm may be triggered by steam, condensation or fumes.

 Don't put your smoke alarm next to or directly above heaters or air conditioning vents.

 Don't fix your smoke alarm to surfaces which are normally much warmer or colder than the rest of the room. These can include uninsulated exterior walls and ceilings (temperature differences might stop smoke from reaching it).

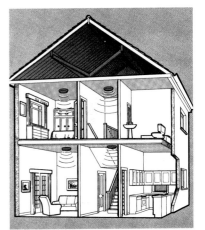

Many readers would find that a helpful and reassuring way of presenting the main points from that section of the leaflet.

EDITING AND PROOF READING

Finally, one aspect of neatness and presentation which you must not forget concerns checking your work. Editing means thinking about issues raised in this and previous chapters such as:

- **audience**: who is this writing for, and what requirements does that imply?
- **purpose**: why am I writing this, and what do I want to get across?
- **topic**: have I included the right information, given the audience and purpose?
- **structure**: is the content presented logically and in the best order?

To those issues we can now add:

- **presentation**: is it easily understood, and does it look right?

Proof-reading means checking for mistakes in the mechanics of your writing: spelling, punctuation and grammar. Look particularly for mistakes which you know you often make, and correct them carefully. In coursework, using a word processor, it is easy to produce a final draft which makes it seem there have never been mistakes. In an examination, simply cross out the error neatly and write the correction above or beside it. Don't worry that the examiner will think your work looks a mess: he or she will actually be impressed that you have proof-read successfully.

WHAT MAKES THE GRADE? ▶

For written work to achieve a Grade C, you should be able to use some of the more obvious presentational devices of the sort we have looked at here. For higher grades, you are expected to experiment with ways of presenting work attractively, and to be aware of how different ways of presenting work are appropriate to different audiences, purposes and topics. While untidy handwriting should not in itself put your grade at risk, remember that you want the examiner to read and understand all you have written: so make his/her job as easy as you can.

Check yourself

QUESTION

Q1

If an examination question gave you a piece of written information on a subject such as smoking by teenagers and asked you to re-present it more attractively for a given audience, what sorts of presentational devices might you think of using? Make a list of up to six appropriate devices, and say why each could be useful. Remember this is in an examination, so you do not have access to IT.

REMEMBER! Cover the answers if you need to.

ANSWER

A1
1) An appropriate title, especially in a different style or size of lettering, attracts the reader's attention.
2) Sub-headings are useful to guide readers through the different parts of the material.
3) Bullet points can clarify lists and also make important points stand out.
4) Simple diagrams, e.g. of a typical school site where there are hidden corners for smokers to gather in.
5) If statistics are used, graphs and charts are an economical and easily understood way of re-presenting them.
6) The whole article could be framed, or written in two columns, to make more visual impact.

TUTORIAL

T1

The title is often forgotten – but it's where people begin to read, and it may either attract them or turn them off.

You might add that using underlining, or frames, or upper case letters for sub-headings is even better.

Remember that you can use different styles of bullet points, indent them differently, etc.
Good – always look for opportunities to 'lift' the writing with appropriate visual material.

Yes – you can draw bar graphs or pie charts fairly accurately by hand.

The overall appearance is often forgotten, and even in an examination answer-book you can make your work leap off the page

CHAPTER 23

USING A WIDE RANGE OF VOCABULARY AND STYLISTIC FEATURES

- In this chapter, you will learn how to expand your range of vocabulary. You will also learn how to use some stylistic features.
- If you can do both these things, your writing will have a more powerful effect on the reader.
- Engaging and sustaining the reader's interest is necessary to gain high marks in GCSE.

WRITING NARRATIVE

If you are writing narratives, or stories, you need to think about successful examples you have read. Why did they work? In particular:

- how did the authors use effective vocabulary in describing settings, characters, ideas?
- what techniques or stylistic devices did they use?

In all your writing you should try to use apt and imaginative vocabulary, choosing words for their precise and appropriate meaning. Most of us use a limited range of words in daily life, especially when talking, but when writing for specific purposes and audiences, it is important that you match vocabulary to their needs and to the settings, characters or ideas you are describing. To extend your own vocabulary you can:

- read widely, checking the meanings of unfamiliar words in a dictionary;
- think about words which have very close meanings: what is the difference between them, and how would you use them appropriately?
- use a thesaurus to find alternatives to words which you overuse, or which do not seem quite right for a particular purpose, and use a dictionary alongside the thesaurus to check the precise meanings of unfamiliar words.

Look at the opening of this GCSE candidate's story called 'Discovery':

The repetitive hum of the helicopter echoed threateningly above them. Their thick, leather boots, toughened by previous use, trekked rhythmically over the difficult terrain. Suddenly they halted, hiding in the shadow of a tree, their hands on the drenched moss, trying to recapture lost breath and regain lost stamina. Rain was beating on the trees above them. A flash of lightning illuminated the forest around them – or was it? Their minds were so confused and exhausted it might have been the strong beam of the helicopter scanning the area for them.

Very few of the words used here are unusual, but all are chosen carefully to give a precise description of the scene and an impression of the feelings of the hunted people. The use of 'repetitive' and 'trekked rhythmically', for example, suggests the weariness of the people and the length of time they have been on the move. Sometimes, just one or two precise, colourful words will achieve their effect by contrast with the plain language around them. The effect of the word 'drenched' is made greater by the plainness of the language around it: it is a small detail which brings the scene to life by involving your sense of touch and it prepares you for the mention of the 'beating' rain later.

157

Pamela by Samuel Richardson, published in 1740, is one of the earliest novels written as a series of letters. The letters are from Pamela, a maid, to her parents and they document her struggle against the advances of her employer Mr. B.

This is an important point to remember. You cannot always be using original, imaginative vocabulary – very few people know great numbers of unusual words, and anyway they would lose their effect if used constantly. Judging when to use a word is as important a skill as knowing the word in the first place.

As well as the language of narrative, think about different ways of presenting stories and what effect this can have on readers. You may have read George Orwell's *Animal Farm*. If so, you will be aware that he uses the apparent structure of a children's story about talking animals to tell a fable or parable about modern society. How could you use a similar technique?

In a piece called 'Love Story', for example, you might write what seems to be a conventional romantic narrative about a handsome young man and a beautiful young woman. But it comes to a sudden and unexpected ending, perhaps when she is mistakenly killed by a member of her own family using a weapon supplied by the man, who turns out to be an arms dealer. Skilfully written, that could be a parable about the weapons trade in the modern world and how much unpleasantness and destruction goes on beneath the apparently calm surface of diplomatic relations.

Another kind of stylistic feature is for a story to be told by two or more characters so that the reader not only gets to know them well, but sees events through two sets of eyes and has to think about where the truth lies. This can be done by using letters or diaries to tell one or both sides of the story. If you were writing about someone confined to one place, such as a prison cell or a hospital bed, or even a boarding school, using a device such as an interchange of letters to tell a story can be realistic as well as effective.

WRITING POETRY

If you have the opportunity to write poems for your coursework, you need to think about poems you have read, and about what works well in them. You need to decide:

- how the vocabulary you use can convey strong feelings or ideas to the reader;
- what use you can make of devices such as metaphor, simile, alliteration to make your vision vivid;
- what form you will use: rhyme or no rhyme? A regular verse-pattern or not?

The following lines which end Seamus Heaney's *Storm on the Island* show the use of alliteration, onomatopoeia, metaphor and half-rhyme to convey a striking idea, that space is frightening simply because it is 'empty', 'a huge nothing':

> Space is a salvo,
> We are bombarded by the empty air.
> Strange, it is a huge nothing that we fear.

The words 'space', 'salvo' and 'strange' are linked by the alliteration which therefore joins the words in your mind and helps to form the idea of the peculiar and threatening nature of space, which you may previously have thought of as mere emptiness. The use of an onomatopoeic word like 'bombarded' strengthens the threatening quality of the lines, in which the air is seen metaphorically as a force which attacks us. The half-rhyme of 'air' and 'fear' is like a discord in music, a jagged sound on which to end an unsettling poem.

When you write poetry, you are aiming to write short, concentrated bursts of language. This GCSE candidate conveys the intense feelings of young love.

The poet starts with an original image: 'passions' ago, rather than days, weeks or months. The image is carried on in the suggestion that the love is so intense that it has burnt up the grass and flowers, and this leads to the idea that love is not built on anything secure – 'erosion', an unusual choice of word in this context, and made to stand out even more by the fact that it provides the only rhyme in the poem. 'Crumble' is again a strikingly unromantic word in this setting, and the last three lines express the poet's guilt or loss of innocence, using a pun in 'greenness', which both refers back to the burnt-up grass but also means innocence. The intensity of the language and the stylistic features used by the candidate mean that in just thirty-four words, the reader has been given much to think about.

There are many ways of writing poetry and you should experiment with form and content and try out several drafts to see what works for you.

> Passions ago,
> we walked on grass
> and flowers.
> They have died
> by our heat;
> we stand on
> erosion,
> our feet
> crumble by hours.
> We have kissed away
> greenness, and the colours
> of uncrushed joy.

WRITING NON-FICTION

When you write non-fiction, it is often presentational features (see Chapter 22, pages 154–5) which contribute much of the effect; however, stylistic devices can be used too. For example, the following headline of an advertisement for banking services to assist Amnesty International uses a metaphor, calling a credit card and cheque book weapons, which is ironically appropriate for an organisation which tries to stamp out torture and abuse and arms dealing:

If you are writing about advertising, or preparing your own advertisement, you need to be aware of language use of this kind.

If you are writing narrative kinds of non-fiction, such as autobiography or travelogue, you need to think about the use of carefully chosen vocabulary and stylistic devices much as you would if writing fictional narrative. For example, here is the start of a GCSE student's memoir of her early life:

> My earliest memories are like the bottom of an old bucket: rusty and damp. Rusty, because I really don't remember them all that well, but damp because I do recall that in our Dartmoor village it seldom seemed to stop raining.

This is a striking opening, not through the use of any unusual words, but because the simile which compares life to a bucket is original and makes you want to read on. The writer has also skilfully chosen three words beginning with 's' at the end of the second sentence, using the alliteration to imitate the sound of the rain which is the chief memory.

WHAT MAKES THE GRADE?

For your writing to achieve a Grade C, you must show that you can use a range of vocabulary, stylistic and structural features which create interesting effects and appeal to readers, involving them in the text. To achieve higher grades, you need to use more unusual or original vocabulary, and to be more ambitious in the effects you create so that the reader's interest is sustained throughout your writing.

Check yourself

QUESTIONS

Q1 As an exercise in using a range of vocabulary, copy out this passage from William Golding's *Lord of the Flies*, filling in the blanks with appropriate words.

Smoke was rising here and there among the creepers that ......[1] the dead or dying trees. As they watched, a ......[2] of fire appeared at the root of one wisp, and then the smoke thickened. Small flames stirred at the ......[3] of a tree and ......[4] away through leaves and brushwood, dividing and increasing. One patch touched a tree trunk and ......[5] up like a bright ......[6]. The smoke increased, sifted, rolled outwards. The squirrel leapt on the ......[7] of the wind and clung to another standing tree, ...[8] downwards. Beneath the dark canopy of leaves and smoke, the fire laid hold on the forest and began to ......[9]. Acres of black and yellow smoke rolled steadily towards the sea. At the sight of the flames and the ......[10] course of the fire, the boys broke into shrill, excited cheering. The flames, as though they were a kind of wild life, crept as a ......[11] creeps on its ......[12] towards a line of birch-like saplings that ......[13] an outcrop of the pink rock. They ......[14] at the first of the trees, and the branches grew a brief ......[15] of fire. The heart of flame leapt ......[16] across the gap between the trees and then went swinging and ......[17] along the whole row of them. Beneath the ......[18] boys a quarter of a mile square of forest was ......[19] with smoke and flame. The separate noises of the fire merged into a ......[20] that seemed to shake the mountain.

REMEMBER! Cover the answers if you want to.

ANSWER

A1

1   festooned

2   flash

3   bole

4   crawled

5   scrambled

6   squirrel

7   wings

8   eating

9   gnaw

10 irresistible

11 jaguar

12 belly

13 fledged

14 flapped

15 foliage

16 nimbly

17 flaring

18 capering

19 savage

20 drum-roll

TUTORIAL

T1

Don't be disheartened if only a few of your answers match the words used by Golding. This is a complex extract and there are many possible words for each gap.

1   *you may have suggested 'covered': 'festooned' gives a more vivid picture of great hanging loops, like decorations*

2   *creates an effective alliterative and visual effect*

3   *you may have put 'trunk'; 'bole' means the same, but is a useful variant*

4   *suggests the animal-like qualities of the fire*

5   *you may have suggested 'climbed': 'scrambled' suggests more effort, and reinforces the comparison of the fire with animals*

6   *a clue to this in the next but one sentence! It is a surprising but apt comparison, given the way squirrels leap about in trees*

7   *alliterative effect*

8   *continues the animal image*

9   *you may have suggested something like 'spread'; 'gnaw' is more menacing*

10 *we now tend to use the secondary meaning of this word (fascinating) more than its first meaning (cannot be stopped)*

11 *the fire is now more fierce than a squirrel*

12 *a stronger, rougher word than 'stomach'*

13 *unusual choice of word: it makes the trees sound like the feathers of a young bird (fledgling) and so reinforces the image of the fire as a jaguar stalking its prey*

14 *notice all the alliterations on 'f'*

15 *an original, precise visual image*

16 *another animal image*

17 *an alliterative word again*

18 *not a common word, but continues the picture of excited, slightly out-of-control boys*

19 *conveys the emotions of the boys and the effects of the fire*

20 *you may have suggested a general word such as 'noise': the use of a word which is a precise noise is much more powerful*

CHAPTER 24

WRITING TO EXPLORE, IMAGINE AND ENTERTAIN

- In this chapter, you will learn the qualities and techniques you need to show in your writing which explores, imagines or entertains.
- You will also learn how to plan and structure a piece of writing, by looking at examples from professional writers and GCSE students.

WHAT KIND OF WRITING IS THIS?

This category includes most 'imaginative' or 'creative' writing, in other words, usually fiction. This writing could be in the form of poetry or a playscript, but prose is usually expected in examination answers, and that is what we will look at in detail here.

The writing need not start with your own original ideas: if you have read a novel or a play and you decide to write an extra chapter, or a 'missing' scene, that would count as writing which explores, imagines or entertains, even though you are using someone else's characters and settings.

This category could also include writing about your own experiences, in other words, non-fiction, if it is used to explore or imagine. For example, if you wrote about work experience and part of the account was an exploration of whether you would actually want to do that job in your adult life, then the piece could come into this category.

QUALITIES OF PROSE FICTION

Let's look first at the beginning of a rather unusual short story and see what it shows us about some of the essential qualities of prose fiction. The story is *There Was Once* by Margaret Atwood.

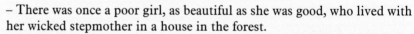

Angela Carter reworked and 'updated' many traditional tales. **In the Company of Wolves,** *based on* Little Red Riding Hood, *was made into a film.*

– There was once a poor girl, as beautiful as she was good, who lived with her wicked stepmother in a house in the forest.

   – Forest? *Forest* is passé, I mean I've had it with all this wilderness stuff. It's not a right image of our society, today. Let's have some *urban* for a change.

   – There was once a poor girl, as beautiful as she was good, who lived with her wicked stepmother in a house in the suburbs.

   – That's better. But I have to seriously query this word *poor*.

   – But she *was* poor!

   – Poor is relative. She lived in a house, didn't she?

   – Yes.

   – Then socio-economically speaking, she was not poor.

What does this extract reveal about writing which explores, imagines or entertains?

It explores:

- the idea of how a traditional fairy-tale might be updated;
- character, by structuring the story through the different viewpoints of two speakers.

It imagines:

- what an updated plot or story might be;
- what an appropriate setting for the modern story might be.

It entertains:

- by making fun of (or 'parodying') a traditional form or structure;
- through the relationship of the characters as shown in their language.

PLANNING A STORY

We can now identify some of the features of prose fiction which you need to consider when planning a piece of writing:

- **plot or story:** what happens? Why? How? In what order?
- **characters:** who are they? How do you bring them alive through description, dialogue and action?
- **setting:** how important is this to the story? How do you create a sense of place through detailed description and the action of the story?
- **ideas:** what is the point of your story? What's it all about? Is there a clear 'message'?
- **structure:** do you tell the story? Is it told by one of the characters involved? Do you use flashbacks? Do you tell part of it through diaries or letters?

Your planning can take the form of outline notes, or you can try to rough out some actual sentences or paragraphs which you might want to include in the finished story. The example below uses the second method to make clear what you should be trying to achieve in a completed story.

Let's use as a title one which was set on a recent GCSE paper:

Write a story about a school trip where something unexpected happened.

PLOT

The starting point for your planning must be, what was it that happened? Why was it unexpected? You cannot write an original best-seller in one hour under examination conditions, but you must aim for some originality. Don't write about a pupil getting lost, or the bus breaking down, or someone being ill or losing all their money: these are not unexpected happenings on a school trip!

On the other hand, don't be absurd – so don't write about a pupil finding a paper bag containing a million pounds which he and his friends get to spend, or a famous film or music star coming by and falling madly in love with one of the pupils.

Instead, think hard about what might happen which is realistic and possible, but not expected. Let's say that a pupil who has always been very shy and quiet performs a heroic deed by helping another pupil, always seen as brave and outgoing, who has become stuck on an ruined castle tower.

Babette Cole in her picture books for young children modernises traditional tales.

The opening page of Princess Smartypants.

A page from Prince Cinders.

163

CHARACTERS

Staying with that example, what about the characters who might be involved? There are certainly two pupils, of contrasting personality: one apparently quiet and shy, the other bold and noisy. You could establish these aspects of their characters through describing part of the bus journey to the castle. Don't just write 'Tom sat quietly while Jack made a lot of noise'. You need to give more detail and in more subtle ways. For example, you might describe an incident such as this, involving description, dialogue and action:

> Tom could hear the noise at the back of the coach. Everyone was laughing at Jack's impersonations of the teachers, and at his jokes. Suddenly he felt a sharp pain on the back of his neck: so it had started, throwing things. Next they'd tease him, try to embarrass him. 'Tommy, oh Tommy'. He could hear them now. It would get worse. He continued reading his book, pretending that he couldn't hear.

Setting the scene is just that: don't spend so long establishing the characters that you have no time left to describe the central incident. Concentrate on bringing the main characters to life through detail, but where other characters are concerned remember that just one or two carefully chosen words will make a description work in the reader's mind. So instead of merely writing 'They went into the castle past the attendant's hut', try something like:

> They went into the castle past the hut where the attendant sat, watching them suspiciously as if they were an invading army returning after hundreds of years to attack the walls again.

That sentence quickly conveys the picture of the attendant who's not very keen on school parties, and suggests some of the noisy, and perhaps aggressive, qualities of the children.

SETTING

If the setting is to be a castle, with ruined towers and high, exposed walls, take the chance to show your powers of description. After all, the setting is crucial to the plot of this story. A poor writer will be content to say something like 'The castle was old and falling down. The walls were high and broken in places. The towers had gaps where you could see right through them'.
If you wish to show your skill at creating an atmospheric setting, you will want to use more complex sentences, more sophisticated vocabulary and images:

> The ancient castle, its harsh grey stone partly covered with green and gold lichen, loomed above them. In places, the walls had tumbled into piles of random boulders, while the towers, still dark and tall against the pale blue spring sky were ragged with holes; they looked like the arms of an old, worn-out jumper stretching towards the clouds.

Make the description of your setting as evocative as possible.

The use of colours in description helps the reader visualise a scene more precisely, and if you can use similes (such as comparing the castle towers with old sleeves) or other figures of speech, that adds even more to the atmosphere.

IDEAS

What is this story about? It is making the point that true bravery does not always make a loud show, or that people's true characters and qualities are only revealed under stressful circumstances. It would not be good to state either of those ideas as a kind of 'moral' tacked on to the end of the story. You have to credit your readers with the intelligence to work that out for themselves, provided you nudge them gently in the right direction. So you might end with a paragraph something like this:

> Tom sat silently in his seat on the coach. Not in the way that he had sat that morning, but with a glow of calm satisfaction. Yes, he knew they were talking about him again; but he knew that they wouldn't be throwing anything and that the talk would no longer be mocking. Jack was sitting quietly too, he noticed.

An understated ending like that leaves the reader to think over what the story has been about, keeping interest engaged right to – and beyond – the end of the written words.

STRUCTURE

In working through this example, the assumption has been that you would tell the story in the order in which it happened and in the third person, that is, as though you were someone outside the action watching it and describing it. There are other ways. You could be one of the characters in the story and so tell it in the first person. If you were writing as Jack or Tom, you could even tell parts of the story in flashback, remembering what happened while you travel back to school at the end of the day.

Be careful, however. An examination answer is often too brief to allow sufficient space for you to show all kinds of clever structural tricks – longer pieces of coursework are really the place for that. In an examination, you will do better to concentrate on showing the range and depth of your vocabulary and your control of different sentence structures, so that you can tell your story in a way which catches and holds the reader's attention.

LANGUAGE

We have already seen in this chapter that when you write to explore, imagine and entertain, you need to display a wide and versatile range of language skills. If you look back at Chapters 1, 2 and 3, you can remind yourself of how professional prose writers achieve their effects on readers. We are now going to look in more detail at how the particular skills of description and dialogue writing can be developed.

DESCRIPTIVE WRITING

When writing prose fiction, you will need to create descriptions which bring people, places and events vividly to life. We have already looked at some ideas in the example above, where descriptions of the castle and of the attendant are made vivid by carefully chosen words and images.

Think about your reader's senses when writing descriptions, and try to appeal to sight or sound, for example. Because of the precise description of angles and movement, it is easy to visualise this scene described by Barry Hines in *A Kestrel for a Knave*:

> A thrush ran out from under a rhododendron shrub and started to tug a worm from the soil between the loose asphalt chips. It stood over the worm and tugged vertically, exposing its speckled throat and pointing its beak to the sky. The worm stretched, but held. The thrush lowered its head and backed off, pulling at a more acute angle. The worm still held, so the thrush stepped in and jerked at the slack. The worm ripped out of the ground and the thrush ran away with it, back under the shrubs.

You can appeal to the reader's sense of sound as well as sight; often the two go together, as this short passage from Susan Hill's *I'm the King of the Castle* shows:

> There was a slight, persistent movement of wind through the yew tree branches, and the elms and oaks of the copse, and a rustling of the high grasses in the field. The moonlight, penetrating a thin pace between two trees, caught the stream that ran through its centre, so that, now and then, as the branches stirred, there was a gleam of water.

If you can visualise scenes in this kind of detail and introduce them appropriately into your writing, it is a sure way of capturing the reader's interest. The use of onomatopoeic words, that is words which sound like what they describe (such as 'rustling' in the previous example), is obviously a very effective technique if you wish to appeal to the reader's sense of hearing. Movement and colour are useful ways of describing people too, especially their faces. This can say a great deal about their character. Look at this extract from L. P. Hartley's *The Go-Between*, which describes a young woman:

> Her hair was bright with sunshine, but her face, which was full like her mother's, only pale rose-pink instead of cream, wore a stern, brooding look that her small, curved nose made almost hawk-like. She looked formidable then, almost as formidable as her mother. A moment later she opened her eyes – and her face lit up.

This use of colour makes the woman sound attractive, but other words such as 'brooding' and 'formidable' and the image of the hawk suggest more menacing qualities. The movement described in the last sentence suggests that she has a powerful presence.

From all these examples you can see that the art of effective description is to observe details – either in reality or in your imagination – and then to use the most precise words and images you can think of to capture those details. Look now at this example of a candidate's work from an actual GCSE paper. It is the start of a story called 'The Dare':

On a midsummer afternoon, the sun was like a burning eye looking down at us, making us sweat like pigs. My brother, my friend Peter, his brother Andrew and I were wandering around the streets, our feet lazily following the intricate track of the pavement like a train. It was too hot to do anything but suddenly Peter shouted out, 'Let's play Double Dare.' This was a game we had devised a long time ago and only emerged when days like this pulled it out by the hand. Everyone's face lit up like a lantern and suddenly we were sitting on the floor spinning a bottle and devising dares to carry out before the bottle stopped.

This candidate was awarded a Grade A in the examination, and some good descriptive qualities are evident in the extract from this story. There is variation of sentence structures, conscious choice of vocabulary and use of imagery to interest the reader. All of these can be seen in phrases such as 'the sun was like a burning eye looking down at us', 'our feet lazily following the intricate track of the pavement like a train' or 'Everyone's face lit up like a lantern'. There is an occasional misjudgement: 'sweat like pigs' is a cruder comparison than any others in the passage. It would have worked better as dialogue, in other words, if one of the characters had said, 'I'm sweating like a pig!'. Nevertheless, this writing shows awareness of the need for description, and some sense of style in achieving it.

WRITING DIALOGUE

Narratives are often more lively and interesting if they contain dialogue – the Margaret Atwood story which we have looked at consists entirely of dialogue, and the story about the unexpected event on a school trip would certainly need dialogue to bring the main incident to life. This is where you have an opportunity to show your ability to use non-standard English in creating lifelike characters. Here is another extract from an examination answer. The candidate is writing a story about a teenage girl whose mother walks out on her family. Karen, the daughter who suspects what has happened, is on the phone to her aunt, Denise:

'Hi, Denise, how are you?'
'Fine, thanks. What's up, Karen?'
'Oh, I was just ringing to speak to mum.'
'Your mum, what would she be here for?'
Karen was shocked by this reply. 'Oh. I, I thought she said she was popping in to see you today.'
'No, I've not seen her for ages. Sorry, love.'
'It's OK. Bye.'

The candidate was awarded a Grade C overall, and this passage shows a sound ability to write a convincing, but not very demanding, passage of conversation. The words sound realistic, using non-standard forms such as 'Hi' and 'Bye' and abbreviations commonly used in speech, but we do not experience a strong sense of two different characters, or of a tense situation, which a better candidate would have been able to suggest.

Let's look at how a professional writer can create character through dialogue. In this further extract from I'm the King of the Castle, two boys, Hooper and Kingshaw, are in a wood. Hooper has been bullying Kingshaw, and is trying to frighten him again:

It was gone eight, they had been in the wood for more than two hours. The thought frightened him.

Hooper was standing a couple of yards away, scraping at the leaf mould with his toe.

'Come on, Kingshaw.'

'I don't want to play this game now.'

Hooper's face puckered with scorn. 'What game? We're tracking deer, aren't we? I am, anyway. You can do what you like.'

'I want to go. It's about time I was getting out.'

'Out where?'

'Of here. I'm going through the fields behind the wood, and then …'

'Then what?'

'Never mind. Nowhere. You'll have to go back, though.'

Hooper shook his head.

'I'm off.'

Kingshaw had stuffed his sweater inside the satchel. Behind him were the bushes, through which they had just come. He went straight on.

'Where are you going?'

'I told you, I've got to go out of here now.'

'Home?'

'Mind your own business. No.'

'Out the other side of the wood, then?'

'Yes.'

'That's not the way.'

'It is.'

'It's not, we were over there. We turned round.'

Kingshaw hesitated. There were clumps of undergrowth all round. He tried to get his bearings. If he went into that clearing to his left, then he would be heading out of Hang Wood. He must be almost on the edge, by now. He walked on, for some way. After a bit, he heard Hooper coming behind him.

The clearing narrowed, but there were none of the tangled bushes here, it was possible to walk upright. The branches of the trees locked closely together, overhead. It was very dim. Kingshaw stopped. It went on being dark for as far as he could see. If it were near the edge of the wood, it would be getting light.

He turned round slowly. But it was the same. Everywhere looked the same.

'What's the matter now?'

Kingshaw heard, for the first time, a note of fear in Hooper's voice, and knew that he was leader, again, now.

'What have you stopped for?'

Very deliberately, Kingshaw inserted his forefingers under the string, and pulled the satchel off his back. He untied his anorak from it, and spread it out on the ground, and then sat down. Hooper stood above him, his eyes flicking about nervously, his face as pale as his limbs in the dim light.

Kingshaw said, 'We're lost. We'd better stay here and think what to do.'

Hooper crumpled. He knelt down on the ground some way off, and began to poke restlessly about among the foliage, his head bent. 'It's your fault,' he said, 'your bloody stupid fault, Kingshaw. You should have done what I said.'

'Oh, shut up.'

There was a sudden screeching cry, and a great flapping of wings, like wooden clappers. Kingshaw looked up. Two jays came flying straight through the wood, their wings whirring on the air. When they had gone, it went very still again at once, and it seemed darker, too. Then, a faint breeze came through the wood towards them, and passed, just stirring the warm air. Silence again. A blackbird began to sing, a loud, bright, warning song. Hooper looked up in alarm. From somewhere, far away, came the first rumble of thunder.

Notice how the dialogue is used to reveal the characters of the two boys, and how their relationship changes as Kingshaw gradually realises it is now Hooper who is the more scared. The dialogue moves the plot on by showing this change, but there is some effective description of the setting as well to underline this. The darkness of the wood, the noises made by the birds and the approaching storm add to the atmosphere of tension and the reader's feeling that this is a significant moment in the boys' relationship. Achieving a balance of description and dialogue while moving the plot forward is very much at the heart of a well-planned story, and the extract shows how you can achieve this balance by describing a small but important incident in detail.

WHAT MAKES THE GRADE?

To obtain a Grade C, writing in this category must show your ability to:

- be entertaining and interesting;
- develop realistic characters;
- describe settings effectively;
- present events or ideas convincingly.

To achieve Grade A, your writing must still have those qualities, but use a wider range of language and structures to achieve more original and sophisticated effects, for example, in using standard and non-standard forms of English to convey character through speech, or in using metaphors and other images in your descriptive writing.

Check yourself

QUESTIONS

Q1 Rewrite the conversation between Karen and Denise (page 167), including detail to make the aunt sound more concerned and the teenager more confused. At the end, add Karen's reflections after the phone call.

Your answer will not be the same as the one given here, but if you have used similar techniques, you will have raised the standard of the passage from Grade C to nearer Grade A.

Q2 In the section 'Planning a Story' (pages 163–5), we looked at how you might draft short pieces of writing which could be included in the final story. You also need to plan the whole story so that you know exactly what is going to happen, who is involved, where it takes place, what the central idea is and how it is going to be told.

Do that now, using the idea of the quiet boy who saves the popular, friendly one from a perilous position on the castle tower. Under each of the headings 'plot', 'characters', 'setting', 'idea' and 'structure' jot down brief notes which would help you write the complete story.

ANSWERS

A1

'Hi, Denise, it's Karen. How are you? Is . . .'

'Fine, thanks. What's up, Karen? You sound different. Is something wrong?'

'Oh . . . no. I was just ringing to speak to mum. Nothing important, really.'

'Your mum? Why would she be here at this time? Isn't she at work now?'

'No. She . . . she said . . . I thought she said she was popping in to see you this afternoon.'

'No, she's not here. Actually, I haven't seen her for ages. I've been a bit worried really, and . . . But I'm sure everything's all right, love!'

'Yes, no problem! It's OK, I must've got the message wrong. See you soon. Bye!'

'Bye, Karen. But are you sure . . .'

Karen had already hung up. She hoped she hadn't sounded too worried to Denise, but her heart was racing. She had the feeling that today was no longer any old Tuesday, but had suddenly become a very special Tuesday, one the family would remember for ever. Bitter memories, they would be.

Plot

A2

- School trip to castle – art class – to sketch the ruins
- Teasing on bus
- Pupils told to keep off dangerous high walls, one pupil ignores this
- Boy stuck on high tower – frightened to move, helped down by quiet boy who he teased on bus
- Both boys quiet on bus on way back but for different reasons

Characters

- Tom – quiet boy
- Jack – the loud, confident one
- some of their friends, who join in teasing on bus
- art teacher – not very strong on discipline
- castle attendant – does not like school parties disturbing the peace

Setting

- the bus journey
- the castle (outside – going in – the inside generally – the ruined tower where Jack gets stuck – going out again)
- the return bus journey

Idea

- that quiet people can be brave
- that some people can behave in very unexpected ways

Structure

- starts on return journey, told by Tom, flashback to earlier events

TUTORIALS

T1

Karen's concern and confusion make her start to ask about her mother before waiting for an answer to her first question.

Denise notices something unusual in Karen's manner.

Karen tries to pretend there's nothing wrong, after being thrown for a second.

Denise is now worried, realising that Karen's mum must have changed her usual routine.

Karen is finding it difficult not to reveal too many of her fears.

Denise expresses her own worries, then realises she ought to be reassuring Karen and changes direction.

Karen also tries to adopt a cheerful attitude and quickly rings off before she is asked any more questions. Denise is still wanting to find out more.

Karen reflects on how she sounded to Denise – has she given away too much? Then she begins to think about her immediate situation, and how – if her fears about her mum are right – their lives will never be the same again.

T2

- *You need to set the scene : why is the trip happening? Who is on it?*
- *Establish the main characters and their relationship.*
- *How does the main incident come about?*

- *What is the central unexpected happening? This needs to be the detailed focus of the story.*

- *An ending which will allow contrast with the start, to convey the 'message'.*

- *Use your plan to work out who is really important: obviously the two boys, some of the other children, and at least one teacher. Including the attendant will bring a second adult into the story and give you extra opportunities for description and dialogue, and he can be part of the plot, e.g. raising the alarm.*

- *Variety gives you more descriptive opportunities again, and bus–castle–bus is a pleasing circular structure. How will your description convey the different atmosphere on the return journey on the bus?*

- *Worth noting how you will convey this, e.g. by the different way the two boys are treated on the return journey.*

- *If attempting a complicated structure, it is worth developing a paragraph plan, so that you do not lose track of the sequence of events.*

- In this chapter, you will learn the qualities and techniques you need to show in your writing which informs, explains or describes.
- By looking at examples from professional writers and GCSE students, you will also learn how to plan and structure a piece of writing.

WHAT KIND OF WRITING IS THIS?

This category could include writing which tells someone how to do something, or how something works, or what it looks or feels like. This is not the kind of describing we looked at in the previous chapter, where the intention was to create character or setting in a piece of fiction; this is describing actual events, places or objects, so that someone can find their way somewhere, learn how to do something, or recognise a feeling.

Writing of this kind is often based on your own experiences and observations. In an examination, you may have to use your imagination, but you will often be given some material you can use in your answer, some indication of the audience you are writing for, and some general idea of the purpose of your writing.

The sorts of writing tasks you might be given within this category could include the following. All are taken from sample GCSE examination papers.

You are a member of your school or college council. The council has recently agreed to try to make the school or college more environmentally friendly. Write a letter to your Chair of Governors in which you inform her/him of the council's decision and explain ways in which you would like to see it carried out. **[This is a task which requires you both to inform and explain. Note that the audience will mean a polite, formal letter.]**

Many poets or novelists write about their earliest memories and how these memories have affected them. Write about a memory and explain how it has affected you. **[This is a task which requires you mainly to explain, but will also involve some describing. If an audience is not given, assume that you are writing for a sympathetic, intelligent adult.]**

Describe a place at two different times of the year or at two different times of the day. It could be a place that you know very well or one that you have imagined. **[This is a task which requires you to describe. Again, no audience is given, so assume you are writing for a sympathetic, intelligent adult.]**

As you can see from the above sample questions, it is often difficult for examiners to completely separate informing, explaining and describing. Take note of which of those words are used in any question, and make sure that you write appropriately for the stated purpose and for any given audience.

Early memories can be very vivid.

INFORMING

This is part of a leaflet published by the Government Information Society Initiative, which informs the public about the uses of information technology, and how they can find out more if they are interested.

So how can I find out more?

There are many different ways you can find out more about IT.

To start, you could become more familiar with some of these technologies. Ask friends. Try things out yourself. Don't be afraid or embarrassed. The 'Information Society' is nothing to be scared about.

Come and take part.

For a handy guide to some everyday IT technologies, take a look at our jargon busters list over the page.

Get the facts for <u>free</u>

Another smart step is to call the free **'IT for All' Information Line on**

0800 456 567

Tell us your name and address and we'll send you a copy of our special booklet, *The Guide To How IT Can Help You,* explaining everyday information technologies in plain, simple language. What's more we'll also keep you informed of any 'IT for All' activities in your area. It won't cost you a penny.

Make the most of IT

Some ideas to think about...

Try out a computer

Today's computers are versatile and fun. Try a friend's or visit one of the high street stores. A home computer is one of the best ways to give your family a flying start in IT.

Experience the Internet

It won't take long to get used to using the Internet, and it is fascinating. Ask if your library can give you a demonstration or look out for an Internet Café. There's one in most major towns.

Learn about the basics

A little knowledge goes a long way. Call the 'IT for All' information line and we'll send you our special booklet, *The Guide To How IT Can Help,* as well as keeping you informed of any 'IT for All' activities in your area.

Read all about it!

The national press and television often dedicate features and programmes to IT topics. With an understanding of just a few basic terms they are easy to follow.

Although it is written in a style appropriate to a leaflet, rather than in continuous prose, it shows some of the approaches you can use in informative writing. And remember, it may be appropriate for you to use similar presentational techniques, depending on purpose and audience (check back to Chapter 22, page 154).

Some techniques this leaflet uses are:

- straightforward, friendly and welcoming language;
- a reassuring tone;
- suggesting alternative ways of obtaining the information;
- refering to where more information is available if required;
- repeating key points.

How does this help you approach a task such as the one about making your school or college more 'green'? It should make you think about:

- the tone of language you use: you are addressing a formal letter to someone you may not know very well, or even at all, and you are suggesting some changes which may be seen as revolutionary! You need to reassure, as well as merely inform;
- suggesting a number of alternative schemes or approaches, so that the Chair feels he or she has some choice;
- using structural devices such as bullet points or headings to make your suggestions clear and immediate;
- using repetition appropriately, to emphasise your reasons for wanting change;
- offering ways in which the Chair could discuss this further with the Council if he or she wishes.

EXPLAINING

PURPOSE AND AUDIENCE

Good explanations begin with an understanding of two issues we have already considered several times in this Study and Revision Guide: purpose and audience. In other words; why are you writing the explanation, and who is it for?

If you are explaining something in writing, you must decide how much your audience needs to know, i.e. for what purpose they require the explanation, and what they may understand or know about the subject already. This will help you decide on the amount of detail to use, and on the appropriate language level.

Suppose someone said to you, 'Write an explanation of the Internet for me.' Your explanation could be a few lines, several paragraphs, two or three pages, or a whole book, depending on your questioner's needs and previous knowledge.

To illustrate this point, compare these two descriptions of the Internet.

The first (on the right) comes from the same leaflet we looked at opposite. It is intended to be an explanation for someone who knows almost nothing about the subject, so it is brief and simply laid out. The language is simple, comparing the Internet to something which every reader will understand ('a huge telephone system'). It gives only basic details; although it tells you how to connect to the Internet and what you can do on it ('make contact with anyone else, anywhere'), it doesn't tell you why you might want to do this.

The second example (on the next page) is taken from a book entitled *Internet Explorer 3 for Windows 95 for Dummies*. The book is obviously not for total dummies, however, as the explanation assumes the reader will understand terms such as 'bean-counters', 'computer networks', 'on-line services', 'accessing' and 'web site'. One of the most common errors in explanatory writing is to assume that your reader knows and understands all that you do – which is why explanations in instruction manuals for all kinds of equipment (such as how to programme video recorders) are often notoriously difficult to follow.

The Internet (or Net)

The Internet (or Net) is like a huge telephone system linking computers from all over the world. This means that you can make contact with anyone else, anywhere, who is also on the Net. With the right equipment, home computers can connect to the Internet on a normal phone line, often to a local number.

173

No one really knows how big the Internet really is...

Come on, 9 million?

The plain fact is, no one really knows just how big the Internet really is. That's because no one really owns the Internet. But several organizations make it their business to periodically try to find out how big the Internet is. The science is far from exact, but these organizations are able to come up with pretty reasonable estimates.

The best known of these Internet bean-counters is *Network Wizards*, which does a survey every year. In January of 1996, Network Wizards found that the Internet connected 240,000 separate computer networks and that more than 9.4 million separate computers existed on the Internet. When compared with 1995's numbers, the 1996 survey shows that the Internet has more than doubled in size in the past year. Or to put it another way, three new computers were added to the Internet *every second*.

Truth is, estimates such as Network Wizards are probably *low*. Consider that three of the largest online services – America Online, CompuServe, and The Microsoft Network – together support more than 10 million users. No one knows exactly how many of these users actually use the Internet. Still, the indisputable point is that the Internet is big – and getting bigger every day. If you find these figures interesting, you can check up on the latest Internet statistics from Network Wizards by accessing its Web site, www.nw.com.

STRUCTURE

Purpose and audience are your starting point, but in addition you must think about the structure of your writing: what is the best, most logical order in which to present explanations so that your reader does not become muddled or confused. Do not throw too much information at your reader at once: technical terms or complicated ideas may need to be repeated several times, and in different ways, to make sure they are understood.

You may find that you are asked to explain not how something works, or what it is, but how something has happened. This is the task in the sample exam question on page 171, about an early memory and how it has affected you. The way to approach this is still the same. Think about:

- who you are writing for, and what they know about you already, if anything;

- why you are writing: to explain why an aspect of your personality has been shaped by that early memory;

- describing the memory in a logical, straightforward way: use the best words and grammatical structures you can, but remember this is essentially an introduction to your explanation, not a developed piece of exploratory or imaginative writing such as we looked at in the previous chapter;

- making your explanation clear by giving examples, for example of how this early memory affects the way you relate to people, or your interests, or your fears – giving several examples will emphasise the effect on you, as well as ensuring the reader understands the point you are making.

DESCRIBING

We have already noted that describing within this category of writing is different from the kind of describing which explores, imagines or entertains. But non–fiction descriptions are often intended to produce an effect on the reader; descriptions of people or places are seldom totally objective, and the same may be true of the description of an object, especially if someone is trying to sell it.

Look at this paragraph from Bill Bryson's *Notes From a Small Island*. From it, you gain a clear description of what has happened to the village of Tyneham over the years, and what is to be found there. However, you are also left with a very clear impression of Bill Bryson's feelings about the way history has treated the village:

> A couple of miles beyond Kimmeridge, at the far side of a monumentally steep hill, stands the little lost village of Tyneham, or what's left of it. In 1943, the Army ordered Tyneham's inhabitants to leave for a bit as they wanted to practise lobbing shells into the surrounding hillsides. The villagers were solemnly promised that once Hitler was licked, they could all come back. Fifty-one years later they were still waiting. Forgive my disrespectful tone, but this seems to be disgraceful, not simply because it's a terrible inconvenience to the inhabitants (especially those that might have forgotten to cancel their milk), but also for poor sods like me who have to hope that the footpath through the firing range is open, which it is but occasionally. In fact, on this day it was open – I had prudently checked before setting off – so I was able to wander up and over the steep hill out of Kimmeridge and have a look round the clutch of roofless houses that is about all that remains of Tyneham. When I was last there in the late 1970s, Tyneham was forlorn, overgrown and practically unknown. Now it's become something of a tourist attraction. The county council has put up a big car park, and the school and church have been restored as small museums, with photographs showing what it was like in Tyneham in the old days, which seems kind of a shame. I liked it much better when it was a proper ghost town.

Think about the sample exam question at the start of this chapter, which was to describe a place at two different times of the day or two different times of the year. You might want to convey your strong feeling that the place is miserable in winter, or threatening at night, for example.

In writing such a description, you would therefore need to:

- observe or remember (or imagine) accurately, and in detail – if imagining, relate as much as possible to real places you know;
- select what is important for your purpose (is it to create a particular atmosphere, or a strong feeling?) and your audience (how formal should your writing be? Are your readers likely to sympathise with your point of view?);
- choose words which describe precisely and accurately, and remember to vary sentence structures and lengths for effect.

A CANDIDATE'S WORK

This is part of an examination answer in which the task was 'Put together a fact sheet on truancy for parents of teenage children. Explain what causes truancy, describe who typical truants are, and inform parents how they can help prevent truancy.' Candidates were provided with some materials to help them, including statistical information.

<u>Fear of French and Petrified of P.E.?</u>

A THIRD OF TEENAGERS TURN TO TRUANCY!!

<u>The Truth behind Truancy</u>

It's time to face up to the facts! Truancy cannot just be ignored, it is alive and well and could be effecting YOUR child. Truancy is becoming serious, with shocking figures that could include your family:

- 1 in 10 fifth formers admitted truanting once a week
- 8% admitted truanting
- ¼ of fifth formers truanted once per month

The figures are real and can't be hidden so it is no use passing the blame – it may be happening near you.

<u>Who Truants – Not Our Family!</u>

I hear you say. This may very well be true but can you be entirely sure? Figures show those most likely to truant school are 16 year old boys and girls followed closely by 15 year old boys then girls. At such a vital age at GCSE level <u>truanting school over a period of 2 years could cost them a qualification for the rest of their life!</u> Is it really worth it? An estimated 200,000 truant during their GCSE year.

The candidate was awarded a Grade A for the overall examination, and the extract from the fact sheet shows good use of:

- information (e.g. the statistics);
- explanation (e.g. the headline which suggests fear of certain lessons);
- description (e.g. who it is that actually truants).

The candidate has also thought carefully about maintaining the reader's interest by using:

- a range of appropriate presentational devices such as headlines and sub-headings;
- different font sizes and styles;
- upper- and lower-case letters;
- underlinings and bullet points.

The language is direct and often poses questions to make the reader stop and think. The headlines use alliteration to eye-catching effect. The purpose of this leaflet is to make its target audience (concerned parents) gain a better understanding of truancy, and the sample response succeeds in this.

To achieve a Grade C , you must be able to inform, explain and describe in a coherent, logical fashion, and show some awareness of adapting the content and format of your writing to its purpose and to the needs of its audience.

We have just looked closely at a piece of examination work which shows top-grade qualities in this category of writing. To achieve a Grade A, you need to use a wide range of precise vocabulary, including images such as similes and metaphors where appropriate, which have the desired impact on your audience. You will also be expected to present your work in an imaginative but suitable way.

Check yourself

QUESTIONS

Q1 Below is an examination answer by a candidate working at borderline C/D level. The task was to write a letter from a school to parents, informing them about a planned trip for pupils, explaining the arrangements and describing the purpose of the activity.

Write such a letter, remembering the qualities this category of writing should display. You may use the example as the basis of your answer if you wish, but try to make your letter much more successful in achieving its purpose!

Anytown Comprehensive School
Anything Road
Anywhere
Blankshire
XX9 9ZZ

10 June 1997

TRIP TO THORPE PARK

Dear Parent/Guardian,

We are planning a trip to Thorpe Park on 5 July, and any one is welcome.

We shall depart at eight o'clock in the morning from the school gates, and are planning to return at five o'clock.

Thorpe Park opens at ten o'clock, the students shall be free to go where they please within the Park as long as they are in a group of at least three.

Everyone will meet up again at twelve o'clock for lunch, may I advise your child to bring a packed lunch, although food can be bought from the cafe.

The coach shall leave at three o'clock, so everyone should be ready on the coach for quarter-to-three.

Your child can go on any of the rides, but I must reccomend Space Station Zero, a fast and exhilerating ride through moving coloured lightes, made more terrifying by the tilt of the seats; I would also advise your child to bring waterproofs, especially if they are planning a ride on Thunder River.

If your child is interested please fill in the attached form along with £7.00 to cover admission and traveling.

Thank you.

Yours sincerely

Miss Candidate Five

ANSWER

A1

Anytown Comprehensive School
Anything Road
Anywhere
Blankshire
XX9 9ZZ

20 June 1997

VISIT TO THORPE PARK

Dear Parent/Guardian

We are planning to take all Year 7 pupils on a visit to Thorpe Park, near Newtown, on Friday 18 July.

We shall leave school at 8 o'clock in the morning, and we intend to be back at school by 5 o'clock in the afternoon. We shall be travelling by Fred Blogg's Coaches, all of which are fitted with seat belts and other safety devices. Six teachers will accompany the pupils, together with several parent volunteers, so that pupils will spend the day in groups of no more than ten, each accompanied by at least one adult.

If your child comes on this visit, s/he will need to bring a packed lunch and a small amount of spending money in case s/he wishes to buy more food and drink or a souvenir of the visit. No pupil should bring more than £5: all the facilities of Thorpe Park are free once inside, and large sums of money may be lost or stolen. School uniform is not necessary; pupils should wear comfortable, casual clothes and footwear suitable for outdoor activities.

Thorpe Park is a centre where young people can try pursuits such as wall-climbing, abseiling, assault courses, canoeing and caving. All activities are supervised by trained centre staff, and specialist clothing and equipment are provided where necessary. We are arranging this visit as part of the pupils' personal and social education programme, so that they can develop their skills of teamwork and supporting and encouraging each other in challenging situations.

We hope that you will agree to your child taking part in this visit. If so, will you please sign and return the slip at the bottom of this letter together with a donation of £7.50 to cover the cost of travel and use of the facilities at Thorpe Park. We regret that we shall have to cancel the visit if insufficient parents are able to support it.

Yours sincerely

TUTORIAL

T1

Your letter will probably be quite different from the example above, but check to see if you have included all these features. If so, your work should be worthy of a Grade A!

Informing *Remember:*
- *where is the trip to?*
- *who is the trip for?*
- *what is the date?*
- *what are departure and return times?*
- *what does it cost?*
- *how do you book a place?*

Explaining *Remember:*
- *what is the method of travel?*
- *safety issues (e.g. travel and supervision)*
- *lunch arrangements*
- *clothing*
- *money*
- *why has this trip been chosen?*
- *what will happen if there is insufficient interest?*

Describing *Remember:*
- *what is there for the pupils to do at Thorpe Park?*
- *what will the pupils gain from the visit?*

Language *Remember:*
- *formal, but friendly – this example ends rather negatively*

Layout *Remember:*
- *the school address*
- *the date (which may be placed left or right)*
- *a heading to say what the letter is about (best placed after 'Dear Parent/Guardian' rather than before as in the examination example)*
- *paragraphs (best to keep them fairly short so that the letter does not look too dense on the page)*
- *if you refer to a return slip, it's a good idea to actually include it, as it is another opportunity for you to show how clearly you can set out the necessary information*

CHAPTER 26

WRITING TO ARGUE, PERSUADE AND INSTRUCT

- In this chapter, you will learn the qualities and techniques you need to show in your writing which argues, persuades or instructs.
- You will do this by looking at text written by professional writers and GCSE students.

WHAT KIND OF WRITING IS THIS?

This category includes writing in which the purpose is to present opinions in ways which make them seem attractive and convincing to the reader. Your intention is to:

- change the reader's way of thinking if it differs from your own;
- strengthen the reader's views if they are similar to yours;
- suggest reasons why it is correct to think in a particular way.

The sorts of writing task you might be given within this category could include the following. All are taken from sample GCSE examination papers.

'The world would be a better place if television had never been invented.' Write an essay in which you argue either for or against this statement. [**This is a task which asks you to argue, but some persuasion will also be involved. You would have to assume that you were writing for an intelligent adult, as no audience is given.**]

Write an article for a teenage magazine about skin problems. Reassure your readers that they should not be so worried about imperfections in their appearance that they become easy prey for advertisers of cosmetics and other products. [**This is essentially a persuasive task, with some elements of instruction and argument. Note that a specific purpose and audience is given, so that you can use appropriate language and presentation.**]

Write an article for primary-school children in which you explain the dangers of too much sugar in their diet and also give some advice about keeping healthy teeth. [**This task calls for instruction, although some argument and persuasion may well be involved. A specific purpose and audience is again given; candidates were also provided with some reading material on another part of this paper to help them with useful information.**]

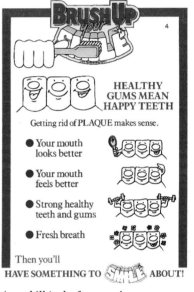

HEALTHY GUMS MEAN HAPPY TEETH

Getting rid of PLAQUE makes sense.

- Your mouth looks better
- Your mouth feels better
- Strong healthy teeth and gums
- Fresh breath

Then you'll HAVE SOMETHING TO SMILE ABOUT!

An uphill task of persuasion.

Because it is so difficult to separate argument, persuasion and instruction, we shall consider them together in this chapter, looking at ways of presenting this kind of writing as effectively as possible.

When you write to argue, persuade or instruct, it can of course help if you have strong feelings on the subject. Sometimes, shocking the reader with the strength of your views is an effective and powerful way of opening an argument before going on to persuade or instruct. Look at the start of this advertisement for Amnesty International.

"The men stripped me naked and assaulted me. I begged them to kill me. Instead, they cut off my hands with machetes." – SALLAY GOBA

DON'T LOOK THE OTHER WAY.

As the start of a piece about Amnesty International's aims, the combination of shocking picture, distressing personal account by the victim and the large black headline which challenges the reader not to ignore it, is undeniably powerful.

Sometimes, however, strong feelings can get in the way of presenting your case logically and coherently. The rest of the Amnesty International advertisement takes up more than a page of small print which presents other case histories. They are still upsetting, but are presented in more detail and are linked to political decisions about refugees made by European governments.

Once the organisation has got your attention, it uses evidence to persuade you that there is a genuine problem, one which you can do something about. This extract is the closing section of the advertisement. What techniques are used here? We will identify some of them in 'Devices and structures' opposite.

No-one wants to be a refugee. People don't want to be homeless any more than you do – tortured, murdered, raped, any more than you do.

They want to be offered a safe haven, as much as you would if you and your family were fleeing for your lives. They long to go home as ardently as you would. When that's impossible, they'd like the chance to make a valuable contribution to their new country, just as you would.

For heaven's sake wake up and help them.

One powerful thing you can do is join Amnesty International and/or donate to our campaign funds.

Help us stop the human rights abuse that creates refugees, and repeal those cruel laws that often deny them help after their lives have been destroyed.

Don't turn away. Please don't turn away. Even a few pounds helps us to intervene on behalf of people who are in terrifying danger, sometimes even to save their lives. Is there a better use for your money? We defy you to think of one. Please join us here and now.

ACHIEVING THE BEST EFFECT

In this kind of writing, you need to present your material powerfully, but not allow strong emotions, or the conviction that your views are right, to weaken your argument: readers may just switch off if you are incoherent, or if they feel they are being preached at. To persuade people, you need to instruct them as well; in other words, to present them with evidence which makes them think about, and perhaps change, their views.

Look at this extract from an examination answer in which the candidate was asked to write a letter to a newspaper, arguing against another letter (from a Mr Glass) which had claimed that drinking and driving is not dangerous:

Mr Glass says that he regularly drives his car when he is over the limit. I don't think that this is anything to be proud about. Although very stupid, he has been a very lucky person not to have had an accident in the 20 years he has been driving. A third of all drivers and motorcyclists who die in UK road accidents have blood alcohol levels above the legal limit.

Mr Glass claims that he feels more alert and alive after he has drunk a few pints, and that his driving improves because of this. Alcohol is a repressant; even small quantities impair reaction times, blur vision and reduce the ability to judge speed and distance. It also gives a false sense of confidence, which explains why he feels a better driver, when in reality he could be swerving all over the road, and being a danger to other drivers.

Another point which Mr Glass has misunderstood is the claim that if you drink with a meal, eating the food will mean you can drink more yet still be safe to drive. Nothing, not food, or coffee or anything can reduce the amount of alcohol in your blood, or the risk of drink driving. Food only delays the absorption of alcohol into your bloodstream, thus delaying the effects of the drink. Waiting half an hour as Mr Glass suggests before driving home is only giving the alcohol time to take effect. It can take 24 hours for your body to get rid of the alcohol you have consumed, meaning that you can still be over the limit driving to work the morning after an evening of drinking.

Will you be responsible this year?

Every year, thousands are killed, crippled and maimed in drink drive accidents by people who felt OK to drive.

Have none for the road.

Controversial views on topics that people feel strongly about are often used to provoke debate.

The letter is argued forcibly and skilfully, taking points raised by Mr Glass one by one and using evidence to support the writer's case that Mr Glass's views are wrong. This is part of an examination performance which was awarded a Grade A overall. The only slight miscalculation in this extract is where the writer calls Mr Glass 'very stupid' – you are unlikely to convert people to your way of thinking if you insult them, so keep cool, whatever the provocation!

DEVICES AND STRUCTURES

TO SHOCK OR NOT TO SHOCK?

'Keeping cool' can be a most effective technique in this category of writing. We have seen the 'shock tactic' approach used by Amnesty International to gain the reader's attention, but what about the following? In Chapter 21 (page 147), we used part of a newspaper article about public executions in Jedda to illustrate an aspect of paragraphing. Here is how that article ends (after the man was beheaded, his female accomplice was stoned to death by the crowd):

> The execution of the man? Well, let us not forget that it was as recently as 1936 that the French held their last public execution. And the beheading was at least humanely and quickly carried out.
>
> But the doing to death of the woman is something which the handful of horrified Europeans in the crowd will not quickly forget.
>
> It took just over an hour before the doctor in attendance, who halted the stoning periodically to feel the victim's pulse, announced her dead.
>
> This double execution took place just the other day.

Given the subject matter, this is indeed a 'cool' piece of writing, yet it is clearly intended to argue that capital punishment is barbaric, to persuade readers to the author's point of view, and to instruct them in what took place in the world when the article was written. There is no gruesome detail of the woman's slow death and no particularly colourful language in the passage ('doing to death' and 'horrified' are the strongest words used): it makes its effect by being purposely detached – note especially the last sentence – and by the short paragraphs which give the reader time to stop frequently and take in just what is being described.

CONSIDERING DIFFERENT POINTS OF VIEW

There is one other important feature shown by the above piece of writing. Although the author clearly believes that the executions were wrong, he nevertheless puts forward some information which, if not actually supporting the events, does make the reader think more carefully about their reaction to them. In pointing out the recent abolition of public executions in France, and the humane speed of the beheading, the author suggests that the Western world may not be blameless in its own involvement with capital punishment. This willingness to see another point of view strengthens the argument, since it makes the reader believe that the author is a reasonable person, not a fanatic willing to consider only one viewpoint. If you are writing to argue or persuade, it is worth including some points of view with which you disagree, or acknowledging that a different point of view from your own may have some virtues. If you can do this, while still persuading the reader to your own point of view, you will be highly rewarded for your writing skills.

PRESENTATIONAL DEVICES

Chapters 22 and 23 looked at a range of presentational and stylistic features, and many of these are useful when writing to argue, persuade or instruct. We have seen how the photograph and headline contribute to the effect of the Amnesty International advertisement. In writing where you are presenting factual evidence, or drawing conclusions from this evidence, any of the following presentational devices may also be useful:

- titles, headings and sub-headings;
- underlinings and frames;
- bullet points;
- graphics, including charts and tables of statistics.

STYLISTIC DEVICES

Depending on the approach you adopt in a particular piece of writing, i.e. whether you are using shock tactics or gentle persuasion, the whole range of stylistic devices might be appropriate. Think about the effective use of:

- precisely chosen individual words, such as 'tortured', 'murdered', 'raped', 'fleeing', 'ardently' to convey horror and desperation in the Amnesty International extract;
- images: in a part of the newspaper report about the Jedda executions not quoted above, the writer says that the faces of the men in the crowd were 'transformed into masks of sadism', which conjures up a vivid visual image;
- direct appeals, such as 'For heaven's sake wake up and help them' in the Amnesty International extract;
- questions, to make your reader think about the views they hold and what they are prepared to do about something: 'Is there a better use for your money?' (Amnesty International);
- repetition, such as 'Don't turn away. Please don't turn away' in the Amnesty International appeal, or 'Nothing, not food or coffee or anything can reduce the amount of alcohol in your blood, or the risks of drink driving' in the candidate's letter;

- appropriate endings: 'This double execution took place just the other day' achieves a chilling effect at the end of the Jedda report; 'Please join us here and now' sums up what Amnesty International want you to do after reading their advertisement; the candidate's letter went on to finish 'As to his suggestion that the government is wasting its money with their drink driving campaign, I don't think they have spent enough if there are still people around like Mr Glass'.

◀ **WHAT MAKES THE GRADE?**

To achieve a Grade C in this category of writing, you must be able to present an argument which is clear and coherent and which is aware of the needs of its audience, for example in judging whether to use strong language and disturbing evidence or a more detached approach. Some use of straightforward, appropriate presentational devices would also be expected.

To achieve a Grade A, you must be able to use a full range of appropriate presentational and stylistic devices; the structure of your writing must be detailed and logical, and you should be able to consider different points of view in reaching your own conclusion, while still constructing a powerful and persuasive argument.

Check yourself

QUESTION

Q1 The following piece of writing is part of an examination answer in which the candidate was asked to write about whether countries should keep nuclear weapons. The whole answer was assessed at just below Grade C.

Rewrite this part of the answer, identifying some of its faults and improving it where you can.

Why does nearly every country in the world compete for Nuclear Weapons? Nearly every country in the world has Nuclear Weapons. Those countries with large economies have bigger and better nuclear weapons, which could destroy the whole world in seconds. Other countries have smaller weapon, but these could still do a lot of damage. Today there are a number of groups which are trying to get every country which owns nuclear weapons to dispose of them safely. We have nuclear weapons to protect our country, we then think we are safe from being attacked by another country. All the main countries with large economies are living in fear because they know that one day they may be attacked and that nuclear weapons will be used in the attack. They may also think that the more weapons they have the less chance they have of being attacked. Today, no country is prepared to be the first country to dispose of their weapons, they say that we couldn't survive if we didn't have nuclear weapons. They think they will be attacked by other countries and they won't have any weapons to defend themselves.

ANSWER

A1

This is not the only way to rewrite the beginning of the passage, but see if you have identified similar problems in the original, even if you have dealt with them differently.

> Why do many countries compete over nuclear weapons? Those with successful economies have more effective weapons than poorer countries, but any nuclear weapon could cause enormous damage. Many economically developed countries live in fear of being attacked with nuclear weapons, and so keep them as both protection and deterrent.
>
> Today, a number of organisations are trying to persuade countries to dispose of their nuclear weapons safely, but no country is prepared to be the first...

TUTORIAL

T1

Content and structure

- *Avoid exaggeration: it is not true that 'nearly every country in the world' competes for nuclear weapons.*
- *The original answer is very repetitive both at the beginning and the end.*
- *The answer needs to be split into two paragraphs and some of the material to be re-arranged, as there are two different ideas here: a description of the problem, and attempts to do something about it.*

[Note: from this opening, it appears that the writer is arguing one side of the question only. Remember that to gain a high grade, the argument would need to consider other opinions and viewpoints, even if they are ultimately rejected.]

Style

- *Starting with a question is good, and worth retaining.*
- *'Nuclear weapons' does not need upper-case letters.*
- *Much of the language of the original is very simple. For example, using 'successful' rather than 'large' economies; 'more effective' instead of 'bigger and better'; 'enormous' instead of 'a lot of'; 'both protection and deterrent' to replace at least two whole sentences; 'organisations' instead of 'groups'.*

Presentation

No presentational features have been added, but it might have been worth considering:

- *a title (perhaps something like 'Nuclear weapons: fear or threat?');*
- *underlined or framed headings for each paragraph (e.g. 'The weapon race' and 'Peer pressure');*
- *bullet-pointing the reasons given in the first paragraph for why countries keep nuclear weapons.*

CHAPTER 27

WRITING TO ANALYSE, REVIEW AND COMMENT

- In this chapter, you will learn the qualities and techniques you need to show in your writing which analyses, reviews or comments.

- By looking at examples from professional writers and students, you will also learn to plan and structure a piece of writing.

WHAT KIND OF WRITING IS THIS?

This is probably the most difficult kind of writing you are asked to do for your GCSE examination. It involves:

- analysing: identifying and describing the particular qualities of something, e.g. a person, a place, an event, a book or an advertisement;

- reviewing: thinking about those qualities and what they tell you about the person, place, event, book or advertisement;

- commenting: putting your ideas into a shape and structure which explains your reaction and why it is significant.

In practice, it is not always easy to separate these three activities, but it will be helpful to bear the distinctions in mind as we work through the examples in this chapter.

WHEN WILL I WRITE LIKE THIS?

You are most likely to write in this way when you are analysing texts, maybe set books for a Literature examination or media and non-fiction texts (such as newspapers or advertisements) when practising for your English examination. Later in this chapter, we will look at some examples of the latter kind of writing produced by actual examination candidates.

The other situation when you will analyse, review and comment is in personal writing, when you reflect on people, places, events or feelings. You may be writing a section of your autobiography – for example, memories of early childhood – or an account of work experience or a foreign holiday. Typical tasks could include the following. Both are taken from sample GCSE examination papers.

Look carefully at the materials from the NSPCC included with this examination paper. They are part of a Christmas appeal. Consider how successful you think this appeal would be in encouraging people to give money. [**This task will clearly involve analysing, reviewing and commenting.**]

Most people at one time or another are involved in some kind of celebration or festivity. This often includes a ritual or ceremony. In your own words give an account of any occasion such as this in which you took part, or which you observed. Comment on why it was memorable. [**This task is directed towards commenting, but will involve some analysis and review.**]

London, my London

Sebastian Faulks

It is 20 years ago to the day that I arrived in London for a job interview in Camden Town. Twenty summers with the length of 20 long winters; and still it seems to me that London is not really appreciated either by the rest of the country or by the phlegmatic people who live there. It is a wonderful city, diverse, un-pushy, a bit tawdry, but a serious place to live, with the vast reserves of historical character and contemporary activity. The rest of England, with the exception of parts of Cornwall and the Yorkshire Moors, is a suburb. In this country there has been no flight from the countryside, as in France, because the towns in England have come to meet the country. The two have joined sticky hands around the in-filled lanes, the street-lit roads and green-site superstores. Compared with Montana, the Marche or the Auvergne, the English countryside is a tarmac non-event. But compared with New York, Rome or Paris, London is unashamed.

PURPOSE AND AUDIENCE

Once again, these are key words in helping you to write effectively in this category. For example, If you were writing about your early childhood memories to entertain a group of young children, you would probably concentrate on things that happened. In other words, describing and entertaining would be more important than analysing, reviewing and commenting. Even in this situation, however, you might round off an amusing account of something you did as a young child with a comment such as 'That was silly of me, wasn't it?', which is an analytic/reviewing comment. If you are writing for a more mature audience, and the purpose of your writing is to introduce general ideas rather than tell a story or describe something, then the proportion of analysis, review and comment will be much greater.

WRITING ABOUT A PLACE

Let's start with an example from journalism. In the extract on the left, Sebastian Faulks, a columnist with *The Guardian*, is writing of his feelings about London. What techniques does he use?

He identifies and describes features of London which he likes – 'vast reserves of historical character and contemporary activity' – and features of the rest of England which he does not like: 'with the exception of parts of Cornwall and the Yorkshire Moors, [it] is a suburb.' In other words, he analyses his feelings about London.

He thinks about those qualities and what they tell him about London: 'It is a wonderful city, diverse, unpushy, a bit tawdry, but a serious place to live …'. In other words, he reviews his feelings about London.

He then puts his ideas into a shape and structure which explains his reaction to London and why it is significant: 'still it seems to me that London is not really appreciated either by the rest of the country or by the phlegmatic people who live there'. In other words, he comments on his feelings about London.

Some of this article is information and description, and part of its purpose is to persuade you of the virtues of London, but for the most part it consists of analysis, review and comment.

Reflective writing needs vocabulary which can precisely describe the feelings and reactions of the writer – note the use here of words such as 'phlegmatic', 'diverse', 'unpushy', 'tawdry', 'unashamed'. Two striking images are used: the idea of the town and the countryside having 'joined sticky hands', and the countryside being 'a tarmac non-event'. These stylistic features give the article a sense of accurate observation (the choice of vocabulary) and individuality (the original images), which are qualities you want to achieve in this category of writing.

WRITING ABOUT A CONCEPT OR IDEA

The following extract is from a Grade A examination answer by a candidate writing about the intrusion of the press into the private lives of rich and famous people, and the proposal that there should be restrictions on newspapers.

> To have your private life splashed across the front pages of national newspapers must be at best humiliating, but it is a risk those in the public eye must take. If they are unprepared to accept this aspect of their position, they should not occupy it. The Royal Family and the government are the representatives of our country, so they are naturally expected to behave responsibly. This is not an unjust expectation and those who do not live up to it must suffer the consequences.
>
> However I think that the issue goes far beyond the invasion of privacy of a handful of people. The public has a right to know what is going on, and the proposed curbs would cut information that is revealed down to a minimum. A free press is what keeps a country as a democracy – otherwise the papers become propaganda and the government a dictatorship, because no one is allowed to question their actions.
>
> In the end it comes down to this: no government has the right to act as God, to say what we should or shouldn't read or indeed, what we should or shouldn't write. As the 'Daily Mirror' says, 'The freedom of the press is... the inalienable right of every citizen to speak his mind in public without fear of penalty, prosecution or persecution.'

What are the qualities of analysis, review and comment which this work shows?

- The analysis of the situation is in the first sentence of each of the first two paragraphs. This shows the candidate has thought carefully about the structure of the answer, and is setting out the main issues at the beginning of each section, after which they are reviewed and commented upon.

- Review is in the third sentence of the first paragraph ('The Royal Family and the government ...') and the third sentence of the second paragraph ('A free press ...').

- The rest of the extract can be described as comment, although as was suggested earlier, it can be a false exercise to try and distinguish absolutely these three aspects of the writing category – the last sentence of the second paragraph, for example, ('A free press ...') is arguably analysis, review and comment all at the same time.

This candidate has successfully tackled the subject by using an appropriate style of writing (impersonal, but still engaged – 'However, I think that ...') and a coherent structure.

WRITING ABOUT EMOTION

Analysing, reviewing and commenting on emotions is challenging, but is a useful skill to develop not only in writing about yourself, but in writing fiction, when you may wish to open up the thoughts and feelings of a character in a story, for example.

Richard Hillary was a fighter pilot in the Second World War. He wrote an account of his experiences and feelings, *The Last Enemy*, from which the following extract is taken. He has just killed his first enemy pilot.

My first emotion was one of satisfaction, satisfaction at a job adequately done, at the final logical conclusion of months of specialised training. And then I had a feeling of the essential rightness of it all. He was dead and I was alive; it could so easily have been the other way round; and that would somehow have been right too. I realised in that moment just how lucky a fighter pilot is. He has none of the personalised emotions of the soldier, handed a rifle and bayonet and told to charge. He does not even have to share the dangerous emotion of the bomber pilot who night after night must experience that childhood longing for smashing things. The fighter pilot's emotions are those of the duellist – cool, precise, impersonal. He is privileged to kill well. For if one must either kill or be killed, as now one must, it should, I feel, be done with dignity. Death should be given the setting it deserves; it should never be a pettiness; and for the fighter pilot it never can be.

You should now be able to identify clear elements of analysis, review and comment in the above passage.

- **Analysis:** the author identifies and describe his feelings of satisfaction, relief and 'rightness'.
- **Review:** he thinks about the situation, and why he has those feelings.
- **Comment:** the last sentence sums up Richard Hillary's reaction to the situation.

How might you use some of these skills in your own writing? In Chapter 21, we looked at some extracts from one student's response to the title 'Journey to my Father'. Here is the ending of another student's response to that same task:

I began to collect together my things; my clammy hands stuck to the handle of my case, and I struggled to straighten my skirt and brush off the various specks of sugar. The remains of the doughnut I had just eaten reminded me to wipe around my mouth, which had been splattered with jam.

What would my father think, his long-lost daughter still had the eating habits he had been familiar with, so long ago? He would be familiar with them now too, I had forgotten about his 'new' children. What happened if they didn't like me, and his wife?

They would all probably hate me and they couldn't ask me to leave. I was going to have to stay with these people for the full holiday, despite how we were going to feel about each other.

As the train pulled into the station, my thoughts stopped in their tracks. I caught a glimpse of a face, familiar to me. But this man was not surrounded by small children or a young-looking blonde as I had imagined. He couldn't have come on his own to meet me. Could he?

I stepped down onto the platform and with trembling uneasy steps I made my way through the crowds to this man. He saw me and came and took my cases, but then put them down. This man had a large grin on his face and his arms were open, he leant over and hugged me. All the thoughts I had experienced on the train left my head. This was my father.

This sophisticated piece of work shows the writer analysing her situation by identifying all the things that could go wrong when she meets her father; she reviews the change in his personal circumstances – the new wife and children – and in the touching final paragraphs, she comments on the reality of the meeting, and what it means to her. Writing about emotions needs to be firmly grounded in action and detail like this, such as wiping the crumbs and jam from around the mouth, to make the feelings seem real to the reader.

WHAT MAKES THE GRADE?

To achieve Grade C in this category of writing, you must be able to distance yourself from the topic (unlike when you are arguing, persuading and instructing) so that you can present and explain opinions, viewpoints and attitudes coherently and logically, even if writing about feelings or emotions. You must also be aware of your audience in judging the balance between analysis, review and comment.

To achieve Grade A requires the same qualities, but also the use of a more sophisticated range of vocabulary, imagery and grammatical structures, together with more searching analysis, detailed review and cogent comment. Remember that 'distance' from a subject does not mean a lack of involvement on your part: you must always engage and sustain your audience's attention, which means you must be interested in, and concerned about, your subject.

Check yourself

QUESTIONS

Q1 Answer this GCSE examination question. Allow yourself about forty-five minutes, and compare what you have written with the model answer and tutorial which follows. Remember that your purpose is to analyse, review and comment on the success of the project.

Your school has been running a very successful project called 'Improving our School'. As one of those involved, you have been asked to write an article about this project for the school magazine. You have made the notes on the right:

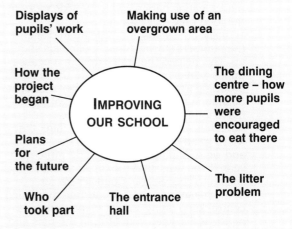

Displays of pupils' work

Making use of an overgrown area

How the project began

The dining centre – how more pupils were encouraged to eat there

IMPROVING OUR SCHOOL

Plans for the future

Who took part

The entrance hall

The litter problem

ANSWER

A1 You probably all remember what a mess the school site looked a year ago. What was wrong with it? Where do I start! Bare patches on the grass at the front entrance, weeds in the flower beds, litter bins broken or overflowing. Yes, you remember!

Inside wasn't a lot better, either: bare walls and echoing corridors don't feel much like home, do they? So a group of us on the School Council decided to change this if we could, and the Improving Our School campaign was launched.

We had someone from each year in the action group, and they all talked to everyone who had anything to do with the school so that ideas for changes wouldn't just come from one part of the community. We didn't have much money to spend, but the Head and the Governors said they could spare about £500 to start us off, and that if the changes worked, we might be able to have more money next year.

We looked at the problems and all the suggestions, and realised that with only £500 to spend, we couldn't do everything. So we decided to concentrate on four improvements: displaying work on the corridors, improving the entrance to the school, encouraging more pupils to eat in the school dining centre, and – the biggest challenge of all – attacking the litterbugs!

The corridors look really attractive now, and I've overheard visitors commenting on them. Of course, they're already impressed by the entrance to the school: the flower beds and what used to be an overgrown area by the car park are tidy and bright with shrubs and trees. I know that doesn't make us a better school, but it certainly gives people a better impression of us.

Once we had persuaded the Cook to survey pupils' eating habits and to provide more of the food they really wanted – not chips, actually, but salads and vegetarian dishes – the numbers staying for school meals shot up. This helped the litter problem, because pupils weren't coming back into the grounds dropping wrappers from food they'd bought outside. A few extra bins in the right places made a huge difference too.

So, it has all gone really well. We think that we've given back some pride to the school, and we're hoping that we can do more next year. If you want that too, make your feelings known to your School Council rep.

In the meantime, keep supporting the dining centre; keep doing all that great work to go on the walls, keep your litter in the bins and keep off the flower beds!

TUTORIAL

T1 The answer uses the notes well to:

- analyse the situation in the school before the improvement campaign started;
- review the process which then took place;
- comment on the end results and possible future developments.

If you have also done this in one way or another, you have fulfilled the main purpose of the task.

The answer is presented coherently and logically, and with a sense of enthusiasm and involvement. The language and tone is appropriate to a school audience. Although it is an easy piece to read, and so would hold the interest of its audience, some of the points made are quite sophisticated (such as the comment 'I know that doesn't make us a better school, but it certainly gives people a better impression of us'). This answer would gain a high GCSE grade.

SECTION III

Speaking and Listening

CHAPTER 28

ORGANISING WHAT YOU SAY AND HOW YOU SAY IT

- **In this chapter, you will learn to:**

  plan *what* you say, so that listeners are more likely to understand you;

  think about *how* you say things, so that listeners are more likely to consider your point of view.

- **If you are confident, fluent and sympathetic when working with different audiences, you will gain a good GCSE grade for Speaking and Listening.**

INFORMAL/FORMAL SITUATIONS

When your speaking and listening skills are assessed for GCSE English, there will be times when an informal approach is appropriate, for example, if you are:

- discussing your first ideas about a piece of writing which you have not seen before;

- in a group, arguing about a controversial issue which has suddenly cropped up;

- role-playing a family situation of some kind.

But there are other times when you need to speak more formally, for example, if you are:

- explaining something to a group which includes people you do not know well;

- welcoming visitors to a school or workplace, and giving them information;

- trying to persuade others to share your point of view in an organised debate.

There are times when speech is informal ... and others where more formality is required.

KEY FEATURES OF SPEAKING

When speaking in any formal situation, it is vital that you think about:

- what you are saying, both in general and in detail (your *topic*);

- why you are speaking (your *purpose*);

- how you are going to make your subject interesting (your *audience*).

In situations like those mentioned above, you therefore need to plan carefully *what* you say so that you:

- include all the necessary information (topic);

- present ideas in a logical order (purpose);

- speak appropriately (audience).

TOPIC AND PURPOSE

Making sure that you don't forget to say something important, getting everything in the best order and keeping your listeners interested is quite easy if you prepare properly. You could try the **BORE** technique:

- **B**rainstorm all the ideas you have on the subject;

- **O**rganise your ideas – use headings, spider-grams or any other method you prefer;

191

Brainstorm all the ideas you have on the subject.

- **R**educe these to brief notes on one side of paper or on a few index cards, with main points highlighted if you wish;
- keep **E**ye-contact with your audience when speaking.

You won't always be able to plan what you say in such detail, nor will this kind of approach suit every situation, but practising in this way when you can will give you confidence in your ability to 'think on your feet' when you need to. Chapters 30–34 go into more detail about different speaking and listening situations.

AUDIENCE

Speaking appropriately to different audiences (*how* you say things) can be difficult. Chapters 29 and 34 go into more detail on this subject, but for now you should remember to:

- use words which are suited to the occasion – not slang if it is formal, not too formal if it is a chat with friends;
- if appropriate, help your audience understand more by using pictures or other visual aids, or by referring to books, statistics, etc.;
- employ non-verbal gestures which help to convey your message – smile, use your hands, perhaps move about – but not so much that you distract listeners.

WHAT MAKES THE GRADE? ▶

To gain a Grade C, people who listen to you speaking formally need to see that you have skills such as:

- speaking fluently and keeping to the point;
- adapting talk to different audiences, using varied vocabulary and expressions;
- putting forward a clear point of view and sustaining the listeners' interest.

To gain a Grade A, you need to develop the ability to:

- explain complicated ideas and issues in detail, using a wide range of language and techniques;
- show sensitivity to other speakers and listeners;
- handle different points of view and cross-reference ideas.

Check yourself

Q1

Prepare a two-minute statement which you might make on a radio phone-in programme for teenagers on the subject of reducing under-age drinking. Try to plan in the way suggested above: **brainstorm**, **organise**, **reduce**. You can use notes if you wish.

Then deliver your prepared statement to a friend or a relative and ask his or her opinion about it. Your friend should just listen to what you say, but not watch you.

If possible, you should tape yourself, and use the descriptions in 'What Makes the Grade?' above to think about the overall quality of your statement: was it nearer to a GCSE Grade C or Grade A?

REMEMBER! Cover the answers if you want to.

ANSWER

A1

A spider-gram brainstorm might look something like this:

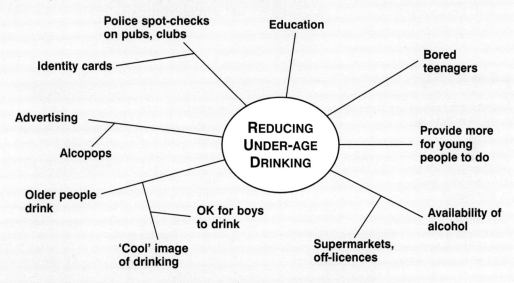

Having organised those thoughts and made some notes, this could be your statement:

> I think there are several problems if you want to reduce underage drinking. For a start, there isn't much for teenagers to do if they live in the country. Even if they live in towns, they probably go to pubs and clubs to listen to music with their friends. Alcohol will be sold there, and the owners aren't usually too fussy about who they sell it to. Because drink has a cool image with some young people, they will buy it in places like that or in supermarkets and off-licences sometimes.

ANSWER

A1

You can't really criticise them, because most of their parents probably drink, and some parents even think it's quite grown-up for boys to get drunk. A friend of mine, Nick, and his sister got really drunk at a party a couple of weeks ago, and their dad thought it was quite funny about Nick, but went mad at his sister. He said that men have to learn to drink but a drunk woman is disgusting. I don't see why it should be any different.

Some people say that new drinks like alcopops are a problem, especially for teenage girls, because they don't taste of alcohol, but I think young people choose to drink and know when they're drinking. Some of them actually enjoy the feeling of being drunk. It wouldn't be any different if there was less advertising – we always know where to get hold of something if we want to.

The only real solution is to make everyone have an identity card so their ages can be checked. I don't see why so many adults are against identity cards. If the police also did more spot checks on pubs and clubs it might help. I don't think more alcohol education in school would make much difference – you don't think about that when you're with your friends and they're all drinking.

More things to do would be some help, but in the end alcohol is a drug which society accepts and so young people are always going to use it. Under-age drinking is just a fairly normal part of growing up.

TUTORIAL

T1

To judge how effective your own statement was, ask your listener(s) these questions:

- How long did it last? (This will show how well you paced your talk.)
- What opinions and ideas was I trying to convey? (This will show whether you actually got your point of view across.)
- Could you follow my argument? (This will show whether your talk was well organised.)
- Did I sound convincing? Why/Why not? (This will show whether you judged your audience well, and whether you used the right sort of language for the situation.)

The model talk above:

- is the right length if spoken at a sensible speed;
- conveys the speaker's attitude that there isn't a simple answer to this problem;
- argues clearly that society has some double standards on the subject of alcohol;
- uses language which is straightforward but to the point, and appropriately informal for the situation (e.g. abbreviations, and words such as 'cool') and makes persuasive use of personal anecdote to reinforce the message (although you might think the speaker veers off the point a little and starts to talk more about male-female drinking than under-age drinking).

Taking all this into account, the model answer shows some Grade A qualities; to be certain of this grade in an overall Speaking and Listening assessment, the speaker would need to remember relevance, and would need to show the ability to use a wider range of vocabulary in more formal situations.

- In this chapter, you will learn to:

  recognise and use standard English where necessary;

  consider what kind of language is appropriate in different situations.

- If you learn to use standard English appropriately in oral work, you will gain higher marks in your GCSE Speaking and Listening assessment

WHAT IS 'STANDARD ENGLISH'?

The National Curriculum defines standard English as 'the language of public communication'. This means that in most activities which are assessed as part of your spoken English work, you must try to use vocabulary and grammar which will be easily understood by most adult English speakers.

STANDARD VOCABULARY

As we will see, this involves using words which have a shared meaning, for example:

- everyone understands 'fun' or 'enjoyable', but slang words such as 'cool' or 'wicked' should be avoided, because they can be misunderstood and because they have a short life-span before becoming unfashionable and meaningless;

- avoid local dialect words such as 'starving' – although it means 'cold' or 'freezing' to a northerner, it means something different (i.e. 'very hungry') in standard English;

- avoid North American usage: because of imported television programmes, many people are now quite comfortable with words such as 'fall' (meaning 'autumn'), but these should be used only for particular effects.

Try to avoid speaking like an American cartoon character.

STANDARD GRAMMAR

Standard English also uses grammatical conventions. For example:

- accurate past or present tenses: 'he come(s) here yesterday' is quite commonly heard, but standard English requires 'he came here yesterday';

- accurate verb forms: for example, in speech we often hear 'they was', when standard English requires 'they were';

- accurate articles and pronouns: informal speech may use phrases such as 'this man said to me' or 'them books are expensive', when standard English requires 'a man said to me' or 'those books are expensive'.

WHEN IS STANDARD SPOKEN ENGLISH REQUIRED?

Think about different ways of describing a collision between two cars, and what this might tell us about the appropriate use of standard and

HI GUV, WOULD YOU BE SO KIND TO SHOW ME A GOOD TIME?

TAXI

Foreign visitors often have trouble knowing when to use standard and non-standard English.

non-standard English. What sorts of things might these people say, and how might they say them?

● a bystander calling the emergency services on 999

● an eye-witness giving a statement to a policemen later that day

● one of the people involved in the accident talking to the representative of an insurance company

● a teenager telling his or her friends about the accident the next day

Which of these people would be speaking standard English? Certainly the bystander, as he or she would want the emergency services to understand immediately what has happened. The eye-witness and the person involved in the accident would probably speak standard English too, because of the formal situations they would be in. Either of them might drift into a less formal style from time to time, especially if they feel some personal involvement, but the questions asked by the police or the insurance firm would probably make them keep to a more formal manner. It is very unlikely that the teenager would use standard English to his or her friends, especially when describing something exciting or upsetting.

WHAT DO DIFFERENT FORMS OF SPOKEN ENGLISH SOUND LIKE?

The four people we have been thinking about might therefore say things such as:

Bystander: There has been an accident in the High Street. Two cars have collided. They have gone into a tree. I think some people may be hurt.

Eye-witness: The blue Escort came out from the side street without stopping and hit the red Cavalier hard. I think the Escort was speeding. The Cavalier was pushed across the road and against a tree. Some of the people inside seemed to be injured, and they were all trapped.

Person involved: I was driving up Church Road, towards High Street. I was driving at about 20 miles an hour. When I got to the junction I slowed right down, looked both ways and pulled out as the road was clear. Suddenly, this red Cavalier appeared from nowhere, and I hit it side-on.

Teenager: This bloke in an XR3 comes shooting out of Church Road, never looks anywhere, smashes into this Cavalier and chucks it into a tree over the road. There was three or four inside it, and they didn't look too clever.

In the first account, the only feature which could possibly be described as non-standard is the use of 'gone into' rather than 'hit'. The words as a whole convey a message clearly and quickly and would be comprehensible to any adult English speaker.

Both the second and third accounts sound a little unnatural. People would not normally speak as formally as that, except in situations (probably talking to strangers) where they are discussing something very important. Even here, standard English is likely to slip when someone becomes involved in what they are saying, so the driver of the Escort refers to 'this' Cavalier, rather than 'a' Cavalier, which would be the standard form, and says that he slowed 'right' down, to give emphasis and make it seem that he did nothing wrong.

FEATURES OF NON-STANDARD ENGLISH

The last example is non-standard in all kinds of ways. For example, the teenager uses:

- 'this' twice when 'a' would be the standard form;

- several slang or non-standard terms, such as 'bloke';

- the present tense to describe events which happened in the past – this is a very common non-standard feature of conversation, as it undoubtedly adds excitement;

- 'never' to mean 'did not', another common non-standard form;

- 'was' instead of 'were' – non-agreement of verbs is a common non-standard feature.

WHAT MAKES THE GRADE?

You do not have to use standard English all the time when you are speaking. It would often sound very odd – even rude – if you did. However, when you are being assessed for spoken English, you should normally use standard English unless you wish to create a particular effect. For example, you might be taking part in a role play exercise in which you have the part of a teenager talking to friends, in which case it would be quite appropriate to use some everyday, non-standard forms of English.

When you are assessed for spoken English, one of the differences between a Grade D and a Grade C in examination board mark schemes is this:

Grade D: increasingly aware of the need for, and use of, standard English vocabulary and grammar

Grade C: competent use of standard English vocabulary and grammar in situations which demand it

In other words, a 'D' candidate is not completely in control; he or she will use some non-standard forms inappropriately and often without realising it. A 'C' candidate, however, is sufficiently in control to know when it is right to use non-standard forms, but at other times will be 'competent' (not perfect!) in using standard English.

To achieve a Grade A, mark schemes say that you must be 'sensitive in choice of speech style' and that your 'use of standard English vocabulary and grammar is mature and assured'.

Check yourself

QUESTION

Q1 Rewrite the teenager's account of the car crash (page 196), putting it into standard English.

.... **REMEMBER! Cover the answers if you want to.** ....

ANSWER

A1 A man in an Escort XR3 came out of Church Road very fast. He did not look. He hit a Cavalier and pushed it into a tree on the other side of the road. There were three or four people inside, and it looked as though they had been injured.

TUTORIAL

T1 *If you have understood the description of standard English, and comments about the non-standard features of the teenager's account, your rewritten version should be very close to the suggested answer.*

Note that non-standard features which have been corrected in addition to those already mentioned under 'Features of non-standard English' are:

- *the reference to an 'XR3': not everyone would realise that this is an Escort XR3;*
- *the words 'shooting' and 'chucks': these are vivid words which add atmosphere to the informal description, but are inappropriate in a more formal situation which requires standard English;*
- *the phrase 'didn't look too clever', which is a slang idiom and one which might not be understood by all English speakers.*

- In this chapter, you will learn to explain, describe and narrate effectively in speech.
- If you develop a wide vocabulary and learn how to interest and involve listeners, you will improve your GCSE grade.

EXPLAINING

In your GCSE English course, you might be asked to explain an interest or hobby as part of a Speaking and Listening assessment. What makes a good explanation?

Look at this brief extract from Barry Hines's A *Kestrel for a Knave*. Billy Casper is telling his classmates about the hawk he has reared and trained:

> I started training Kes after I'd had her about a fortnight, when she was hard penned, that means her tail feathers and wing feathers had gone hard at their bases. You have to use a torch at night and keep inspecting 'em. It's easy if you're quiet, you just go up to her as she's roosting, and spread her tail and wings. If t'feathers are blue near t'bottom o' t'shaft, that means there's blood in 'em an' they're still soft, so they're not ready yet. When they're white and hard then they're ready, an' you can start training her then.

What can you learn from this?

- Billy uses one technical term, 'penned', which he explains to his audience; other terms such as 'roosting' or 'shaft' he assumes they will understand;
- he includes personal anecdote in his explanation when he talks about inspecting the hawk's feathers at night;
- when he has explained the detail of the feather shafts hardening, he then returns to his main subject – training Kes.

These are good techniques to use when explaining:

- challenge your listeners, but give them some help as well;
- talk about your own involvement;
- don't allow details to sidetrack you from the main subject.

DESCRIBING

The secret of successful describing is to use precise language and a clear overall structure. Let's look at another part of Billy's account of hawking, where he describes how you attach the hawk to a lead:

> ... when she stands on your fist, you pull her jesses down between your fingers ... Then you get your swivel, like a swivel on a dog lead, press both jesses together, and thread 'em through t'top ring of it. T'jesses have little slits in 'em near t'bottom, like buttonholes in braces, and when you've got t'jesses through t'top ring o' t'swivel, you open these slits with your finger, and push t'bottom ring through, just like fastening a button.

This illustrates good practice in describing. Note how Billy:

- uses examples which his audience will understand to help make a point, when he mentions dog leads, braces and buttons;
- uses words like 'when', 'then', 'and' to make clear the sequence of events;
- repeats key words, such as 'jesses', which may be unfamiliar to the audience.

NARRATING

Telling a story may involve explaining and describing, but the emphasis is on creating an atmosphere or a feeling rather than on conveying information. Here is Billy again:

> It wa' one Friday night, an' when I got up next morning I thought right, if she flies off, she flies off, an' it can't be helped. So I went down to t'shed. She wa' dead keen an' all, walking about on her shelf behind t'bars, an' screamin' out when she saw me comin'. So I took her out in t'field and tried her on t'creance first time, an' she came like a rocket. So I thought, right, this time.
>
> I unclipped t'creance, took t'swivel off an' let her hop on to t'fence post. There was nowt stoppin' her now, she wa' just standin' there wi' her jesses on. She could have took off an' there wa' nowt I could have done about it. I wa' terrified. I thought she's forced to go, she's forced to, she'll just fly off an' that'll be it.

Dramatising events and using vivid words can make your listener share your emotions.

Notice how Billy involves the listeners, making them share his fear and excitement by:

- dramatising the events: he tells us what he was saying to himself at the time;
- using vivid words to describe the hawk ('keen', 'screamin', 'rocket');
- using a sudden short sentence ('I wa' terrified.') to create tension;
- using repetition to build suspense ('she's forced to go, she's forced to').

WHAT MAKES THE GRADE?

Explaining, describing and narrating all involve similar skills:

- using language precisely and vividly to explain an idea, to describe something, or to create an atmosphere or feeling;

- challenging listeners, to capture their interest;

- using knowledge or understanding that listeners already have to sustain their interest;

- using personal references or anecdotes to bring a topic to life;

- explaining details, but keeping a clear overall structure;

- using different sentence lengths, repetition, etc. to make listeners share your feelings.

What distinguishes a Grade C performance from Grade D in this aspect of Speaking and Listening is your ability to use detail and an overall structure which between them keep listeners interested. Grade A performance depends on a mature use of vocabulary and expression to create a range of qualities such as humour, irony, suspense or pity.

Billy uses a lot of non-standard forms of English (see Chapter 29), but this is appropriate as he is talking to his peers. However, it is generally a good idea to use standard English when explaining or describing, although a careful use of non-standard forms can bring a narrative to life, as in the example above.

Check yourself

QUESTIONS

Q1 Explain how to tie a shoelace to someone who must follow your instructions exactly, or tape your explanation and follow it exactly yourself. Try to give your explanation without using notes or any kind of visual aid, and do not spend more than two or three minutes preparing it.

Q2 Describe this picture on the right to a friend so that he or she is able to make a copy of it. You are only allowed to use words, and your friend must not ask you any questions!

Q3 Choose an event from your own life – such as your first day at school – which created strong feelings in you and which you can still remember. Narrate this event either to a friend or onto tape.

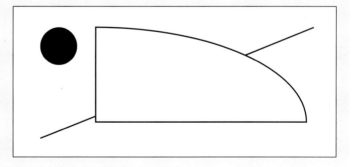

ANSWERS

A1 Make sure that the two ends of the lace are an equal length – if not, adjust them so that they are. Hold the left-hand end of the lace in your right hand, and the right-hand end in your left hand. Take the right-hand end under the left-hand end, then over and under again; pull tight, so that you are now holding what has become the left-hand end of the lace in your left hand and what has become the right-hand end of the lace in your right hand. Make a loop with about two-thirds of the left-hand end of the lace, leaving the rest of it hanging free. Hold the base of the loop between the thumb and forefinger of your left hand. With your right hand, take the right-hand end of the lace over the loop, then with your left-hand thumb and forefinger pull a loop in this end back through to the left while your right-hand thumb and forefinger take hold of the original loop. Pull both loops tight to complete the bow.

A2 The picture is in a rectangular frame about nine centimetres wide and four centimetres high. Half a centimetre in on the left-hand side and half a centimetre below the top edge is the centre of a black circle about one centimetre in diameter. Half a centimetre to the right of the right edge of this circle, and starting level with the top of the circle, a vertical line runs to a point one centimetre above the bottom of the frame; from this point, there is a second straight line parallel to the bottom of the frame, which goes to within one centimetre of the right-hand side of the frame. This point, and the point where the vertical line started to the right of the circle, are joined by a curving line. From the right angle where the two straight lines meet, a straight diagonal line goes towards the corner of the frame, but stops half a centimetre short of the corner.
A continuation of this line leaves the curved line and goes towards the top right-hand corner of the frame, but stops one centimetre short of the corner. The whole picture could represent the sun in the sky with an iceberg tip protruding from a flat, calm sea.

TUTORIALS

T1 *Judge how well you did in this exercise by the success of the experiment! If your listener cannot follow your instructions easily, compare what you said with the answer opposite, and think if you:*

- *made your terminology easy to follow?*
- *gave the sequence of actions in the correct order?*
- *missed anything out?*

T2 *How successful was your friend in copying the picture? Ask what made it difficult (or easy) to follow your instructions. Did you say something like the answer opposite? If your friend found it difficult to reproduce the drawing, did you:*

- *use appropriate words to describe the shapes?*
- *make relative sizes and positions of objects clear?*
- *try to give a description of the whole picture as well as the parts?*

ANSWERS

A3 It was enormous: a huge redbrick building with windows like so many pairs of eyes glaring down at me. 'Don't leave me here,' I remember saying to my mum, 'don't leave me.' I didn't know what would happen inside that building; I didn't know what school was – after all, this was my first day! Then it happened. As mum went out through the gate the evil clanging sound of a bell rang out across the damp playground. Most of the children hurried into lines. I didn't know where to go. My face sank onto my chest and I began to cry, quietly at first, then great racking sobs.

TUTORIALS

T3 *You may have chosen a different event, and in any case your memories will not be the same as the ones described here! However, you can judge how well you did by considering whether your account was as successful as the sample answer opposite, by asking yourself:*

- *Did I make the event sound dramatic through my choice of words (e.g. 'glaring', 'evil', 'clanging', 'racking')?*
- *Did I make the event seem vivid by describing important details (e.g. the size of the building, the sound of the bell, mum leaving, the damp playground, the fact that most of the other children seemed to know what to do)?*
- *Did I convey my feelings by using different sentence lengths, or repeating words, or any other suitable device (e.g. comparing the windows to eyes, repeating 'don't leave me', the short sentence 'Then it happened' which creates tension)?*

- In this chapter, you will learn to explore, analyse and imagine through speech.
- If you are able to analyse and communicate ideas and information effectively, you will improve your GCSE grade for Speaking and Listening.

WHAT EXACTLY DOES IT MEAN?

Exploring, analysing and imagining is quite different from explaining, describing or narrating. While audiences are usually necessary to hear explanations, descriptions or narrations, they do not need to be actively involved – they are essentially listeners who may sometimes ask questions; if they do, they are seeking information rather than participation. Exploring, analysing and imagining can be done without any audience at all (particularly imagining), but if there is an audience, it will usually be an active partner in the process.

Much of the exploring, analysing and imagining you are asked to do for GCSE Speaking and Listening assessment is likely to involve working on texts with one or more partners. You will explore the meanings of those texts, analyse how authors have created and shaped those meanings and imagine what lies behind the texts and your responses to them. Much of what you have learned from Chapters 1–17 of this book is therefore relevant to this group of Speaking skills.

EXPLORING

Exploring through talk really means having a dialogue with one or more partners who will comment on and develop your ideas about texts and contribute thoughts of their own. In Scene 6 of George Bernard Shaw's *St Joan*, Joan of Arc is on trial for blasphemy and turns on her accusers with these words:

> You promised me my life; but you lied. You think that life is nothing but not being stone dead. It is not the bread and water I fear: I can live on bread: when have I asked for more? It is no hardship to drink water if the water be clean. Bread has no sorrow for me, and water no affliction.

How would you explore her situation? You might ask questions such as:

- why is she so angry? Apart from the obvious fact that she has been imprisoned, she feels she has been lied to, because she has been promised 'life' but does not feel that she has any kind of life simply by being alive;
- what is the problem? She says she is not complaining about having to live on bread and water – so what point is she trying to make about the conditions she is kept in?

ANALYSING

Analysing means looking closely at situations, characters, language or ideas in texts and beginning to tease out their significance, often with the same partner(s) who first helped you explore the text. Joan's speech continues:

But to shut me from the light of the sky and the sight of the fields and flowers; to chain my feet so that I can never again ride with the soldiers nor climb the hills; to make me breathe foul damp darkness, and keep me from everything that brings me back to the love of God when your wickedness and foolishness tempt me to hate Him: all this is worse than the furnace in the Bible that was heated seven times.

This is where exploration needs to move into analysis. Following your initial exploration of her situation, you can now begin to analyse what makes Joan's imprisonment so unbearable to her. To analyse effectively, you need to pose questions or raise issues which:

- interpret central issues, for example, discuss Joan's feeling that the worst aspect of prison is to be shut away from an outdoor life;

- examine how the author communicates Joan's ideas through language, for example, discuss how the repetition of 'to shut', 'to chain', 'to make' builds up the feeling of oppression Joan suffers, how the alliteration of 'fields and flowers' emphasises these pleasures to which Joan now has no access;

- help you reflect effectively on Joan's experience, for example, discuss what you know about her state of mind here: how her faith is being tried by her punishment, which seems to her worse even than anything she has read about in the Bible.

IMAGINING

Imagining what led to the creation of the text, or what you might do in a similar situation to that described, may be something private and personal or may still involve partners in helping to define and describe your response as clearly as possible. The last issue raised above brings you close to imagining. This will become clearer by looking at the rest of Joan's speech. She goes on to say:

I could do without my warhorse; I could drag about in a skirt; I could let the banners and the trumpets and the knights and soldiers pass me and leave me behind as they leave the other women, if only I could still hear the wind in the trees, the larks in the sunshine, the young lambs crying through the healthy frost, and the blessed blessed church bells that send my angel voices floating to me on the wind.

Here effective imagining would raise issues such as:

- what this passage tells you about Joan's past experience: for example, you can work out that she likes to be with the soldiers, that she loves nature, and that she thinks angels speak to her, so you may imagine that she is a disturbed person, that her state of mind is a strange mix of love for nature, love of God and love of fighting;

- how the language moves and involves you by reminding you of relevant personal experience: you will not have been in Joan's situation, of course, but it may remind you of times you have felt mentally imprisoned, or in despair, or deprived of something important to you.

**WHAT MAKES
THE GRADE?**

A Grade D performance in this aspect of Speaking and Listening would be shown through straightforward understanding and interpretation of texts, but moves into Grade C territory if more difficult ideas are involved and if the language used to interpret them is orderly and precise. To achieve Grade A, you would be expected to cross-reference and prioritise complex ideas or information and to come to perceptive conclusions, including some relevant, focused personal response.

Check yourself

QUESTION

Q1 Read the following diary entries, all written on January 1st in different years.

1785

Whether this be the last or no, may it be the best year of my life!

John Wesley

1915

What a vile little diary! But I am determined to keep it this year.

Katherine Mansfield

—1850—

Cold, & foggy, & dismal the New Year opens. I pray most earnestly that I may never see the commencement of another. May I soon, very soon, lie in that grave where lie my Joys & Recollections! I am heart sick of everything, & long only for that peace which is nowhere but in the grave.

Edward Leeves

1980

'Another year ... another deadly blow' – so Wordsworth, but not so me. I enjoyed 1979 and expect to enjoy 1980. Resolutions? Two. First, to keep up this diary. My last attempt – a failure – was when, aged 11, I exchanged Charles Letts' 'School Boys'/Girls' Diaries' for Christmas with my cousin Angela. After I had completed the personal particulars I gave up. Second resolution? To try not to cheat. I resolve to stick to what happens and not to drag in more interesting events of previous years to make for better reading. Dull or enjoyably uneventful days exist and will be noted.

Hugh Casson

If you were asked to explore and analyse these entries, and to imagine why their authors wrote them as they did, what notes would you prepare to take to a discussion? Write down two or three questions you might want to discuss under each of the headings: explore, analyse, imagine.

ANSWER

A1 **Explore**

- Do the entries fall into groups such as happy/sad; humorous/serious?
- Is the date (New Year's Day) significant to all the diarists?

Analyse

- What does each entry actually say?
- What state of the writer's mind does each entry suggest?
- What individual words or ideas are significant, e.g. why does Katherine Mansfield use the word 'vile' and what does Hugh Casson mean by 'enjoyably uneventful'?

Imagine

- Why is Edward Leeves (and Wordsworth, as reported by Hugh Casson) so unhappy at the prospect of another year?
- Why do John Wesley and Hugh Casson seem so content?
- What exactly is Katherine Mansfield's state of mind?

TUTORIAL

T1 The suggestions opposite are all good questions to take to a discussion, and would give plenty of opportunities to start an excellent discussion. Notice how:

- the exploring questions look for patterns or comparisons in the texts – this is often a good way in when you have more than one text to deal with;
- the analysing questions are to do with actual meaning and implied meaning, i.e. what lies 'between the lines' or what unusual words and phrases might mean or imply;
- the imagining questions take you a stage further and invite you to speculate about what lay behind the diary entries – what may have caused the writers to say what they did, and how were they really feeling (and why) at the start of another New Year.

How would you record last New Year in your diary?

CHAPTER 32

DISCUSSING, ARGUING, PERSUADING

- **In this chapter, you will learn to discuss, argue and persuade fluently through speech.**
- **If you are able to make thoughtful contributions to discussion and promote points of view effectively, you will improve your GCSE grade.**

DISCUSSING

Discussion is not easy to practise on your own! But you can learn ways of presenting information or ideas to help you take part in discussions with greater confidence.

Let's take an example from a book to identify some basic techniques. At the start of George Orwell's *Animal Farm*, old Major speaks to the other animals:

> Now, comrades, what is the nature of this life of ours? Let us face it: our lives are miserable, laborious and short. We are born, we are given just so much food as will keep the breath in our bodies, and those of us who are capable of it are forced to work to the last atom of our strength; and the very instant that our usefulness has come to an end we are slaughtered with hideous cruelty. No animal in England knows the meaning of happiness or leisure after he is a year old. No animal in England is free.

Although this is part of a long speech delivered by Major, it has many of the qualities you should aim for in contributing to a group discussion. We can see:

- use of a question which does not expect an answer (this is known as a 'rhetorical question'): this makes listeners think, and involves them in the issues straight away;

- use of descriptive language, which is more effective than plain statements: for example, see how Major puts three words 'miserable, laborious and short' together to build an effect, and how he uses the powerful phrase 'slaughtered with hideous cruelty' rather than the plainer word 'killed';

- use of repetition for emphasis: read the passage out aloud to yourself, and note the power of the repetition of 'No animal … No animal …' in the last two sentences;

- varying sentence length for dramatic effect, for example the last sentence of the extract.

You will often make shorter statements, or ask briefer questions, in a genuine discussion. But if you intend to state a point of view, give information or put forward ideas, careful use of Major's techniques will help you.

There are other discussion techniques. Among the most important are:

- asking questions which develop the subject: for example, in a discussion on capital punishment, don't ask somebody 'Do you agree with hanging?', but rather 'Why do you think hanging is the best way?'

- asking for explanation or clarification: for example, 'I'm not sure. Could you explain that again?' or 'What does that mean exactly?'

- taking different views into account and summarising: for example through statements such as 'Right, so what we've said so far is that … '

- supporting other people, either by using brief statements such as 'Yes, I agree' or by developing what they say, for example through statements such as 'Yes, and why don't we also think about … '

If your discussion is chaired effectively, then there should be opportunities for everyone to contribute. If you are in an informal group, or a group which is badly chaired, be sure that you make contributions, but without dominating.

ARGUING

Many of the points about discussing apply equally well to arguing: it is what you say that is different, rather than the way you say it. Remember that arguing in this context does not mean a heated disagreement, but expressing a point of view forcefully!

In fact, an argument can often be strengthened by the use of humour rather than anger, especially ironic humour, which has a tinge of anger within it. In one of the plays from Alan Bleasdale's *Boys from the Blackstuff*, an employee of the Department of Employment wants to prosecute someone for claiming unemployment benefit while working. His manager, who is becoming disillusioned with her life, says to him:

> I can hear the laughter and outrage now. First of all, we manage to crash all our vehicles into a council wagon at the start of the raid, then a man is killed who is only killed, whatever we might say, because he is trying to escape from us, and finally for good measure, we are trying to arrest unemployed men who are busy building an unemployment exchange.

Another important feature of arguing is the use of evidence. Do not overdo this, or you may sound like a walking encyclopaedia, but if you are able to cite events, people or (a few) statistics to support a case, then that may confirm the strength of your argument.

PERSUADING

Successful persuading again depends very much on techniques we have already identified in this chapter, i.e. the skilful use of:

- questions;
- repetition;
- varied structure and length of sentences;
- powerful, vivid vocabulary;
- humour;
- evidence.

The other major techniques in persuasion are aspects of what the next two chapters (pages 212–16) consider in detail: listening, and body language. It is very hard to persuade others to your point of view if they don't think *you* have listened to *them* and their opinions; you are also less likely to be persuasive if you make poor use of non-verbal communication skills.

As far as discussion, argument and persuasion is concerned, GCSE mark schemes are quite clear that to gain a Grade C rather than a Grade D, you must be able to:

- make a *significant* contribution to discussion;
- *engage* with other people's views, and recognise any assumptions they make or biases they show;
- *promote* a point of view.

In other words, it is all about involvement! To gain a Grade A, you must show that you can also:

- *initiate and sustain* discussion;
- respond *persuasively and engagingly*.

If, in addition to that, you are able to express yourself powerfully and make thought-provoking contributions to any discussion or argument, then you will be rewarded with the very highest marks.

Check yourself

QUESTION

Q1 Write part of a discussion between four young people on the subject of whether compulsory school uniform is a good idea or not. In it, try to make them demonstrate some of the good features of contributing to discussion which have been identified in this chapter.

Does uniform encourage uniformity?
Always a thorny subject for debate.

ANSWER

A1 The content of the following example will probably be quite different from what you have written, but see if your discussion illustrates the same features in a similar way. If so, you have understood this chapter well and should be able to ensure that you make valuable contributions to classroom discussion.

1	Jon	I think uniform's a good idea, a really good idea, because it means you don't have to think every morning should I wear this, should I wear that?
2	Nereeka	But uniform's so unfashionable! Dull colours, outdated styles, ties and jumpers which are so uncomfortable and restricting in hot weather.
3	Emma	Yes! And you know, uniform's impractical for lessons like science or art. It's dangerous if you're using technology equipment.
4	Wesley	Why's it so bad? It's cheap to replace if it gets damaged.
5	Nereeka	Cheap? You obviously never go to buy it.
6	Emma	Exactly. Expensive. Nasty. Uncomfortable. That's school uniform for you.
7	Jon	So you two would prefer us to wear our own clothes, would you?
8	Emma	Uh, huh.
9	Nereeka	I would, and most pupils in this school think so too. I did a survey in maths, you know, and three out of four pupils I asked wanted to get rid of uniform.
10	Wesley	How many did you ask? Four?
11	Emma	Very funny. But go on, tell us what's so good about uniform then.
12	Wesley	It makes us all the same so that ...
13	Nereeka	Exactly! Uniform makes us uniform, and I thought education was supposed to develop the individual or something.
14	Jon	Well, wearing uniform doesn't seem to have stopped you having your own opinions, does it?

TUTORIAL

T1 *Let's look at the discussion techniques used here.*

1 *Jon uses repetition to reinforce his opinion that uniform is a good idea.*
2 *Nereeka uses some good vocabulary: unfashionable, dull, outdated, uncomfortable, restricting.*
3 *Emma supports and develops Nereeka's view.*
4 *Wesley asks a question to open up and develop the discussion.*
5 *Nereeka uses a rhetorical question (one that doesn't need an answer) and repetition to emphasise how she disagrees with Wesley.*
6 *Emma backs up Nereeka's emphatic view by a succession of one-word sentences.*
7 *Jon summarises others' views by asking a question which will develop the discussion in a new direction.*
8 *Emma makes an encouraging sound of agreement.*
9 *Nereeka offers some evidence to support her case.*
10 *Wesley uses ironic humour to try to undermine Nereeka's claim.*
11 *Emma asks for more explanation or clarification of the pro-uniform view.*
12 *Wesley begins to add detail to his previous opinion.*
13 *Nereeka interrupts and refers to a new idea which supports her case.*
14 *Jon humorously turns that argument back on her.*

In this discussion, Emma and Wesley both:

● *make significant contributions;*
● *engage with other people's points of view;*
● *promote their own point of view;*

sufficiently to be performing at a sound Grade C level. Jon and Nereeka additionally:

● *initiate or sustain the discussion;*
● *respond persuasively or engagingly;*

and so are performing at a level closer to Grade A.

CHAPTER 33

LISTENING SKILLS

- In this chapter, you will learn how to show you are a good listener by the way your listening skills are demonstrated in discussion groups.
- If you are able to listen sympathetically and respond to a range of speaking, your GCSE grade will improve.

HOW IS LISTENING ASSESSED?

Effective listening can be difficult for teachers to recognise and reward. Clearly, it goes on inside your head, and the only ways in which it can be identified are through:

- any verbal signals you can give to show that you are listening;
- the non-verbal signals you give to show that you are interested and involved;
- how you show that you have listened by the way it influences what you later say.

The non-verbal aspects of listening will be discussed in the next chapter. Here we will concentrate on verbal signals and on how you show that you have listened through the way it influences your speaking, both in one-to-one situations and in larger groups.

VERBAL SIGNALS

In many situations, we listen in absolute silence: it would be quite inappropriate, for example, not to be quiet while listening to instructions about an examination, or some church services, or a court case.

At other times, we listen 'actively', in other words we show that we are listening by the occasional use of speech which has little or no meaning in itself, but which indicates to the person speaking that you are still interested in what he or she is saying. Think about listening on the telephone, for example. If you are completely quiet for too long, the person speaking at the other end is likely to ask 'Are you still there?' So what we usually do when listening on the phone is to say 'Yes' or 'Uh huh' or 'Really?' or some such word to encourage the speaker.

This is a useful technique when you are being assessed for GCSE Speaking and Listening. It may feel a little awkward or false at first, and you must not overdo it, but the use of a telephone-style listening technique will show that you are involved with the activity, even if you are not speaking at the time. From the speaker's point of view (and remember that sometimes that will be you!) it is encouraging to hear 'active listening' of this kind.

LISTENING TECHNIQUES

Showing that you are listening is only the first step. To genuinely hear and understand what others are saying, you need to:

- be aware of the speaker's tone of voice: does it match the words? If not, the speaker could be using irony to make a point (see Chapter 32, page 209), or misleading you;
- be aware of the speaker's body language, and what it tells you about the point being made (see Chapter 34);

Verbal signals let the other person know you are listening.

- concentrate on the content of what the speaker is saying, so that you can understand the ideas or opinions being expressed, even if you disagree with them. When you speak, you will then be able to support or argue against the points made;

- note any bias, contradictions, misuse of evidence, etc. in what is said so that you can challenge these, either at the time (see the following point) or later;

- ask for something to be explained if you don't understand: this is a particularly useful technique, as it serves two purposes: it helps your understanding, and shows that you are following what is being said. However, don't interrupt constantly: if you do, it will annoy others, break up the flow of any discussion, and make you seem an unsympathetic and unintelligent member of the group!

HOW IS LISTENING SHOWN THROUGH SPEAKING?

Let's assume that you have listened carefully to part of a discussion, using the techniques suggested above. Now you are about to speak: how do you continue to show that you have listened effectively? You might:

- reply to the main points made by other speakers: recap briefly what they have said to show that you have listened and understood, then add your own ideas and opinions;

- question any bias, wrong information, etc. which you think other speakers have conveyed: ideally, refer directly to who said it, to show again that you were listening to individuals and trying to understand their viewpoints;

- try to use other people's ideas together with your own to reach a conclusion or a turning-point in the discussion, and ask others if they agree with you in the light of what they said earlier.

Chat-show hosts should be skilful listeners.

WHAT MAKES THE GRADE?

Listening requirements in GCSE mark schemes are brief but clear. At Grade D, you would be expected to 'listen carefully and make responses which show some understanding'. If you take note of, and practise, all the techniques suggested above, you should have no difficulty in advancing to the requirement for Grade C: 'listen closely and sympathetically, responding as appropriate'. For even higher grades, the only additional requirement is that you listen and respond to a range of demanding speech.

Check yourself

QUESTION

Q1 Look back at the discussion in the 'Check yourself' section of Chapter 32 (page 211). Read through it carefully and jot down any examples of good listening skills which are explained in this chapter.

ANSWER

A1
2 Nereeka answers Jon's point.
3 Emma uses and develops Nereeka's idea.
4 Wesley asks for an explanation.

6 Emma sums up what she and Nereeka have said.
8 Emma makes an encouraging sound to show she's listening.
10 Wesley looks for any possible flaw in Nereeka's evidence.
11 Emma asks for explanation.

13 Nereeka shows she is listening carefully by seizing on what she sees as a mistake in Wesley's argument.
14 Jon answers Nereeka's point, indicating a contradiction in what she has said.

TUTORIAL

T1
A *basic listening skill*.
A *more advanced skill*, which moves the discussion on.

This shows he has been listening, and allows him to add an idea of his own.
This shows that she has been listening sympathetically to all that has been said.
This indicates her continuing involvement appropriately, even if she has nothing to add at this point.
This shows he has been listening critically and with understanding, not just in a casual way.
This shows her trying to stay involved by returning the discussion to the main issue.
This shows involvement and sustained listening.

This shows sophisticated listening skills which allow Jon to make an important point in the discussion.

- In this chapter, you will learn how body language, or 'non-verbal communication', plays a part in speaking and listening activities.

- If you can use techniques of non-verbal communication effectively, it will help improve your GCSE grade in Speaking and Listening.

WHAT IS NON-VERBAL COMMUNICATION?

Some of the attitudes we convey to others come not from what we say, or from how quietly we listen, but from how we say it and from what we are actually doing while listening. In other words, the way we stand or sit, what we do with our hands, how our facial expressions change and how our eyes move: all these give powerful messages. Non-verbal communication works both ways in speaking and listening activities. If you get it right, it enhances your own skills and achievements; but equally you can encourage other speakers, and make it easy for other listeners, by employing features of non-verbal communication in a supportive way.

THE BODY LANGUAGE OF LISTENERS

Think about how these features might affect your view of someone listening to you:

- body posture: someone literally on the edge of their seat will suggest great interest in what you are saying, while someone slumped back with hands in pockets will convey total boredom;

- facial expressions: smiles encourage, frowns discourage!

- gestures or movements: nods of the head, or clasping the hands together suggest involvement, whereas biting nails, tapping a pencil or other fidgeting indicate lack of interest;

- eyes: if they're on you, you have the listener's attention; if they're wandering or closed, so is the listener's mind!

- arms: tightly folded suggests an uninterested listener, while relaxed arms suggest an open, relaxed mind.

When you are the listener, think carefully about the messages you are sending. For the purposes of GCSE assessment, you want to show that you are an encouraging and supportive listener – not least because you will want others to listen sympathetically to you!

Body language can tell you a lot about your listener's attitude.

215

There are a lot of non-verbal techniques you can use when speaking!

THE BODY LANGUAGE OF SPEAKERS

When someone is speaking, most of the body language issues from listening are relevant, together with a few more:

- body posture: you convey a great deal by the way in which you sit or stand – the straighter, the better if you want to be heard;

- facial expressions: sometimes frowns will be appropriate, as your expression needs to match what you say: if it doesn't, listeners are likely to doubt your sincerity;

- gestures and movements: some gesturing (if speaking from a sitting position) and/or some moving around (if standing up) can help to keep listeners' interest; on the other hand, too much of this can be a distraction, or downright annoying. It is usually a question of scale: if talking to a small group in a small space, limit your movements; if talking to a large group in a large space, more use of gesture and movement can be a way of keeping attention on you;

- eyes: look at all your listeners, not just one, and vary the sequence of looking at them. Skilful use of eye-contact is the single most important aspect of successful non-verbal communication;

- tone and pitch of voice: you might say that this is verbal communication, but it's not about what you say, rather how you say it. Some people talk at the same volume, the same speed and the same pitch all the time, regardless of whether they are excited, amused, sad, angry or whatever. Make your voice match the mood of what you are saying or – as in the case of misjudged facial expressions – your listeners simply won't believe you!

- use of silences: an underused technique. Think of teachers trying to quieten a noisy class, or to gain attention: shouting usually fails, while silence works! When you have made a complicated point, or if you have asked listeners to think about something, give them some time to take in what you have said;

- visual aids: sometimes it will be appropriate to use objects appropriate to what you are saying. Be careful not to overdo this: remember, you are assessed for the quality of your speaking, and listeners may be distracted from what you are saying if there are too many other things to look at.

WHAT MAKES THE GRADE? ▶

Very few aspects of non-verbal communication are directly mentioned in GCSE mark schemes, but it will be difficult for you to achieve a good grade if you do not:

- speak clearly and audibly, with appropriate speed and emphasis, using gestures and eye-contact;

- show a range of listening skills which support other speakers.

Remember, the better your body language, the more encouraging it is for others!

Check yourself

QUESTIONS

Q1 If you have access to a video camera, repeat the talk about under-age drinking you gave for 'Check yourself' in Chapter 28 (page 193) and ask someone to videotape it for you. If you prefer, you could use the model answer.

Q2 Each of the following drawings below illustrates one of the features of body language explained above in the 'The body language of listeners'. For each drawing, write a two-sentence caption which might be going through the listener's mind, given the body language displayed.

a) b) c) d) e)

REMEMBER! Cover the answers if you want to.

ANSWERS

A1 When you gave the talk this time, you will have been confident about the content, and should have concentrated on your delivery. If you communicated your opinion well (and you will need to be quite self-critical about this or – better still – allow someone else to comment on it), you will certainly have used some of the techniques discussed above. In other words, did you:

TUTORIAL

T1 All the techniques listed can be practised and improved. Don't try to do it all at once, but take one aspect – for example, eye-contact – and decide to improve that over a period of, say, one week. Then really concentrate on maintaining eye-contact in all your speaking and listening situations during that time.

If you do not find it easy to use gestures, try to develop this skill when you feel it is most natural, for example if you are talking to someone about an object which you are holding, or to which you can naturally point. If you develop your confidence this way, you will find that you gradually come to use gestures quite unselfconsciously. Clarity, audibility, pitch and tone can all be practised using a tape recorder. Varying pitch and tone can feel awkward, like using gestures, if it does not come naturally to you. The trick again is to concentrate on developing these skills in situations where you tend to use them naturally, for example, if you have the opportunity to take part in drama sessions where you can attempt to portray different characters and moods through the pitch and tone of your voice.

ANSWERS

A1
- speak clearly?
- speak audibly?
- speak at an appropriate speed?
- emphasise points you make by varying the tone or pitch of your voice?
- employ gestures and movements which hold the interest of listeners?
- maintain eye-contact?

A2 You won't have come up with exactly the same as these suggestions, but if your answers are similar, then you understand this aspect of body language well, and should be able to use it as a check on how well you are keeping listeners involved when you speak.

a) I wish he'd hurry up and finish. This is the most boring talk I've heard in ages.
b) I'm enjoying this. I hope she has some more to say about that.
c) I'm really worried about that maths homework I've got tonight. I wonder if Ali can help me?
d) Yes, I agree with that. I think she's made a number of good points.
e) I don't agree at all. I wouldn't ever go along with that.

TUTORIAL

T1 In fact, almost everyone does vary the pitch and tone of their voice in different daily situations; next time you have the opportunity, try to listen to yourself when you are being sympathetic to someone and contrast it with the sound of your voice when you are angry or agitated about something. Again, you can practice with a tape recorder by performing a simple sentence such as 'I can't come to see you until next week', or 'Have you heard the news about John?' in ways which show different emotions, e.g. anger, disappointment, frustration, amusement, etc.

T2 a) The slumped posture is a give-away. If you are talking and you see some of your audience looking like this, you need to regain their attention. Perhaps you need to pause for effect, or vary the tone of your voice, or ask a question.

b) The smile shows that the listener is interested in what you are saying, and that he wants more of the same. Use signals of this kind to encourage you and give you confidence when speaking.

c) Nail-biting suggests that your listener's mind is elsewhere. It may not be your fault – it may well be that he or she is faced with a problem which seems more important than what you're saying. One tactic you can try here is to try and establish eye-contact with the person, so that they feel you are speaking directly to them. It is then much harder for them to lose concentration on what you are saying.

d) When a listener returns the eye-contact you have made, this signals that they are interested in what you are saying. It will usually also mean that they are sympathetic to your point of view, although it could mean the opposite – that they disagree entirely and are trying to unnerve you by 'staring you out'! The clue, of course, is in the facial expression which goes with the eye-contact: is it welcoming or challenging? Either way, you have the listener's attention, which is what you want.

e) The folded arms do often suggest a closed mind – not necessarily someone who has listened to what you have to say and has disagreed with it, but someone who had made their mind up from the start (or even before that) and will not be shifted. Your only tactic with listeners such as this (who don't really listen at all, of course) is to use eye-contact to try and draw them into the discussion and to speak directly to them when you are making particularly strong arguments. You can also try throwing in a comment such as 'You may disagree completely with that, but I can assure you that ...', and then make your point again in a different way. Expert use of gestures and voice tone/pitch can be helpful also in at least gaining their attention.

SECTION IV Examination Practice

SECTION Ⅳ

Examination Practice

CHAPTER 35

EXAMINATION TECHNIQUE

GENERAL PRACTICAL GUIDANCE

BEFORE YOUR ENGLISH EXAM

- Read the Chief Examiners' reports on previous years' exams. These highlight where students have performed well and badly and will give you a good idea of where marks are won and lost.
- Study the mark schemes published by your GCSE Examination Board.
- Look at the kinds of questions you are likely to be asked by studying previous papers or examples produced by your GCSE Examination Board.
- Practise writing to the time limits of the exam.

IN YOUR ENGLISH EXAM

1 Read the *instructions* on the exam papers carefully so that you can:
   - establish how many questions you need to answer (all? a choice? different sections?);
   - work out how long to spend on each question. To do this, you need to apportion time to each question *in proportion* to the marks available;
   - check which text(s) or parts of them to use in answering reading questions;
   - check whether you are being asked to use your imagination/experience as well as/instead of text(s) in answering writing questions.

2 Read *each piece of text* carefully and make brief notes on:
   - your first reactions to events/setting/characters in the case of fiction texts;
   - your first reactions to information/facts/opinions in the case of non-fiction texts;
   - ideas and concerns that strike you;
   - initial thoughts on language, technique and presentation.

3 Read *each question* carefully so that you can:
   - make sure you understand exactly what information is required. Think about key words in the question title such as 'How' and 'How far ... ?' You could underline or circle such words so that you remember to address them in your answer;
   - use any prompts provided with the question to help you focus and structure your answer. Remember that they may be listed in order of difficulty;
   - argue the question: refer to it at various points or make very clear that you are mentioning something or quoting something specifically because it is relevant to the question.

4 Plan your answer in *note form*. This ensures that you:
   - don't rush to write until you've got a good idea of what you want to say;
   - decide on the overall structure of your answer (How many paragraphs?, Which will be the key points/ideas in each?, etc.);
   - decide what you want to use from the text(s) to support your ideas when answering reading questions. It is a good idea to mark these key sections of the text(s) before you start writing your answer.

Practise writing to the time limits of the exam.

219

5 Check your final answers – have you:

- expressed yourself clearly?
- spelt difficult words correctly?
- punctuated your writing correctly?
- set out quotations accurately and clearly?
- included all the material you prepared?
- numbered your answers accurately?
- completed the correct number of questions?

PRACTICAL GUIDANCE ON READING AND RESPONDING

THE FIVE BASIC ASSESSMENT OBJECTIVES TESTED

There are five basic skills or assessment objectives which will be tested. These are your ability to:

- show that you can read and respond to fiction texts with insight and engagement. This means showing that you enjoy and understand texts and can explain their meaning by referring to details in them;
- recognise facts and opinions and how writers present ideas;
- follow an idea or argument, understanding the writer's implications or inconsistencies;
- select and use appropriate references or quotations from a range of sources;
- understand and comment on how writers achieve particular effects through using words, images and other devices.

The first seventeen chapters of this book break down these five basic assessment objectives into their smaller, more manageable parts, each chapter focusing on one specific aspect in relation to fiction (Chapters 1–9) and non-fiction (Chapters 10–17).

GAINING HIGH MARKS FOR READING IN YOUR EXAMINATION

Grades up to D are awarded for knowledge of what is in the texts. In the case of responding to fiction, this means being able to explain *what* situations occur, *what* characters are like and *what* they do. In the case of non-fiction, this means being able to say *what* a non-fiction text is about.

Knowledge on its own is not going to lift you above a Grade D. Knowing the story and the characters or the subject matter amounts to *literal* knowledge, not *literary* knowledge. For a Grade C or above, you have to show understanding of *how* the writer achieves effects (the techniques he or she uses) and *how* the text reveals the writer's concerns, attitudes and ideas. Your appreciation needs to be about *how* the writer uses language and forms to make you gain knowledge, understand an idea, or feel an emotion. You also need to explain *how* you responded to a text and formed any views as a result. If Grade D is about describing what you have read, then Grades C and above are about reflecting on, exploring, analysing and evaluating what the writer has done and how he or she has done it. The 'What makes the grade?' sections at the end of each chapter have been written to let you see exactly what you need to do to raise your written response from a C to a B or an A.

READING UNSEEN TEXTS IN TIMED CONDITIONS

- Read any instructions carefully so that you understand what you are reading and why.
- Read the questions to help focus your understanding.
- Read the text(s) slowly and carefully.
- Underline or circle words or phrases which seem interesting or important. Also mark any passages or phrases that puzzle you, as you may need to spend longer re-reading these.
- Identify any quotations you may be able to use in your answers.
- Think what the text means to you, and why and how it has that effect on you.
- Read the questions again and begin to plan your answer(s).

PREPARING PRE-RELEASED MATERIAL

- Read any introductory or explanatory material as this may help you to:
  - relate different texts to one another by theme or subject matter;
  - understand some of the background to the texts or authors;
  - prepare for the kinds of questions you are likely to be asked.
- Annotate your copy in the way allowed by your Examination Board. This normally means that you can underline words or phrases in the text and put a note in the margin which explains their meaning or cross-reference them to something else. Highlight important words, phrases or sections of text, maybe where a significant idea or description of a character appears, or where the use of language is particularly interesting.
- Decide what you think about each text and consider how other people might respond, so that you can write about different possible interpretations.
- Make separate notes on the texts (not on the copy) under headings such as:
  - text(s) I enjoyed and why;
  - text(s) I disliked and why;
  - thematic connections between texts;
  - interesting or unusual uses of language in texts;
  - interesting or unusual ideas in texts;
  - interesting or unusual writing techniques or devices;
  - main points of interest in relation to character/setting /theme;
  - similarities and differences between texts in relation to themes, ideas, techniques, purpose, audience, language.
- Remember to take your annotated pre-released material into the exam, but not any other notes.

Remember that you can only take your annotated pre-released material into the exam.

AVOIDING COMMON MISTAKES

Every year, candidates fail to do themselves justice because of one or more of these common faults:

- Narrating or describing rather than commenting: telling *what* happens in a fiction text or the contents of a non-fiction text, rather than *why* something is significant or *how* it made an impact on you.
- Describing action not motivation: showing recall of events, but not of what caused them, or how they showed something about people.
- Not using selective quotation: unloading prepared quotations even if they're not relevant to the question.
- Treating prompts as though they were separate questions: the prompts should guide you as to what to include in the answer; you should address the actual question asked.
- Failing to read beneath the more obvious surface meanings.
- Failing to comment on specific details of language or presentation which convey thoughts, feelings, attitudes or information.

Some phrases to avoid:

The writer describes the scene so you can almost imagine you're there.

Easy to say. Explain how!

What the writer's trying to get across is ...

Writers are usually successful in getting ideas across – it is the readers who have to try to respond.

There is a lot of punctuation in this part. or
There are lots of bullet points and headings.

What *effect* does this have? If nothing special, then it's not worth mentioning.

There are lots of hidden meanings in the poem.

There are meanings in the poem. The poet hasn't attempted to hide them. If they are not immediately obvious, it is because they are implied, and need more subtle reading. Don't blame the writer for your lack of discovery!

This advertisement is obviously very powerful.

You mustn't assume anything on the part of the examiner reading your answer. You have to qualify and support such a statement. *Why* is it powerful? Is it the words, the picture or what? *How* does it achieve this effect on you?

PRACTICAL GUIDANCE ON WRITING

THE FIVE BASIC ASSESSMENT OBJECTIVES TESTED

There are five basic skills or assessment objectives which will be tested. These are your ability to:

- communicate clearly and appropriately for different purposes and audiences;

- use and adapt forms of writing to achieve particular effects;
- organise ideas into sentences, paragraphs and whole texts;
- spell and punctuate accurately and present work neatly;
- write accurate standard English and use a wide range of vocabulary to express meanings clearly and precisely.

Chapters 18–27 of this book break down these five basic assessment objectives into their smaller, more manageable parts, each chapter focusing on one specific aspect of writing.

GAINING HIGH MARKS FOR WRITING IN YOUR EXAMINATION

Writing to explore, imagine and entertain

- Decide on the ideas, feelings and situations you want to explore in your writing.
- Imagine the sort of behaviour, dialogue and reactions to others that will make your characters believable.
- Remember that in order to entertain you don't have to amuse: readers can be entertained by suspense, surprise, doubt, conflict as well as humour.

Writing to argue, persuade or instruct

- Think about the *position* you adopt. Is it to be powerfully one-sided or a rational consideration of different points of view?
- Think about the *language* you use. Will it achieve its effects by being shocking, or by being distanced?
- Think about the *evidence* you can use to support your case and affect the reader's response.

Writing to analyse, review and comment

- Convey the special qualities of a place, book or performance by *analysing* what had an effect of you, why it had this effect and how it achieved this.
- Collect evidence, weigh one aspect against another, so that you *review* the issue thoroughly.
- Describe your thoughts and feelings through carefully worded *comments*.

Writing to inform, explain or describe

- Think *purpose*. What is the point of the information or explanation you are providing/the description you are putting together?
- Think *audience* – age, gender, interest, experience, needs, ambitions, anxieties. How will these affect the tone and style you use to inform/explain/describe?
- Think *response*. Do you want your reader to feel privileged, challenged, amused, reassured, educated? Your choice of language will affect this.

Generally

- Think *presentation*. How does your use of sentences and paragraphs and your choice of presentational devices help convey your message?
- Think *accuracy*. Does accurate spelling and thoughtful use of punctuation and grammar make your information/argument/review clear and easy to read?
- Always consider *purpose* and *audience*, especially when you are writing about your own feelings and opinions.

WRITING: PURPOSE AND AUDIENCE

Your purpose is to have an effect upon your reader. This means thinking about what you write and how you write it.

Managing your own opinion: Practical suggestions

Don't rely on assertion, simply stating your own opinion. Your reader may disagree with you. Clashing opinions will produce resistance, not agreement. So concede that your view is only one of many:

It's only my opinion, but....
Most people would say, but I think...
Even if I'm in a minority of one, I still think...

Accept that your reader may have an opinion opposite to yours. Show that you respect the reader's different opinion or point of view:

I can see why some people would ban cars from the city centre, but...
I know some people who have to travel to work need to drive into the centre, but...
Banning cars from the city centre would get rid of pollution but...

Show that you have already thought of what the reader may be thinking. Try to pre-empt opposition by giving an answer to an objection the reader may be about to make:

The usual argument against this is that Park and Ride is too inconvenient for shopping, but...
People may say this won't work because it's too expensive, but...
Commuters and shoppers will object to this because they..., but...

Give validity to your opinion by basing it on personal experience:

I know this because it's happened to me...
When I have the choice, I always...
Three of my friends all said that...

...or by referring to other people's experience:

It has been proved that...
There is a lot of evidence to suggest that...
The result is likely to be a loss of services...

Show that you can handle conflicting opinions or points of view. Use these words to link and evaluate:

Although... Alternatively,... Also,...
because... Despite... Even if... However,...
On the other hand,... Perhaps... Therefore...

Managing your audience: Practical suggestions

Develop variety and reader-appeal in your writing. Use these devices to relax, amuse or interest your reader:

● use anecdote – a brief amusing story which makes a point, e.g.:
Children sometimes don't understand what adults mean, such as the disappointed small boy who was told to "wait here for the present" and then complained that "they never gave it to me."

● use irony – saying something opposite to what you mean, e.g.:
Some people have such a conscience and want to do something to help that they generously put as much as 5p in the collecting tin.

- use hyperbole – highly exaggerated description, e.g.:

Hundreds of millions of angry letters would not make me change my mind ...

- use rhetorical questions – make your reader feel personally involved and challenged, e.g.:

Is it really more important to dump shopping on your back seat than to save our planet for our grandchildren?

- use rapport – make the reader feel that you are on the same side by sharing a thought or feeling, creating a sense of mutual agreement, e.g.:

If we are honest, we'll admit that we all tend to put our own comfort before what we think is right for the world.

AVOIDING COMMON MISTAKES

Every year, candidates fail to do themselves justice because of one or more of these common faults:

- Reproducing irrelevant writing which has been done earlier. Keep to the specific task.
- Trying to tell a complicated story in two or three sides. Keep it simple.
- Letting the imagination go out of control. Keep it believable.
- Getting the tone wrong for the audience. Keep it suitable.
- Missing the point of the task. Keep it focused.
- Appearing biased or simplistic. Keep it balanced.
- Being vague. Keep it precise and bring in evidence.
- Writing impersonally where you own feelings are important. Keep involved.
- Making straightforward spelling, grammar or punctuation mistakes. Keep checking.
- Being untidy. Keep it neat.

You should always collect evidence to support your case and weigh up the arguments carefully.

WRITING IN TIMED CONDITIONS

- Make sure that you understand how to use any stimulus material.
- Make notes about the content of your writing, bearing in mind the length you are aiming for.
- Make a paragraph plan so that you can keep a structure in mind all the time you are writing. This is helpful in almost all types of writing, even imaginative writing.
- Consider drafting your opening and closing paragraphs in some detail to make sure they are effective.
- Write at your normal speed, taking care over accuracy and legibility.

CHAPTER 36

EXAM PAPER 1

This chapter is designed to help you to prepare for a typical final examination paper. It is in two sections: the first tests your reading of a prose passage, and the second tests your ability to write in a particular way. Each of the questions is cross-referenced to earlier chapters in this book, so that you can revise particular skills before attempting the exam.

Section A of the paper specifically tests your ability to:

- read prose with insight and engagement;
- understand and evaluate devices to create character (Chapter 1);
- understand and evaluate purposes in the use of settings (Chapter 2);
- read beneath the surface (Chapter 7);
- make effective comparisons (Chapter 8);
- select and use textual references (Chapter 9).

Section B of the paper specifically tests your ability to:

- write to explore, imagine or entertain (Chapter 24);
- use accurate spelling and punctuation (Chapters 18 and 19);
- use a range of grammatical constructions (Chapter 20);
- structure your work in sentences and paragraphs (Chapter 21);
- use a wide range of vocabulary and stylistic features (Chapter 23).

You should allow yourself two hours for this paper, spending one hour on each question.

- Read the paper first.
- Then read the advice.
- Then write your answers.
- Then compare them with the answers given, and use the examiner's comments to help you decide whether your own answers incorporate most of the positive features in the answers.

Section A

Q1 The following extract is the start of a short story. How does the writer try to interest a reader in what is to follow? You should consider:

- character;
- setting;
- language.

(30 marks)

Vernon Wedge didn't want to see the old man. Olga, his secretary, gave Blesker a sub-zero reception, but he sat on in the attorney's waiting room. His shoulders were rigid, his crooked fingers inter-laced, his chalky face a portrait of stubbornness and determination. Finally, Vernon had to yield.

'Sit down, Mr Blesker,' he said wearily, pointing to the leather chair in his office. 'I know why you're here; my phone's been ringing all morning. Four newspapers, a youth worker, even a settlement house. What have you got, anyway, an organisation?'

The old man looked befuddled. 'Please,' he said. 'I just come about my boy.'

'Yes, I read the newspapers. And I suppose you think your kid's innocent?'

'He is!'

'Naturally. You're his father. Have you talked to him since it happened?'
'I came from the prison this morning. They're not treating him good. He looks skinny.'
'He's only been in custody a few days, Mr Blesker, I doubt if they're starving him. Look,' Vernon said testily, 'Your boy is accused of knifing another kid in the street. That's what happened. You know how many witnesses there are? You know what kind of evidence the district attorney has?'
'I know he's innocent,' the old man said. 'That's what I know. Benjy's a good, serious boy.'
'Sure.' Vernon frowned. 'They are all good boys, Mr Blesker, until they start running with a street pack. Then they're something else.' He was almost shouting now.
'Mr Blesker, the State will pick an attorney for your son. You don't need me.'
'I have money,' Blesker whispered. 'The family, we all got together. I run a fuel oil business; I'm selling the big truck. I can pay what you ask, Mr Wedge.'
'It's not a question of money–'
'Then, it's a question of what?' The old man was suddenly truculent. 'Whether he's guilty or not? You decided that already, Mr Wedge? From reading the newspapers?'
Vernon couldn't meet the challenge, it was too close to the truth. He had prejudged the case from the newspaper stories, and knew from the accounts that this was one client he could live without. His record was too good. What was worse, he had lost his last client to Ossining. Every criminal lawyer is allowed a few adverse verdicts; but two in a row?
'Mr Blesker,' he said miserably, 'will you tell me why you came here? Why did you pick me?'
'Because I heard you were good.'
'Do you know what happened in my last case?'
Obstinate. 'I heard you were good, Mr Wedge.'
'You told every reporter in town that you intended to hire me. That puts me in a very compromising position, you know that? And you, too. Know how it'll look if I turn you down? Like I think your boy is guilty, that the case is hopeless.'
'I didn't mean any harm,' the old man said fumblingly. 'I just wanted to get the best for Benjy.' He was getting teary. 'Don't turn me down, please, Mr Wedge.'
Vernon knew a lost cause when he saw one; perhaps he had known from the start how this interview would end. His voice softened.
'I didn't say your boy is guilty, Mr Blesker. All I say is that he's got a bad case. A very bad case.'
Motionless, the old man waited.
'All right,' Vernon sighed. 'I'll think it over.'
The police blotter had Benjy Blesker's age down as seventeen. He looked younger. The frightened eyes gave him a look of youthful bewilderment. Vernon wasn't taken in by it; he had seen too many innocent, baby-faced, icy-hearted killers. The boy's cell was clean, and Benjy himself bore no marks of ill-treatment. He sat on the edge of the bunk and kneaded his hands. When Vernon walked in, he asked him for a cigarette.
Vernon hesitated, then shrugged and offered the pack. 'Why not?' he said. 'If you're old enough to be here.'
Benjy lit up and dropped a tough mask over his boyish features. 'You the lawyer my old man hired?'
'That's right. My name is Vernon Wedge.'

'When do I get out of here?'

'You don't, not until the trial. They've refused bail.'

'When's the trial?'

'Don't rush it,' Vernon growled. 'We need every minute of delay we can get. Don't think this is going to be easy.'

Benjy leaned back, casual. 'I didn't cut that guy,' he said evenly. 'I didn't have anything to do with it.'

Vernon grunted, and pulled a sheet of handwritten notes out of his pocket.

'You admitted that you knew Kenny Tarcher?'

'Sure I knew him. We went to Manual Trades together.'

'They tell me Kenny was a member of a gang called The Aces. You ever run with them?'

'With that bunch?' Benjy sneered, and blew a column of smoke. 'I was a Baron. The Barons don't mix with those bums. You know who they take into that gang? A whole lot of—'

'Never mind,' Vernon snapped. 'We can talk about your social life later. You were a Baron and Kenny was an Ace, so that made you natural enemies. You had a rumble last month, and this Kenny Tarcher beat up on you pretty good. Don't give me any arguments about this, it's ancient history.' Benjy's mouth was quivering.

'Look, Mr Wedge, we don't have that kind of gang. You know Mr Knapp?'

'The youth worker? I just came from him.'

'He'll tell you about the Barons, Mr Wedge, we're not a bunch of hoods. We got a basketball team and everything.'

Vernon smothered a smile. 'Why do you carry a knife, Benjy?'

'It's no switchblade, Mr Wedge. It's more like a boy-scout knife; I mean, they sell 'em all over. I use it for whittlin' and stuff like that.'

'Whittling?' It was hard to hide the sneer. The end of Benjy's cigarette flared, as did his temper.

'Look, whose side are you on? I didn't stick Kenny, somebody else did! I swear I didn't kill him!'

'Take it easy. I'm not making accusations, kid, that's the court's job. Now sit back and relax. I'm going over the story, from the police side, and then you can tell me where they're wrong. Every little thing, understand?'

Benjy swallowed hard. Then he nodded.

from *The Test* by Henry Slesar

Section B

Q2 Write about a situation in which someone is faced with a problem of doing what they think is right. You should think about:

- character;
- setting;
- motives;
- feelings.

(30 marks)

SECTION A

Q1 This question needs close attention to details about the characters and the situation, to show that you can select appropriately and comment on meaning. You should also comment on information not given if you think this creates some mystery making the reader want to go on. Notice also that the question is about what 'a reader' will find interesting. You are a reader, so your own response is valid, but you may also need to imagine the response of 'a reader' who is not yourself. Try to show how this start to a story may appeal to a range of readers.

SECTION B

Q2 There is likely to be some link between the topic of this writing task and the reading that comes before it, but you don't need to take the reading material as a model. In this case is not necessary to write about a legal situation. The important thing is to show that you can write a structured piece which shows that you can adapt your language and form to a specific purpose. Do a brief plan of your writing first, to show that you can structure your material. Remember to leave time at the end to check for errors.

ANSWERS & EXAMINER'S COMMENTS

SECTION A QUESTION 1

Examiner's Comments

CHARACTERS
Your comments on the characters should give details about each, and about the way they relate to each other. This relationship is surprising in the first place because an old, weak man seems to have the ability to make a powerful, wealthy lawyer do as he wants. This helps to make the reader curious, as does the fact that in all three characters, the author hints about conflicts within them, and holds back information about the crime so that the reader is encouraged to read on.

Here are some details which you should have noted:

Vernon Wedge
He is a realist, not a sentimental man – he thinks fathers tend not to see the faults in their own sons, and good boys often change when they are in a crowd.

He has no illusions about people – he's seen innocent-looking youngsters who have been 'icy-hearted killers'.

When he deals with Benjy, he's very confident and able to make him listen, and he's not taken in by Benjy's claims of innocence or show of toughness.

However, for a powerful man, he finds it hard to get rid of Mr Blesker, or to talk him out of hiring him. He speaks 'wearily' as if he's already been worn down and 'had to yield', and the old man's challenge that he's prejudged the case makes him very uneasy.

Mr Blesker
He is an 'old' man, with 'crooked fingers' and a 'chalky face' and he speaks 'fumblingly' and becomes 'teary'. However, he is 'stubborn', obstinate and 'determined' and can be assertive when necessary – 'suddenly truculent'.

These strengths are apparent in his clever way of forcing Wedge to take the case. Although he seems weak and miserable, he has power over Wedge. He is willing to sacrifice his business to help his son, so it makes the reader wonder what else he will do for him.

Benjy
He is a mixture of youthful fear and bewilderment, worried about being in jail – 'kneading his hands' – but putting on a show of confidence – 'He dropped a tough mask over his boyish features'. He sneers and protests and tries to seem casual and confident, but when Wedge describes how others will see his case, he stops pretending, 'swallows hard' and nods agreement to listen. He denies the murder, but he admits carrying a knife which he claims to use for whittling. Wedge thinks this is not convincing, so the reader wonders which character is going to be right in the end, and how much of the truth Benjy is telling.

SETTING
The passage creates character and relationship without making the setting important. There is very little description of the attorney's office or the cell. The setting is more to do with legal processes than with a physical place. Wedge's worry about his reputation and anxiety not to lose another case makes the reader interested in how he will react if he looks like losing this one. Although he wants to be successful, he accepts this case that looks hard to win because he doesn't want his refusal to make people think the boy is guilty. He has a conscience. The reader will be interested to see how his conscience and his wish for success struggle in the course of events. Also, interest is created by referring to a court case in which the accused may be innocent.

LANGUAGE
Your answer should try to read beneath the surface to pick up any hints in the language which make the reader continue to be curious and read on. For example, the fact that newspapers, a youth worker and a settlement house have contacted Wedge suggests that this is going to be a high-profile case with lots of public interest. This may be because the father is someone special, or because the crime was very unusual. When Benjy says he wasn't in 'that sort of a gang' and quotes Mr Knapp the youth worker, there is a hint that there is more at stake than ordinary teenage gangs. Details such as 'Benjy's mouth was quivering' and his temper 'flared' may also be hints to nervousness and character faults which are important in the story.

SECTION B QUESTION 2

Sample Student's Answer

Captain Lou Alvarez strode into the precinct office, his young companion half-running to keep up. Various officers looked up from their desks as the two of them strode past.
Alvarez reached his desk, took off his jacket, loosened his tie and slung his leather shoulder holster with its customised .44 Biretta on the desk. He sank back in his chair, scanned the paperwork littering the desk, drawing deeply on his cigarette and let the smoke filter through his nostrils before he waved the youngster behind him into a seat.
'That DA has got to be the most ignorant jerk on the South side.'
His assistant, who was called Dan Jensen, nodded.
'Right sir', he said. No way was he going to disagree with the most respected officer in the San Francisco Police Department, not when he had only joined three weeks ago and spent all his waking moments and some of his sleeping ones too thinking how lucky he was to be assigned to Captain Lou

Vincente Carlos Alvarez, a living legend on the street and in the courtroom. No sir.

Suddenly the phone rang. Alvarez picked it up, cradling it between his neck and shoulder as he drew on his cigarette and scanned the sheaf of papers on his desk.

'Yes ... sir ... No ... Sir. That's not my impression, sir, I think the guy's a ... No sir. No sir. Yes sir. Immediately ... sir.'

Alvarez replaced the phone on its stand and a frown creased his forehead.

'Youngster,' he said, leaning forward, taking a last deep draw and screwing his cigarette butt into the ash tray, 'remember this. You want to make it in this business, know when to back off and let the big villains go.'

'You mean you're going to give up on the Columbian Squad?' said Jaspers, his young eyes widening with surprise and disappointment.

The older man looked at him and a crazy half grin played about his lips.

'The hell I am!' he said, 'You have a career ahead of you. Me, I'm going nowhere. Or at least,' he corrected himself, 'I'm going to the fifteenth floor to be told by the Commissioner to start taking an interest in traffic violations.'

Alvarez straightened his tie, put on his jacket and walked through the glass doors towards the lift. Jensen watched as he strode across the floor and through the partition as the doors closed.

It was not twenty minutes later when Jensen pulled up outside the office of the Columbia Trading Co. The heavy on the door phoned through when he showed his SFPD pass, then strode in front of him, his wide shoulders blocking Jensen's view. Suddenly, he was in the main office, facing the head of the Columbian Squad which ran the drugs cartel under the cover of the lawful trading company.

'Sit down, kid. Sorry you lost the case — ha ha ha. No hard feelings, huh?'

Jensen smiled.

'Take a drink. Alvarez send yuh?'

Jensen smiled again.

'No. I came on my own business.'

'Hey, you looking for a share? Smart guy. I never figured you'd be smarter than Alvarez.'

'Not smarter. I'm not looking to make Captain. I've decided I'm into Justice, not the law.'

Then he pulled out his standard issue revolver and pulled the trigger. The bullet smashed into the forehead above the horrified gaze and — crumpled to the floor. Within seconds, gunfire and smoke filled the air and Jensen joined him in a blood-spattered heap.

When Alvarez arrived on the scene, the Pathology crew were there, and the Columbian Squad had gone. He looked at the young face of the recruit on the floor, took a long draw on his cigarette and muttered,

'So long, youngster. You couldn't back off, now you can't get on. Who loves a dead hero, huh?'

Examiner's Comments

This is a confident, skilful but rather cliché-ridden story. It has all the presentational skills of a Grade-A performance, but too little variation of vocabulary or attention to character to be a very strong example of grade A work.

The characters and situations are clearly imagined, though it is, in structure and detail, very dependent on TV/film models, making it rather stereotyped rather than original. Nevertheless, it does explore an issue with choices posed about doing what you believe in and the limits of the law. It has the ability to entertain those who look for simple characters and simplified actions and stereotyped dialogue, but it does not really explore motivation or make the characters believable complex human beings. For example, the head of the cartel is sketched very simply, with stereotyped dialogue, and there is little to make Jensen believable other than being new, naïve and determined to defend justice. It is an imitation of a familiar genre rather than an original, good exploration of motives and effects. It does adapt a literary genre for a specific purpose but may not be well judged as to audience. The ending is ambiguous, perhaps intentionally, not making it clear whether the reader should share the character's view of Jensen as foolish to be a dead hero, or whether he is heroic. There is exploration of a theme here, but some uncertainty about how to develop it.

It is very accurate in spelling, including complex irregular words. It uses adverbial phrases to support the mood and manner of a character's dialogue and it is assured in its handling of tense and agreement.

It is well structured with accurate punctuation of sentences and effective paragraph breaks.

It attempts to give an authentic American style through specific references to officials and use of idiom. There is some variation of vocabulary but also a dependency on repeated words – 'strode' for example, is overused as a verb of movement, and the repeated 'drawing' on the cigarette becomes clichéd. The use of 'suddenly' twice is a weak way of creating a sense of speed in events. Some narrative details are obtrusive and overexplicit, such as the description of Jensen's 'young' eyes widening in 'surprise and disappointment' when the dialogue and context allow the reader to understand this implicitly.

This chapter is designed to help you to prepare for a typical final examination paper. It is in two sections: the first tests your reading of poems, the second tests your ability to write in a particular way. Each of the questions is cross-referenced to earlier chapters in this book, so that you can revise particular skills before attempting the exam.

Section A of the paper specifically tests your ability to:

- read poetry with insight and engagement;
- understand and evaluate sound effects and imagery (Chapter 4);
- understand and evaluate purpose, tone and attitude (Chapter 5);
- read beneath the surface (Chapter 7);
- make effective comparisons (Chapter 8);
- select and use textual references (Chapter 9).

Section B of the paper specifically tests your ability to:

- write to explore, imagine or entertain (Chapter 24);
- use accurate spelling and punctuation (Chapters 18 and 19);
- use a range of grammatical constructions (Chapter 20);
- structure your work in sentences and paragraphs (Chapter 21);
- use a wide range of vocabulary and stylistic features (Chapter 23).

You should allow yourself two hours for this paper, spending one hour on each question.

- Read the paper first.
- Read the advice.
- Then write your answers.
- Then compare them with the sample student's answers, and use the examiner's comments to help you decide whether your own answers incorporate most of the positive features in the sample student's answers.

Section A

Q1 Both these poems involve death and whales.

Compare the two poems, paying attention to:

- attitudes and ideas;
- use of language and poetic devices;
- purpose and effects on readers.

(30 marks)

Death of a whale

When the mouse died, there was a sort of pity:
The tiny, delicate creature made for grief.
Yesterday, instead, the dead whale on the reef
Drew an excited multitude to the jetty.
How must a whale die to wring a tear?
Lugubrious death of a whale; the big
Feast for the gulls and sharks; the tug
Of the tide simulating life still there,
Until the air, polluted, swings this way
Like a door ajar from a slaughterhouse.
Pooh! Pooh! Spare us: give us the death of a mouse
By its tiny hole; not this in our lovely bay.
– Sorry we are too, when a child dies:
But at the immolation of a race, who cries?

John Blight

Killing a whale

A whale is killed as follows;
A shell is filled with dynamite
And a harpoon takes the shell
You wait until the great grey back
Breaches the sliding seas. You squint,
Take aim
The cable snakes like a squirt of paint
The shell channels deep through fluke
And flank, through mural softness
To bang among the blubber,
Exploding terror through
The hollow fleshy chamber
While the hooks fly open
Like an umbrella
Gripping the tender tissue.

It dies with some panache,
Whipping the capstan like
A schoolboy's wooden top
Until the teeth of the machine
Can hold its anger, grip.
Its dead tons thresh for hours
The ravished sea,
Then sink together, sag,
So air is pumped inside
To keep the corpse afloat,
And one of those flags that men
Kill mountains with is stuck
Into this massive death.

Dead whales are rendered down,
Give oil.

David Gill

SECTION B

Q2 Write about an encounter with an animal which has a powerful effect on a person or people.

(30 marks)

ADVICE FOR YOUR ANSWERS

SECTION A

Q1 Some candidates prefer to write about one poem at a time, in effect writing two parts to the answer. This is not wrong, but most successful candidates tend to link the two in paragraphs clearly structured on separate features - for example, subject matter, language, literary devices, authorial purposes, personal response and relevance to you or others today. It gives shape and focus to your answer if you use each paragraph to comment on similarities and differences between the poems.

SECTION B

Q2 There is some freedom for you to choose the form and content of your writing. Again, the important thing is to show that you can adapt language and form for a specific purpose. Do a brief plan of your writing first, to show that you can structure your material. Remember to leave time at the end to check for errors.

ANSWERS & EXAMINER'S COMMENTS

SECTION A QUESTION 1

Sample Student's Answer

Both of these poems are about whales. They make you think a lot about your feelings because whales are big but people are cruel to them and making them extinct. The first whale (in 'Death of a Whale') isn't killed by people, because it's died. The poet compares a mouse dying with a whale dying and says it's easy to feel sorry for a little mouse that's died, but a whale is so big we don't care. I think this is like the way people feel sorry about small things and don't make a fuss about bigger things. When he says 'Pooh!' it's people thinking 'Yuk this is big and smelly' and not feeling sorry for the whale because it's messing up their beach. I think this is a good point. People don't feel sorry for things that interfear with their lives. For example at the end he says we don't care about what happens to a whole race far away because we can't see them. When we see pictures of people starving or injured by landmines we feel sorry for a bit then forget. We only care about what's near to us. The way the poem ends with a question, makes the reader think about his/her own behaviour. This is a good way of making you say people are wrong but am I the same as the rest of them?

The other poem is more about wasting the life of a whale just for oil. It really makes you sorry for the whale because of the horrible discription of the harpoon 'banging in the blubber' and the hooks and tender tissue. This poem asks a big question. Is it worth all this distruction just so humans can have oil?

They are both about whales but they make you think about the way we go on. They make you think human beings are not so good. I liked the second one because of gory words like 'bang among the blubber' and 'hooks open like an umbrella' which is a simile, and you can understand it more. The other one uses words like 'lugubrious' and 'immolation' which people don't know. But it's more about humans than whales. 'Killing a Whale' is a sort of Greenpiece poem.

Examiner's Comments

This answer is written with honesty (e.g. the student admits to not knowing some of the vocabulary) and some energy, which results occasionally in an informal, colloquial style. This however, does not interfere with the writer's sense of engagement. It has Grade C qualities of understanding and response, but it lacks structure and detail.

Read with insight and engagement

This is a good response to the meaning of both poems with some strong statement of differences as well as similarities. There is some insight into attitudes and ideas with some response to language and the feelings it can produce, though this could be more sustained. There is clear engagement with ideas and their implications for readers.

Select and use textual reference
There is some appropriate use of references and some attempt to cross-reference.

Make effective comparisons
The answer would be better if it had been more structured, using paragraphs to compare the poems: a first paragraph dealing with similarities in attitudes and ideas, then one on differences; then one on similarities in language and purpose, then one on differences. It could comment on whether the rhyme scheme was a help or a hindrance in *Death of a Whale*, and comparison with the blank verse of *Killing a Whale* would show awareness of the writers' choice of structural and presentational devices. For example, avoiding a standard line length allows the poet in *Killing a Whale* to set some lines on their own to make them stand out, especially at the end.

Understand and evaluate purpose, tone and attitude
The answer could develop its contrast between the poems as about whales and about people, commenting on implications and relevance to life today. For example, there could be reference to the attitudes of people in England to major events in Northern Ireland, Africa, or Malaysia compared to their attitudes to minor events closer to home. There could also be reference to global environmental concerns. The answer could engage the writers' purposes, allowing some *developed* comment in the way the writers influence their readers. For example, *Killing a Whale* uses graphic detail to shock readers into realising that the manufacture of the oil they use may cause brutal suffering. The comments on the question at the end of *Death of a Whale* are developed, showing awareness of the effect of a change in tone and address.

Read beneath the surface
Some close analysis to support this development could include reference to the poet's use of 'we' in the last two lines. For example, it could show how it includes the reader (and the writer) in the uncaring attitudes of other people in the rest of the poem. This may suggest that the poet feels guilty at his own feelings or may have carefully planned the switch to 'we' to engage the reader after judging others.

Understand and evaluate sound effects and imagery
It could explore the meaning of 'one of those flags that men kill mountains with' and say more about the purpose of each poem rather than describe one as a 'Greenpeace' poem. For example, it could *analyse* details of word choice for sound effect like 'bang among the blubber', or for emotional impact, such as 'tiny', 'delicate' and 'lovely' as things which gain our sympathy.

SECTION B QUESTION 2

Sample Student's Answer

'I'm sorry, Carrie, but it's just not on. I don't want to say no, but it's just not practicle.'

Carrie looked down at her clasped hands, not wanting her Dad to see the tears welling in her eyes.

'But ...' she said, swallowing hard, determined to try one last shot, 'but you said you'd talk about it with Mum, you said you'd see, and Sam says definately she'd look after it if we went away.'

'Well we have talked about it, and we both agree it's not feasible. It's not just feeding it and so on. It's the mess and scratching furniture and all of that. And it would have to get out during the day and you know what the road is like. I'd hate you to get attatched to it and then have it run over.'

He leaned over and held her hand. Carrie took it back instantly and turned to look out of the window. Why did adults always try to tell you they were saying no because they were really thinking of you?

'Perhaps when my job's more sorted and Mum can work from home, we'll think again,' he said. He hated it when she wouldn't look at him, and moved to hold her hand again, but he knew she wouldn't let him. She always held his hand when they went to the park when she was smaller, but not now.

Carrie stood angrilly in front of the big window, peering inside. The cheerfull face of the pet-shop owner looked up from the hutch he was re-stuffing with straw. he came out to her on the pavement.

'Whats the decission then?' he said, then he looked at her and, without waiting for an answer, added, 'Well, never mind. Cheer up,' he said, 'worse things happen at sea! What about a stick insect?'

Carrie looked at him and didn't answer. Why did adults always use stupid expressions like that? She turned her back and walked away from the window where the handwritten sign announced 'New litters - black and white, tortoiseshell and tabby.'

A stick insect! You might as well have a pet rock.

Carrie walked on, then turned sharply to cross the road into a shopping mall.

When she got back, her Mum was on the telephone, as usual. She waved as Carrie went passed her to the kitchen.

'So we'll get it to Design by the end of the week and have samples by the 14th. OK. Keep in touch.'

Where've you been?' She said as she poured herself some coffee. Carrie watched her drain the mug as she rummidged through documents and samples in her brief case.

'Shopping.' she said.

'Anything good?' said her Mum

'Uhuh.'

'What's that then?', she said, looking at her watch.

'A Tamagotchi'

'A what?'

'A Tamagotchi.'

'What on earth is that?'

'Its a cyber-pet'

'A cyber-pet? I dont know what youre talking about.'

Carrie showed her. Her mum read the leaflet.

Then she looked up.

'O Carrie' she said, and she looked at her. Carrie dident look back, but she took the leaflet from her mother's hand and went out of the kitchen up to her room.

That night, Carrie's Dad called up the stairs.

'Can you come down, Carrie.' he said.

Carrie closed her door and came down. They were in the kitchen.

'We've been talking, Carrie, and well . . . we think . . . on the whole we can have a cat as long as you look after its food and litter tray and all that.'

'But what about the mess and furniture and Mums work and everything?' said Carrie.

'We'll manage, somehow' said her Mum, 'Wont we?' she said to Carrie's Dad, and he nodded.

'We'll manage' he said.

'Thanks Dad,' she said, and gave his hand a little squeeze.

Examiner's Comments

What you write in this section will usually be connected in some way with what you have been reading in the other section. The connection you make will be up to you. You will *imagine* a setting, characters and events which allow you to *explore* a theme or idea with some purpose. This should *entertain* a reader in order to make him or her read on.

Likely responses to this question may present the impact of people on the environment, or present a situation in which someone is moved to compassion by an experience, or use an animal as something which changes a person's views or relationships.

Generally, this response is well-controlled and well-presented, with some errors and a tendency to a sentimental portrayal of a teenager. However, there is some originality in making the cyber-pet an animal which has an effect on the adults, and the focus on the adults' feelings gives the story more range and subtlety. This story is an acceptable interpretation of a task which is to imagine, explore and entertain. It is purposeful, structured writing in the Grade A/B area.

Specifically, the story is communicated very clearly, with well-imagined and explored feelings, relationships and events. The writer adapts narrative forms for the specific purpose of showing how a child's needs are important, and how adults may have to change to accommodate them. It is written mainly for an audience of younger readers who would sympathise more with the child than the parents but it also shows understanding of the adult world of work, and of conflicting adult priorities and the anxieties of parents.

Ideas are well organised into sentences and paragraphs, and the whole text develops through narrated events and through dialogue. The repetition of Carrie's thoughts about adults helps the coherence of the story, and the attention to the mother's and father's feelings stops it being a sentimental story about a poor child, with no awareness of other people, especially adults. The ending is predictable and rather sentimental, but it develops with the theme of relationship by the linking reference to hands. There could be some development of the idea that the father's feelings about his daughter not being so close are important, and there could be some development of the conflict suggested between the mother's involvement in her career and in her family.

Spelling is generally accurate, though some standard endings 'cheerful' and 'practical' are incorrect. Some irregular words are incorrect, such as 'attached', 'decision' and 'rummaged'. Punctuation is generally sound, though there are several apostrophes missing, and on one occasion 'didn't' is written as 'dident'. This weakness tends to be more obvious as the story goes on, perhaps because the writer is working against time. It is worth noting that some complex words are written accurately: 'determined', 'feasible' and 'announced'. Speech is accurately marked and sentences, with one or two exceptions, are started with capital letters. Grammar is generally sound, though there is confusion of 'past' and 'passed'.

There is skilful structure in creating a situation and relationship without specifying what is being discussed until later. There is confident use of narrative which avoids totally explicit description, as in the visit to the shop to buy the tamaguchi. Also, the dialogue is occasionally well tailored to suit character, such as in the father's use of the word 'feasible'. There is not much range or selection of vocabulary for particular effects, but there is skilful use of dialogue to move the story on, allowing the reader to understand from implied meaning.

CHAPTER 38

EXAM PAPER 3

This chapter is designed to help you prepare for a typical final examination paper. It is in two sections: the first tests your reading of non-fiction, the second tests your ability to write for a particular purpose and audience. Each of the questions is cross-referenced to earlier chapters in this book, so that you can revise particular skills before attempting the 'exam'.

Section A of the paper specifically tests your ability to:

- collate materials from different sources and make cross references between texts (Chapter 13);
- distinguish between fact and opinion (Chapter 10);
- evaluate the different ways in which information is presented (Chapter 11);
- follow an argument, identifying implications and recognising inconsistencies (Chapter 12);
- comment on writers' use of language (Chapter 14);
- evaluate structural and presentational devices in texts (Chapter 15).

Section B of the paper specifically tests your ability to:

- use accurate spelling (Chapter 18);
- use appropriate punctuation (Chapter 19);
- use a range of grammatical constructions (Chapter 20);
- structure your work helpfully in sentences and paragraphs (Chapter 21);
- present your work neatly and clearly (Chapter 22);
- write to inform, explain or describe (Chapter 25).

You should allow yourself two hours for this paper, spending about one hour on each section.

- Read the paper first.
- Then read the advice.
- Then write your answers.
- Then compare them with the sample student's answers, and use the examiner's comments to help you decide whether your own answers incorporate most of the positive features in the sample student's answers.

Section A

Read carefully the two leaflets, *Camp America* and *Au Pair in America*. Answer all the following questions, remembering to check your answers for accuracy and clear expression.

Q1 Look again at the section of *Camp America* headed 'Do I Qualify?' and the section of *Au Pair in America* headed 'Can I Apply?'. Using these sections only, list:

   a one requirement of the *Au Pair in America* scheme which is not necessary for the Camp America scheme;

   b one requirement of the *Camp America* scheme which is similar to, but more demanding than, one for *Au Pair in America*;

   c three requirements for the *Au Pair in America* scheme which are similar to, but more demanding than, those for *Camp America*.

   (5 marks)

Q2 Look again at the section of *Au Pair in America* headed 'The Opportunity of a Lifetime'. From this section copy:

   a one complete sentence which is factual;

   b one complete sentence which conveys an opinion rather than a fact;

   c one complete sentence which is a mixture of fact and opinion.

   In each case, explain briefly why you consider each sentence to be factual, an opinion, or a mixture of fact and opinion.

   (6 marks)

Q3 Which of these leaflets would most make you want to join the scheme? In your answer you should compare them, writing about:

   • how much detail you are given;

   • how clearly each leaflet is expressed;

   • how attractively each is laid out;

   • what audience you think they are aimed at, and which of the two would be most successful.

   (9 marks)

Section B

Choose one of the following tasks to write about.

Q4 Write an article for a teenage magazine in which you outline the *Camp America* and *Au Pair in America* schemes. You should advise your readers which of them offers the most appealing opportunities, and why.

   (20 marks)

Q5 Imagine that you are taking part in either the *Camp America* or the *Au Pair in America* scheme. Write a letter to your parents describing a typical day.

   (20 marks)

Camp America provides:

▮ Free London — New York — London Flight

▮ Full board and lodging whilst at camp or with a family

▮ Pocket money from US$150 – US$450

▮ Time for up to eight weeks independent travel (at your own cost)

▮ Help in securing J-1 cultural exchange visa

▮ 21+ years experience

▮ Additional departures available at extra cost from Amsterdam, Frankfurt, Glasgow, and Manchester.

CAMP AMERICA

Summer Jobs in America

So what is Camp America all about?

▮ We enable you to spend 9 weeks of your summer working on an **American Summer Camp.**

▮ After the successful completion of your 9 week commitment you will be free to spend up to 8 weeks for independent travel around the United States.

▮ We place over 6000 people a year on over 800 camps and you could be there too...

▮ We also make placements with American families on our 10 week International Family Companion Programme.

Do I Qualify? Yes ... if you are

▮ Interested in working with children

▮ Available no later than June 30 and free until August 20 (minimum 9 weeks is required)

▮ Aged 18+ (by June 1st)

▮ Able to speak english fluently

CAMPAMERICA

Camp America programmes:

▮ **Counsellor:**
Think you can handle children? Put your childcare skills to the test in an environment where you will live, eat and play with young children. Nowhere in our literature will you see your time at camp described as a holiday **...but it is fun.**
We seek people with particular sporting and performance art skills and people experienced working with the handicapped. If you have a medical background, placement chances as an Infirmary Assistant are excellent.

▮ **Campower:**
If you're not so keen on the parental role at camp why not try this challenging programme. Campower workers are the backbone of camp. They keep the camp fed, the place tidy, the clothes clean and the office running smoothly. **It is a visa requirement that campower applicants must be students** (this rule does not apply to the Counsellor Programme). Campower work is not necessarily skilled. We particularly want general kitchen workers – no previous experience required – just the ability to work hard and have fun.

▮ **International Family Companion:**
If hundreds of children at a summer camp sounds a bit much, there's always the more personal approach of being an International Family Companion. Share an American family's home as their summer help, supervising the children and sharing the chores and the fun! **It is a visa requirement that family companion applicants must be students.**

Interested...?

experience the most rewarding year of your life.

au pair AMERICA

A year abroad. A lifetime of memories

join the first legal & most successful child care programme to the USA.

Spend a year you'll remember for the rest of your life.

CAN I APPLY?

To qualify for the Au Pair in America programme you must:

- be aged 18-26 and hold a current Western European passport
- have practical experience in caring for children
- speak English to an acceptable standard
- be able and willing to commit to a full year
- hold a valid driving licence
- be a secondary school graduate or equivalent
- not have a criminal record
- attend an Au Pair in America interview
- agree to the programme's code of conduct and rules
- not have previously participated in an au pair programme to the USA

DON'T DELAY, APPLY TODAY!

THE OPPORTUNITY OF A LIFETIME.

We will give you the unique opportunity to spend a rewarding and fulfilling year as an au pair in America. A year that will allow you to experience a new culture, build life-long friendships, improve your child care skills and study part-time.

As part of our distinguished cultural exchange programme, you will learn about the American way of life while providing your host family with a valuable insight into European culture.

Au Pair in America was the first programme to legally bring young people from Western Europe to the United States to provide child care for carefully selected US families. It is now the largest and most respected programme of its kind with over 3,500 participants every year.

Our programme is sponsored by two distinguished non-profit American foundations, the American Institute for Foreign Study Foundation (AIFS) and the American Heritage Association (AHA), who are responsible for ensuring that the stringent requirements for Au Pair in America are adhered to.

WHY CHOOSE AU PAIR IN AMERICA?

- Au Pair in America places the highest number of au pairs of any organisation - over 75% of all applicants.
- Over the last decade Au Pair in America has established a network of highly experienced Community Counsellors in over 170 US locations to provide help and support to you in your community.
- Joining the largest au pair programme of its kind ensures that you will have a group of au pairs in your area to regularly meet with and develop life long friendships.
- You will have the resources and support of AIFS, the leading organisation in international educational exchange for over thirty years.
- Regular publications will keep you in touch with over 3,500 other European au pairs throughout the United States, who want to be pen friends or travel companions.

IN RETURN FOR PROVIDING A MAXIMUM OF 45 HOURS PER WEEK OF CHILD CARE, YOU WILL RECEIVE:

- the opportunity to spend 12 months living with an American family in New York, Boston, Detroit, Atlanta, Chicago, San Francisco or 170 other USA metropolitan areas
- $135 weekly payment ($115 if caring for children over 2)
  - an exchange visitor J-1 visa
  - four day Orientation in New York City
  - 12 month support from a local Counsellor
  - a $500 tuition allowance
  - free comprehensive medical insurance
  - a private room and meals
  - at least one complete weekend off every month (Friday evening to Monday morning)
  - two separate weeks of paid vacation
  - careful screening of your host family to ensure a safe and comfortable environment
  - a $500 Completion Bonus at the end of your year
  - an optional 13th month to travel throughout the USA
  - free return flight to a major European destination
  - access to a 24-hour toll-free helpline in the event of a emergency
  - regular contact and social activities with other au pairs
  - a quarterly newsletter, TEAM (The Europeans in America Magazine), containing helpful advice and interesting articles
  - discounted flights to the USA for visiting friends and relatives if you join our exclusive Club Au Pair
  - the opportunity to improve your English language fluency if you are not a native speaker of the language
  - and many more exciting benefits!

au pair AMERICA

☐ **Please rush me your brochure & application form**

Name _____

Address _____

Postcode _____

Country _____

Tel. No. _____

Send to:
Au Pair in America, 37 Queen's Gate, London SW7 5HR
Telephone 0171-581 7311 Fax 0171-581 7355

au pair AMERICA

ADVICE FOR YOUR ANSWERS

SECTION A

Q1 This is not a difficult question, but it requires you to pick out relevant details from the appropriate leaflet by comparing both of them. You should re-read the two sections mentioned a couple of times to make sure that you are choosing the best information. Note that 5 marks indicates 1 mark per requirement.

Q2 Again this is a fairly straightforward question, but do be careful not only to distinguish fact from opinion but also to choose your examples only from the named section of the leaflet. Any examples chosen from elsewhere would not gain marks. Note that 6 marks shows you will be given 1 mark for each correct example you choose, and another mark for explaining why you have chosen it.

Q3 It is up to you which leaflet you think is more attractive or appealing, but remember to tackle each of the four bullet points in your answer. You do not need to spend an equal amount of time on each, but you should pay some attention to detail, language and layout as well as to overall general effect. If you do not refer to actual examples in the leaflets but write only generally, you would be unlikely to gain more than 4 marks out of 9.

SECTION B

Q4 Both writing tasks on this paper are designed to test your ability to inform, explain and describe. Make sure, therefore, that in answering this question you make clear what each scheme offers, what the main differences between them are, and which you would recommend to your readers (with your reasons). Clarity is most important, and so you will need to end your article with a firm recommendation for one scheme or the other.

You are writing a magazine article for teenagers, so an appropriate headline would help, and sub-headings can be useful to help structure the information. Think also about the range of your vocabulary and the tone of your writing.

Q5 This is perhaps an easier choice than the previous question, but an examiner would therefore expect more of the answer! A task like this can easily trap you into writing what is a vague, imaginative narrative rather than a clearly focused description based on some material you have read. You can – and should – be imaginative, but within the realistic limits which these leaflets suggest.

Remember that you are writing to your parents, so the tone will be informal, but not too 'slangy'.

ANSWERS & EXAMINER'S COMMENTS

SECTION A

Sample Student's Answers

Q1

a   You must hold a valid driving licence.

b   You must be able to speak English fluently.

c   Have practical experience in caring for children.
    Be aged 18–26 and hold a current Western European passport.
    Be able and willing to commit to a full year.

Q2

a   'Au Pair in America was the first programme to legally bring young people from Western Europe to the United States to provide child care for carefully selected US families': This is factual because it states information about the scheme, that has happened rather than an opinion about what you will do, or how you will enjoy it.

b   'We will give you the unique opportunity to spend a rewarding and fulfilling year as an au pair in America': This is opinion because it is the company's belief, and they are trying to get you interested, but your year may not be rewarding and fulfilling, this is not definite.

c   'It is now the largest and most respected programme of its kind with over 3,500 participants every year': This is a mixture of fact and opinion, because it is only an opinion that it is the most respected programme, because this is what people think about it, but it is a fact that there are over 3,500 participants because these have been counted.

Q3

The leaflet that makes me want to join the scheme the most is Au Pair in America. The reason for this is because it gives me much more comprehensive information about the scheme. It tells me more about what the job entails, and how I will benefit from it. This leaflet also tells me more of the things I will receive, and more details about what qualifications I need. The best thing about this leaflet is that it provides a form to send off for further information.

I find the layout of the Au Pair leaflet more attractive than the Camp America leaflet also. This is because it is less cluttered, and more spaced out. The photographs of the Au Pairs are appealing and interest you more than the picture in the Camp America leaflet.

The Au Pair leaflet uses catch lines to attract you, such as 'experience the most rewarding year of you life' and 'A year abroad. A lifetime of memories'. Both of these are found on the front cover, along with photographs and instantly attract you more than the front cover of Camp America which simply says 'Summer jobs in America.'

Both leaflets use bullet points to express information. This is a good idea, as it makes it more clear, but there are more points made in the Au Pair leaflet. Both leaflets also use subtitles which are questions you may ask, such as 'So what is Camp America all about?' and 'Why choose Au Pair in America?'

Au Pair in America sounds more attractive because as well as stating facts about the job, it tells you additional information such as the facts that you will be experiencing new culture, building friendships and improving your childcare skills. The Camp America leaflet says 'Nowhere in our literature will you see your time at camp described as a holiday'. This statement would actually put me off going there, and following it by '... but it is fun' seems only like an afterthought, but you already have the impression of hard work and no fun!

Camp America does not tell you about what holidays you are entitled to, or what time off you can have. All it tells you about what it provides are the essentials, such as flights and board. Au Pair in America tells you about your holidays, payment, the location insurance and many other benefits.

Although both leaflets use colour, the Camp America leaflets look more tacky because it only uses red and black on a white background. Au Pair in America uses a colour background with a more sophisticated maroon colour, and font.

Both leaflets are aimed at 18-year-olds or above, as this is the minimum age you can join each scheme. I think Au Pair in America would reach this audience more effectively, because the front cover looks more grown up. The picture on Camp America looks a bit childish. Also, Au Pair in America is less patronising in the language it uses and gives the opportunity of getting in touch with other Au Pairs which is a chance young people would appreciate.

Examiner's Comments

Q1   **a**   An alternative answer could be 'not have a criminal record' or 'be a secondary-school graduate or equivalent' or 'agree to the programme's code of conduct and rules' or 'not have previously participated in an au pair programme to the USA'.
      b   There is no alternative answer.
      c   There are no alternative answers.

Overall, these answers to Question 1 would gain the full 5 marks.

Q2   **a**   This is a factual sentence (if we assume they are telling the truth about being the first legal programme of its kind!) and the reason given is adequate. There is no alternative answer.
      b   This is a good choice, well explained. An alternative answer could have been 'A year that will allow you to experience a new culture, build life-long friendships, improve your child-care skills and study part time', as none of those things will necessarily happen. A further alternative would be the second paragraph, beginning 'As part of our distinguished …' and ending '… a valuable insight into European culture', as again these things might not happen, and people might not respond in the way described.
      c   A well-chosen example and a good explanation. An alternative answer could have been the final paragraph beginning 'Our programme is sponsored …' and ending '… stringent requirements for Au Pairs in America are adhered to' – the support of the foundations is fact, but the words 'distinguished' and 'stringent' are opinions.

Overall, these answers to Question 2 would gain the full 6 marks.

Q3   This is a full, detailed answer which would gain at least 8 and possibly the full 9 marks. The reasons for this are:

- the first paragraph makes a clear statement of preference, with a general reason relating to the first prompt in the question (that is, a comment about the amount of detail and helpful information given in the *Au Pair in America* leaflet);

- the next three paragraphs deal in detail with the next two prompts in the question, that is, the clarity of each leaflet and the attractiveness of the layout. The answer considers a range of features such as:

     – the use of space
     – the use of photographs
     – the use of catchy phrases to gain attention
     – the use of bullet points
     – the use of questions and answers

In all these cases, the answer not only describes these features, but comments on the effect they have;

- the final paragraph on this page then picks out additional features (such as the extra detail in the *Au Pair in America* leaflet) which impress this reader;

- the answer also points out how the *Camp America* leaflet might actually have the opposite effect on the reader to the one intended;

- this point is then developed into a more detailed examination of what the *Camp America* leaflet does *not* tell the reader in comparison with the *Au Pair in America* leaflet;

- the comments on colour and font are good, but might have been better placed in the paragraph where other layout features were discussed. However, this comment is related to the explanation of audience, which is the last prompt in the question, so the overall structure of the answer is perfectly sound.

(Note that one of the impressive qualities of this answer is that it continually compares the two leaflets, referring to details in one and then the other. This is a much better approach than writing all about one leaflet first, and then the other.)

Overall, then, this is a very complete answer which uses the structure given by the prompts in the question, but still sounds interesting and lively, and conveys a genuine personal response to the leaflets.

For Section A of this paper, the answers would gain 19 or 20 marks out of the 20 available.

SECTION B

Sample Student's Answers

Q4

Magic America

Looking for a holiday job with a difference?

Why not join one of the following schemes which allows you to spend time working and travelling in America, as well looking after children.

Camp America

This scheme is best if you can't give up a whole year to go to America. To apply for one of the Camp America programmes you must be interested in working with children, aged 18+ (by June 1st) and able to speak English fluently. Also, you must be available no later than June 30th and free until August 20th, to work a minimum of 9 weeks.

There are over 800 camps in America, where 6000 people are placed every year with Camp America. Alternatively they provide a 10 week scheme with an American family. If you opt for this programme you can be an International Family Companion, and be a family's summer help, as well as supervising their children. To follow this scheme you must be a student to get a visa.

If you choose to go to a camp then you can be a counsellor or Campover. To be a counsellor you must have skills in sports, performing arts, care of the handicapped or medical areas. A Campover keeps the camp tidy, clean and fed. As with being an International Family Companion, you must be a student to obtain a visa for a Campover. You need no particular skills or experience except the ability to work hard and have fun.

Camp America provides flights and full board as well as pocket money, help in securing a J-1 cultural exchange visa and 21+ years experience. After you have completed the scheme you can have up to eight weeks independent travel at your own cost.

Au pair in America

This scheme probably gives the best opportunities. You spend a whole year working with an American family in one of over 170 USA metropolitan areas, then you can spend another month travelling around the USA.

247

Q4

As well as building a friendship with the family you work for, with the Au Pair in America scheme you have the chance to meet with other au pairs in your area, and also get in touch with other 3,500 other European au pairs throughout the States.

Following this scheme you will get a \$115–\$135 weekly payment, a J–1 visa, a four day orientation in New York, support from a local counsellor, a \$500 tuition allowance, medical insurance, a private room and meals, a \$500 completion bonus, free flights, access to a 24-hour free help line and a quarterly newsletter. As well as the optional month's travel at the end, you will have at least one free weekend a month, two seperate weeks of paid vacation and discounted flights to the USA for your friends and relatives to visit you.

To apply for this scheme, you need experience in care, a Western European passport, to be aged between 18 and 26, to be able to speak English to an acceptable standard and a free year to commit to the scheme. You also need a valid driving licence, to be a secondary school graduate (or equivalent), to attend an interview and to agree to the code of conduct and rules. Also you must not have previously participated in an American au pair scheme, or have a criminal record.

Although there are more requirements for the latter scheme there are also more benefits, than there are with Camp America. It really depends on how much time you have, as to which scheme you would apply to, but we really do recommend that if you have a year to spare and are interested in children and travel, then Au Pair in America is an opportunity which should not be missed!

For more information on either or both of these schemes, send an SAE to our usual address marking your envelope with the name(s) of the scheme(s) that you would like more information about.

Q5

Mum,

Well it was up early again this morning as Bethany jumped on me in bed– I'm sure that I wouldn't have done that to a virtual stranger! I've only been here for a week and yet the children trust me already!

Today was the first day the family left me totally alone all day with the children, so I had to think up some good activities to do. I didn't want the children telling their 'mom' that I was no fun!

The weather was quite good (although a little misty) so after wrapping up warm we went to the park. Whilst the children played on the round about I talked to a mother (who was watching her children). She told me about the time she had had an Au Pair, but it hadn't worked out. I was just about to ask her why when Thomas called out, 'Megan, help!' Worst case scenarios raced through my mind.

'What is it?', I called out as I raced over, 'I've lost *Bluber Man*,' he cried. It was alright then. I've told you about *Bluber Man* before haven't I? It's the latest craze over here — from the cartoon '*Bluber Man's adventures*.' That crisis sorted out we headed home just in time for dinner. I cooked that crispy veg. salad that you sent me the recipe for. It's such a hassle having 2 vegetarian kids, but I suppose I know the background of it after Ruth's extensive lessons!

Whilst the children napped after dinner I did my chores. Instead of the usual ironing, today I had to dust the lounge. It didn't take too long so I got time to think what we could do next.

Both Bethany and Thomas love hands-on activities so I decided we could do some cooking. As they are 3 and 4 I thought they might have done some before. How wrong could I be — I spent the whole afternoon explaining what utensils and ingredients were! By the time we were actually ready to begin cooking Julie came home from work and said she'd take over.

So that was it — my first day alone. I enjoyed it, but think that next time I want to plan an activity I will have to consult with Julie as to what they have done before!

I think tomorrow we may try some water play if it isn't too cold outside — spring takes so long to come here!

I'd better go I think I can here Thomas coming — looks like its bedtime story time! I hope you write soon.

Love Megan

Examiner's Comments

Although only one question from Section B has to be answered, sample responses to both questions have been included to allow you to compare whichever you attempted with a good model.

Q4 This answer would gain a high mark because it is written appropriately for the given audience, and because the clear layout and use of detail achieves the purpose of conveying information and opinion.

- The use of a headline shows that this is written in the style of a magazine article.

- The brief introduction, starting with a question to the reader, is interesting and captures attention.

- The use of subheadings is appropriate to this style of writing, and is helpful in structuring all the information.

- The main features of the *Camp America* scheme are effectively summarised, always in a direct, straightforward style, keeping the reader involved by constantly addressing him/her as 'you'.

- At the end of the section on *Camp America*, the article has not come down in favour of one scheme or the other, but is simply summarising details.

- The second subheading is helpful in signalling to the reader that a different scheme is about to be explained.

- The *Au Pair in America* scheme is summarised in a clear and comprehensible way. The reader is still addressed as 'you' to retain interest and involvement.

- One of the very few technical errors is the misspelling of 'separate'.

- It is not good style to being a sentence with 'to' (as in 'To apply'): this makes it sound like an afterthought.

- A further subheading before the final paragraph would have been helpful to indicate that the writer's recommendations and conclusions are about to be offered.

- A good conclusion which reinforces the writer's awareness of purpose and audience.

Overall, although the writer shows a few signs of tiring towards the end of this very detailed answer, a high mark would be appropriate for this response – probably in the region of 18 out of 20.

Remember that the kinds of writing tested in Section B of this paper are informing, explaining and describing. Question 4 was focused mostly on informing and explaining, requiring you to represent information in a different way for a specified audience. The alternative, Question 5, is more a test of describing, and offers the chance to write imaginatively, while still referring to the general framework of one of the leaflets.

Q5 This answer would gain a good mark. It is written in an appropriate style for a letter from a child to a parent, and, while showing imagination, clearly describes experiences which could arise from participation in the *Au Pair in America* scheme.

- If you are asked to write a letter, it is a good idea to show that you know how to set out a letter. This answer would have started more strongly if there had been an address at the top right-hand corner of the page, and if 'Mum' (or 'Dear Mum') had not been squeezed in as an afterthought.

- Although the style is appropriately 'chatty', a good range of vocabulary is used (e.g. 'scenario') and different sentence structures are apparent.

- The inclusion of speech (correctly punctuated!) is a good way of making an account livelier.

- The paragraph beginning 'Whilst the children napped …' shows that the writer has understood from the leaflet that au pairs will have to help around the home as well as look after children.

- A good stylistic touch in 'How wrong could I be', which sounds very much as though the writer is talking directly to the reader.

- More good choice of vocabulary in 'utensils' and 'ingredients'.

- One of the very few technical errors occurs in the last section: 'here' should be 'hear', and there's an apostrophe missing in 'it's' (short for 'it is').

As in the Question 4 answer, this writer shows a few signs of tiring towards the end, but the letter would gain a mark of 15 or 16 out of 20.

The combination of the mark for Section A with either of the Section B marks would certainly qualify for a Grade A.

This chapter is designed to help you prepare for a typical final examination paper. It is in two sections: the first tests your reading of non-fiction, and the second tests your ability to write for a particular purpose and audience. Each of the questions is cross-referenced to earlier chapters in this book, so that you can revise particular skills before attempting the 'exam'.

Section A of the paper specifically tests your ability to:

- distinguish between fact and opinion (Chapter 10);
- follow an argument, identifying implications and recognising inconsistencies (Chapter 12);
- collate materials from different sources and make cross references between texts (Chapter 13);
- evaluate the different ways in which information is presented (Chapter 11);
- collate materials from different sources and make cross references between texts (Chapter 13);
- comment on writers' use of language (Chapter 14).

Section B of the paper specifically tests your ability to:

- use accurate spelling (Chapter 18);
- use appropriate punctuation (Chapter 19);
- use a range of grammatical constructions (Chapter 20);
- structure your work helpfully in sentences and paragraphs (Chapter 21);
- present your work neatly and clearly (Chapter 22);
- write to analyse, review or comment (Chapter 27).

You should allow yourself two hours for this paper, spending about one hour on each section.

- Read the paper first.
- Then read the advice.
- Then write your answers.
- Then compare them with the sample student's answers, and use the examiner's comments to help you decide whether your own answers incorporate most of the positive features in the sample answers.

Section A

Read excerpts (a) and (b) carefully. They both describe visits to Weston-super-Mare, a seaside resort in Somerset. Extract (a) is from Bill Bryson's *Notes From a Small Island*, and extract (b) is from Paul Theroux's *The Kingdom by the Sea*. Then answer all the following questions, remembering to check your answers for accuracy and clear expression.

List:

Q1 • three facts that you have learned about Weston-super-Mare from these passages, choosing at least one from each. Letter them (a), (b) and (c), and after each put (B) if it comes from the Bryson excerpt or (T) if it comes from the Theroux excerpt;

• two opinions, one from each passage. Letter them (d) and (e) and after each put (B) if it comes from the Bryson excerpt or (T) if it comes from the Theroux excerpt.

(5 marks)

Q2 What sort of a place is Weston-super-Mare, according to each of these writers? Think about what they choose to describe and discuss, referring to details in each passage to support your views.

(7 marks)

Q3 Which of these passages did you prefer reading? Give reasons for your answer by referring in detail to the content and language used by both writers.

(8 marks)

(a)

I went into a pub called the Britannia Inn, which was unfriendly without being actually hostile, and had a couple of lonely pints, then ate at a Chinese restaurant, not because I craved Chinese but because it was the only place I could find open. I was the only customer. As I quietly scattered rice and sweet and sour sauce across the tablecloth, there were some rumbles of thunder and, a moment later, the heavens opened – and I mean opened. I have seldom seen it rain so hard in England. The rain spattered the street like a shower of ball-bearings and within minutes the restaurant window was wholly obscured with water, as if someone were running a hose over it. Because I was a long walk from my hotel, I spun out the meal, hoping the weather would ease off, but it didn't, and eventually I had no choice but to step out into the rainy night.

I stood beneath a shop awning next door and wondered what to do. Rain battered madly on the awning and rushed in torrents through the gutters. All along the road it poured over the sides of overstretched gutters and fell to the pavement in an endless clatter. With my eyes closed it sounded like I was in the midst of some vast, insane tap-dancing competition. Pulling my jacket above my head, I waded out into the deluge, then sprinted across the street and impulsively took refuge in the first bright, open thing I came to - an amusement arcade. Wiping my glasses with a bandanna, I took my bearings. The arcade was a large room full of brightly pulsating machines, some of them playing electronic tunes or making unbidden *kerboom* noises, but apart from an overseer sitting at a counter with a drooping fag and a magazine, there was no one in the place so it looked eerily as if the machines were playing themselves.

(b)

Down the promenade, I saw that the wind had whipped the water into troughs. Even in this poor light there was a wonderful view – of Wales, of the two black islands, Flat Holm and Steep Holm, and at the end of the beach a curved loaf-shaped landspit called Brean Down. The beach was long and mostly empty and very grey, and it was flatter than the water. Parked on the sand, as in a cartoon of desert mirages, were a red Punch and Judy booth, and two yellow huts, one labelled *Tea-Stall* and the other *Shellfish Bar*. A flapping pennant said *Donkey Rides – 20 pence*. The few people on the beach lay heavily bundled-up on the sand, like war wounded on a beach-head. Their faces were tight with discomfort. A fat old lady with wild hair, wearing a winter coat but barefoot, stood and howled, *'Arthur!'* The donkeys stamped and shuddered in a little group, looking thoroughly baffled. And here on the promenade, hunched-over ladies with big handbags tipped their stoutness into the wind and breathed loudly through their teeth. Across the street at the Winter Gardens people were buying tickets for tonight's show, 'Cavalcade of Song'. Beyond the donkeys, beyond the fat barefoot lady and the Punch and Judy booth, a new island surfaced and sprouted trees. Then I saw it was a ship going by.

I was so unaccustomed to a place like Weston-super-Mare that with a little concentration I saw it in a surrealistic way. What were all these different things doing there? They had accumulated over the years, slowly, piling up like the tide-wrack, and because it had happened so slowly, no one questioned it or found it strange. And this was also why I could spend days in the seaside resorts fascinated by the way the natural coast had been deranged and cluttered. It did not matter much whether a town was pretty or ugly – although ugly ones were often the most telling. The image of the tide-wrack was accurate in some places. Other towns were like river mouths where, mounting like silt, a century of pulverized civilization had been deposited, often floating from the darker interior of England.

Section B

Choose one of the following tasks to write about.

Q4 Write a short radio script for a family magazine programme in which you consider the facilities and attractions of a holiday destination. You may base this on a real or imaginary place, and on real or imagined experience.

(20 marks)

Q5 Write an account of an incident from your life which has had a profound effect on you. Try to convey the significance of the event to the reader.

(20 marks)

ADVICE FOR YOUR ANSWERS

SECTION A

Q1 This is a straightforward question – the hardest part is probably following the instructions, so make sure you do exactly what you are told: present the information in a lettered list, using and identifying the two passages as instructed. When looking for facts, look for the obvious. And note that you are asked to choose facts about the place, not about the weather, or the author.

Q2 This is a more searching question, which requires you to decide on each writer's theme or approach: why do they choose to describe particular aspects of Weston-super-Mare? What are the implications of their choices? What is the tone of each passage – serious, humorous, happy, depressed? You can deal first with one passage and then with the other, but one sign of a really good candidate is the ability to cross-refer between passages.

Remember to keep focused on the question – the answer does not need to be long, but it must be detailed and relevant. A sentence or two at the beginning and end of your answer which set out your overview of both passages is a good structural approach.

Q3 There is no 'right' answer to a question like this; you can be honest about which of the passages you prefer, or if you find both equally (un)interesting. It is generally easier to compare passages, however, if you decide that one is more effective than the other in some way. And don't fall into the trap of dismissing both passages as 'boring' – even if that's what you really feel! You need to look closely at the writing skills used to show that you are aware of the techniques employed by authors.

Notice that you are asked to refer to content here. You will have taken a close look at the authors' feelings and attitudes in Question 2, and there is a danger that you could repeat here what you have already said. Don't fall into this time-wasting trap. A brief summary of content is sufficient here, as the main emphasis should be on the writers' linguistic skills.

SECTION B

Q4 Both writing tasks on this paper are designed to test your ability to analyse, review and comment. Don't therefore spend too much time worrying about the radio script aspect of this task: that is just a context to provide purpose and audience for what you do. Just remember that your language should be quite formal - you are not talking to a friend at school.

Your main challenge is to choose a holiday destination which you can describe briefly, and about which you can then make comments based on an analysis and review of the facilities and attractions it offers.

As with several of the tasks on this paper, it is important for you to 'top and tail' your answer carefully, so that it is coherently and logically structured.

Q5 This should be a fairly straightforward task, but there is a trap - you are asked to tell about the incident from your life for a particular purpose, to convey its significance to the reader. In other words this, like Question 4, is an analyse, review, comment task. If you prefer you can choose to imagine an experience rather than to relate something that has happened to you.

Whichever you choose to do, be careful not simply to write a narrative of a memorable occasion. That may be interesting and entertaining, but it will not meet the requirements of this task.

So keep the account of what actually happened to a minimum, and include plenty of reflection: what did you feel like? Why? How has the incident affected your personality or attitudes?

The range of vocabulary you use will be crucial to the success of your answer. The words you choose must analyse your feelings and engage and retain the interest of the reader through the originality of how you review the incident and comment on it.

ANSWERS & EXAMINER'S COMMENTS

SECTION A

Sample Student's Answers

Q1
a   There is a pub called 'The Britannia' in Weston-super-Mare (B).
b   There is an amusement arcade (B).
c   There is a spit of land called Brean Down at the end of the beach (T).
d   The Britannia 'was unfriendly without being actually hostile' (B).
e   'Even in this poor light there was a wonderful view' (T).

Q2
Both writers seem to think that Weston-super-Mare is a miserable sort of place, but Theroux finds it a more interesting experience to be there than Bryson.

Bryson did not enjoy the pub, or his meal, or the weather: he describes the rain as some of the hardest he had ever seen. The weather is also poor for Theroux, but he is still able to find pleasure in the view he gets across the water. It is windy, rather than wet, for Theroux's visit, and unlike Bryson he describes how it affects others as well as himself. In Bryson's account, the amusement arcade overseer seems unaware of his surroundings or the rain outside, but other people, and the donkeys, are as affected by the wind as Theroux.

From Bryson we get just a general impression that he did not like Weston and that he felt something of an outsider. Theroux seems much more sympathetic to it, although he is also conscious of not belonging, and is fascinated by the town as an example of a typical cluttered English seaside resort which may be ugly, but which represents important aspects of the national character.

Neither writer particularly likes Weston, but the tone of Theroux's description is serious and thoughtful, while Bryson's seems humorous in a bitter kind of way.

Q3
I much preferred the passage by Paul Theroux. Bill Bryson seems obsessed with himself and his own discomfort, but Theroux is aware of others and is interested in things other people do and what this reveals about the place.

Having said that, Bryson is an amusing writer. He creates a vivid picture of a lone eater spinning out his meal, 'quietly scatter[ing] rice and sweet and sour sauce across the tablecloth', and his description of the rain makes an original appeal to our sense of hearing — it 'spattered the street like a shower of ball-bearings'. He sustains this image later when he writes 'With my eyes closed it sounded like I was in the midst of some vast, insane tap-dancing competition'.

Theroux's imagery is more subtle and visual. He writes that 'hunched-over ladies with big handbags tipped their stoutness into the wind' and that 'a new island surfaced and sprouted trees. Then I saw it was a ship going by'.

Bryson does not seem to have a particular purpose to his writing other than to write a humorous description of the place. Theroux uses his description to reflect and comment on seaside towns in general. His ideas make you think for yourself, and you are more likely to remember his writing than Bryson's, which is momentarily amusing but soon forgotten.

Examiner's Comments

Q1 The only real alternatives to 1(a), (b) and (c) are 'there is a Chinese restaurant' (from Bryson), 'there is a promenade', 'there are donkeys on the beach' or 'there is a theatre called the Winter Gardens' (from Theroux); 'it was raining' (Bryson) will not do, as it is about the weather, not the place. Most of Theroux's comments are opinions, e.g. about the beach, the view and the people. The sample answer would gain the full 5 marks.

Q2 The first paragraph of the answer gives an overview of both passages, showing how they are similar yet different. The second and third paragraphs then show how each writer's choice of detail gives a different impression of the place. Constant cross-referencing between the passages like this would score highly. The brief conclusion is good, because it rounds the answer off by once again comparing an overview of the passages, but now with a clearer understanding of the writer's attitudes which have led to their individual reactions to Weston-super-Mare. This answer would gain the full 7 marks.

Q3 Notice how the opening paragraph of the answer does not repeat what has already been written in the answer to Question 2, but builds on it. Although the candidate does not especially like the Bryson extract, there is a recognition that he is a skilled comic writer, and detailed references to the language illustrate this well. There is also a detailed response to Theroux's greater subtlety, and a conclusion which again draws the two extracts together and compares their overall effect on the reader. The perceptive comparison and the use of textual detail mean that the full 8 marks would be awarded to this answer.

SECTION B

Sample Student's Answers

Q4 Riverhead is on the south coast, set in a delightful bay about three miles wide, where the sands are golden and the sea sparkling blue. Rolling green hills lead down to steep, rocky cliffs, and Combe Island with its teeming birdlife lies just a few miles offshore in the middle of the bay. In short, an idyllic English holiday resort of the sort you might think exists only in children's storybooks.

But is it? What does it have to offer families? And what if – as I'm afraid was the case during part of my visit – it rains hard and long?

For a start, there is plenty of accommodation to suit all tastes and all pockets: from a four-star hotel where the guests are expected to dress for dinner, through a multitude of bed-and-breakfast establishments to several camp-sites, all with wonderful views. You would find it hard not to return home relaxed and pampered from a stay in any of them.

The beach is supervised by lifeguards and so bathing is safe for all. I did notice, though, that swimmers often had to move swiftly out of the way of surfers and body-boarders – this could be dangerous for young children, or indeed for anyone not alert to all the activities taking place around them in the busy waters.

And this is the drawback of Riverhead, really: it's mostly a young person's place, where the night life is long and loud but there's little in the way of family entertainment. All the youngsters spend their time getting wet anyway, so nobody has thought about providing indoor attractions for those who want to stay dry, and on dry land.

So I'd have to say: great, if you could guarantee the weather, or if you're just a water baby at heart. But for families, and given our unpredictable English summers, I'd say that Riverhead needs to provide more.

Q5 I was ten at the time. Just an ordinary person, living with a normal family in a quiet street in an average town. It was a Friday, in July, near the end of the school term. I wasn't very happy at school; I didn't make friends easily and I was looking forward to spending the summer holidays with my dad. He could be at home more than most dads, because he sold insurance and had a small office in our house. We used to play cricket together and go for walks and ...

... well we did, up until that summer. I came home from school, and I knew something was wrong when I tried to open the door but couldn't. Mum or dad was always there, but not today. Then Mrs Rose, Aunt Rose I used to call her and thought it was such a pretty name, hurried up beside me and said, 'Come with me, Sam.'

I followed her into next door, into the kitchen where she sat me down and was too busy getting me a drink of milk and some biscuits to answer my questions about mum and dad. I remember suddenly being afraid when she brought me my drink and I saw she was crying. Seeing grown-ups cry always scared me. Mum used to cry lots. I didn't know why at the time; now I think she was always unhappy with dad, but I can't think why. To me he was so kind, so willing to give me his time, so ...

'It's your dad, Sam,' said Aunt Rose. 'He's very ill in the hospital.'

'Is mum with him?' I remember asking.

'No. We don't know where she is,' said Aunt Rose. 'You'd better stay with me while we sort things out.'

Sort things out! That's always everyone's ambition in life, isn't it – to sort things out. Nobody told me the truth until years later, when I suppose they thought I could cope with it. Mum had walked out on us that morning – I never saw her again – and dad had overdosed on aspirins when he found her note.

He died a few days later. I never saw him in hospital, and I've always wondered what he looked like, lying there.

Mum and dad sorted themselves out all right. Me, I never have done. Why? Well, I've seen their ways of doing it and I don't much fancy them. Mum's gone, good and proper, even if she's still alive somewhere. But dad – I still feel he's with me sometimes, really with me. I talk to him, you know, and I think I can sometimes hear him answer me. Am I so silly? It gives me a little happiness, and there's no one else to talk to here.

Examiner's Comments

Q4 This is a good answer, because the content is appropriate and the tone and language sound right for the given audience. The introduction sets the scene, using a large number of descriptive words to convey the atmosphere and qualities of Riverhead. This then allows the dramatic questioning in the second section. In its turn, this allows the writer to then compare what Riverhead has and what it lacks, in an even-handed way, rather than just listing facilities separately. This kind of cross-referencing shows sophisticated writing skills, in the same way that it showed higher reading skills in Questions 2 and 3. The conclusion rounds off the script appropriately, by highlighting Riverhead's main attraction and its main drawback. This answer to Question 4 is skilfully structured and appropriately written, with accurate technical skills. It would gain a very high mark - probably 19 or 20 out of 20.

Q5 This candidate has opted to relate an imaginary experience. This is a powerful piece of writing, although it comes perilously close to overdoing the tragedy, which is always a potential problem if you opt to write about events of this kind. What rescues this answer is the almost self-mocking tone of the central character – who is this person, and where are they? We don't know where 'here' (the last word) is, we don't know how old he or she now is, or whether he or she really 'talks' to the dead father or not. The writer has created a genuine air of mystery through the persona of this character. The vocabulary is fairly plain – the writer's skill is in the varied and complex sentence structures, for example at the end of the second paragraph and beginning of the third. The control of tone is also excellent: from 'normality' at the start, through confusion and fear to bitterness and then a sort of acceptance at the end. This shows a sophisticated control of the reader's reactions.

This answer has many good qualities, but the language is plain and the story is not very original. However, because of the candidate's structural and atmospheric skills it would be awarded a high mark, around 17 or 18 out of 20.

CHAPTER 40

EXAM
PAPER 5

This chapter is designed to help you prepare for a typical final examination paper. It is in two sections: the first tests your reading of media texts, and the second tests your ability to write for a particular purpose and audience. Each of the questions is cross-referenced to earlier chapters in this book, so that you can revise particular skills before attempting the 'exam'.

Section A of the paper specifically tests your ability to:

- follow an argument, identifying implications and recognising inconsistencies (Chapter 12);
- collate materials from different sources and make cross references between texts (Chapter 13);
- evaluate the different ways in which information is presented (Chapter 11);
- comment on writers' use of language (Chapter 14);
- evaluate structural and presentational devices in texts (Chapter 15).

Section B of the paper specifically tests your ability to:

- use accurate spelling (Chapter 18);
- use appropriate punctuation (Chapter 19);
- use a range of grammatical constructions (Chapter 20);
- structure your work helpfully in sentences and paragraphs (Chapter 21);
- present your work neatly and clearly (Chapter 22);
- write to argue, persuade or instruct (Chapter 26).

You should allow yourself two hours for this paper, spending about one hour on each section.

- Read the paper first.
- Then read the advice.
- Then write your answers.
- Then compare them with the sample student's answers, and use the examiner's comments to help you decide whether your own answers incorporate most of the positive features in the sample answers.

Section A

Read carefully the articles *Canny kids splash out on food, drink and fashion with £8 in their pocket* and *Having money makes you feel independent* which first appeared in the *Independent*. Then answer all the following questions, remembering to check your answers for accuracy and clear expression.

Q1 **a** Explain in your own words the meaning of the paragraph in the article *Canny kids ...* which begins 'Some items were bought more often than others ...'

(4 marks)

b Why is this paragraph important to the argument of the article?

(2 marks)

Q2 Does the article *Having money ...* merely repeat what you learn from the article *Canny kids ...* , or does it contradict or add to it in any way? Give examples to support your answer.

(6 marks)

Q3 What linguistic, structural and presentational techniques are used in this feature to make it interesting and attractive to the reader?

(8 marks)

Section B

Choose one of the following tasks to write about. You may use information from the newspaper articles and/or ideas of your own.

Q4 Write a letter from an elderly person to the *Independent*, arguing that young people today have too much money to spend, and waste it on unnecessary purchases.

(20 marks)

Q5 Write an article for a secondary-school magazine, advising young teenagers on how they might learn to manage their money.

(20 marks)

Canny kids splash out on food, drink and fashion with £8 in their pocket

Glenda Cooper
Socials Affairs Correspondent

Pocket money today is a lucrative affair, with British children spending on average £8.40 a week on food, toys and clothes, according to the first official investigation into how they handle their cash.

The biggest spending was on food, which included sweets, crisps, soft drinks, ice cream and school meals which the child bought – accounting for on average £3.20 a week. Next down were leisure goods – toys, compact discs and sports goods – which cost £1.60 a week. The third most popular items inducing children to part with their cash were clothing and shoes.

Liquid assets: Pocket money is now big business, a survey shows, with the nation's children splashing out an average of £3.20 a week on food.

How they spend it

	Boys	Girls
Food/soft drinks	£3.20	3.10
Leisure goods	2.10	1.10
Clothing	0.70	1.50
Leisure services	0.90	0.70
Household goods	0.50	0.60
Personal goods	0.20	0.80
Transport	0.40	0.40
Other	0.30	0.30
TOTAL	8.40	8.50

All amounts in survey are rounded to the nearest 10p

Other items popular with children included spending money on participating in sport, pets, make-up and fares to school. Thirty pence a week was also spent on 'other items', defined as alcohol, tobacco, stamps and subscriptions.

For the first time data on children's spending habits has been collected by the Office for National Statistics as part of the Family Expenditure Survey. The children – more than 2,000 in total – were asked to keep diaries of their daily expenditure over two weeks and the figures were derived from this data.

Older children spent far more than younger ones, with 15-year-olds spending on average more than four times as much as 7- and 8-year-olds. They also spent their money differently, with clothes becoming a higher priority for fashion-conscious teenagers while 7- to 12-year-olds preferred to buy toys or spend their cash on admissions charges.

While boys and girls spent the same money overall, they spent it differently. Boys spent most of their money on food, leisure goods and leisure services. While girls spent almost the same amount on food, they spent twice as much per week on clothing and footwear.

Girls also spent four times as much on personal goods and services – including toiletries, make-up and jewellery – averaging around 80p per week. Boys in comparison would only part with 20p.

Some items were bought more often than others – while more often nine out of ten children bought food, only 13 per cent bought clothes and footwear. So those who bought such items were spending on average £8.70 a week. Similarly, children who bought household goods spent on average £1.40 a week.

Alison Whitmarsh, a statistician, said: 'The actual amount of money passing through children's hands was very interesting. I'm sure I never spent £8.40 a week when I was a child, but then we're not aware of any comparable surveys, so it is hard to say'.

'Having money makes you feel independent'

Young journalists from *Children's Express* show that exercising their spending power goes far beyond the local sweet shop.

"Money makes you feel independent even if you are not," explained Aminah Carter, 13. "When you're out shopping and you've got the money in your hands and you're by yourself, you feel independent."

The importance of managing your own money was clearly recognised, and despite advertisers' attempts to tap the youth market, all the children were wary of their influence. "I don't buy things just for the hell of it. My money goes on day-to-day living, nothing extravagant," Moynul Mustafa, 15, said. And Momtaz Begum Hossain, 16, said: "I have got a bank account – but I only joined so I could get a free gift."

The junior world is divided between those who subsist on parental pocket money and those who help earn their keep. "If you go into the real world and get yourself a job, that's when you're going to prove you're independent ... If you're not hard working, it's not actually your own money," Denis Shukur, 15, said. He acknowledged the attendant responsibilities. "If parents see a child isn't reliable, he or she shouldn't get their own money. They might go out and buy things like drugs."

As they grow up, many believe that getting a part-time job is a valuable step towards greater responsibility. "I work to pay my mobile phone bill and my share of the phone bill at home. It's fair because I can't expect my mum to do everything for me now," teenager Julia Press said. Daniel Blackwood, 15, agreed: "It's right that once you reach a certain age you should earn it yourself."

Where parents are the main source of income, attitudes were mixed. For Mehrak Colestan, 13, financial handouts come complete with trust. "If I ask for extra money, she wants to know what it's for. But she wouldn't say, 'Oh, I don't think that's good, I'm not going to give you money for it' because she respects me." Yet for Momtaz Begum Hossain, shopping sprees quickly turn into show-and-tell: "Every time my mum gives me money, she wants to know what I've bought with it. Then she wants to see it, which is even worse."

Some welcomed greater involvement from their parents – usually mothers. "I don't get pocket money every day," explained Mehrak. "I tell my mum to keep my money for me because I know if I have it, I'll just use it for things I'll regret later such as silly magazines." Nicola Smart, 13, prefers to use banking facilities to control cash flow.

Children appear adept at making their income stretch. While Momtaz hoards concessionary vouchers for the cinema and scours markets for bargains, Mehrak shops for records at the beginning of the week "when singles are 99p", and Stuart strikes a deal with his mother, putting "sometimes £10 towards a really expensive shirt."

ADVICE FOR YOUR ANSWERS

SECTION A

Q1 **a** 'In your own words' does not mean you cannot use any of the language of the original, but avoid copying whole phrases or sentences. Think, for example, of words you could use instead of 'bought' and 'footwear', or how you could express '13%' differently.

b For 2 marks, this does not need to be a complicated answer – one clearly expressed sentence will do.

Q2 Make rough notes first under the headings 'repeat', 'contradict' and 'add'. Remember that you should not only think about factual information here: what about the tone of the two articles? Does one of them seem more sympathetic to young people, and if so, why?

'Give examples to support your answer' in this kind of question does not mean extensive quotation as it might in a Literature examination. It simply means refer to actual details, don't just make generalised unsupported statements. You might still want to quote an occasional word or phrase if it strengthens a point you are making.

Q3 As long as you cover all the aspects mentioned in the question, you need not tackle them in that order. In a question like this, it is often easier to start with comments on presentation, since the layout and appearance of the material is what tends to strike you first. Then go on to the structure of the articles, and deal with the language last – by now, you will have been working with the articles for some considerable time, and will have noted features of the language which merit comment.

As this question carries the most marks in this section, you should allow time to answer it in detail. You will also need to think about how to present the information clearly; there is no need to use presentational devices yourself, but you should at least ensure that your answer is easy to follow by making your points in a logical order and by using paragraphs effectively.

Remember to sum up your answer at the end by stating briefly whether you agree that the feature is attractive and interesting, and why. A comment about the audience is often a good idea in your conclusion.

SECTION B

Q4 This is a letter, so remember to start and end properly (there's no need to invent addresses) and to write in an appropriate tone. This person is concerned, perhaps even angry, but will try to write in a controlled way if he or she wants the letter to be published.

It's a good idea to pick up some details from the reading material (for example, the things children spend their money on) to show that you have thought about your reading.

It could also be a good idea to write as a grandparent, or the neighbour of a family with teenagers, so that you can give examples of young people whose spending patterns you know well.

The writing question will usually be the one single question which carries most marks on an examination paper. Leave yourself time to plan your answer properly. You do not need to write a huge amount, but what you do write should be interesting, accurate and relevant to the task.

263

Q5 This task asks you to write for a specific audience, and you should only choose an alternative like this if you feel you can write in the appropriate style and in a suitable tone. A succession of ordinary, standard English paragraphs will not do: you need to show a feeling for popular journalism, for example using puns, alliteration and informal vocabulary, together with some simple layout features which you can reproduce on an examination paper, for example headings, bullet points, upper-case letters.

Content is less important than style and presentation here, but remember you can always use suitable material from the reading passage in Section A. Length is not too important either: spend plenty of time planning, so that you write just enough, of a sustained quality, to show you understand the requirements of the task and have the necessary writing skills.

ANSWERS & EXAMINER'S COMMENTS

SECTION A

Sample Student's Answers

Q1 a Not all children in the survey bought every item. Although most children purchased food, only a small percentage bought clothes and shoes. Those who did therefore spent nearly £9 a week on these items, many times more than the average amount. Children who bought household goods spent more than twice the average amount on these items, as fewer than half of the children actually purchased them.

b This paragraph is important because it reminds the reader that average spends on items may hide large variations in actual spending patterns.

Q2 The second article repeats very little information from the first, except to reinforce the fact that young people do spend their money on clothes and CDs. It also implicitly agrees that older children spend more, since most of the young people interviewed about their spending habits are 15 or 16 years old.
While none of the information in the second article contradicts that in the first, the tone is different. The writer seems to be suggesting that, on the whole, young people are very sensible in the way they handle money, using words like 'responsibilities' and 'reliable'. The quotation which ends the first article sounds as though the statistician was rather shocked by the amount spent by young people, and is almost disapproving: 'I'm sure I never spent £8.40 a week as a child ...'

The second article adds quite a lot to the first, as it interviews young people and reports their attitudes as well as their spending patterns. It points out that they think about managing their money as well as spending it, that they are conscious of how advertisers try to 'tap the youth market', and that they often earn money for themselves and do not just accept it from their parents.

Q3

This feature on children's spending is made interesting and attractive to the reader in various ways. Firstly, your eye is caught by the colour photograph which shows two happy children (a boy and a girl to keep a gender balance) opening a can of drink. The picture perhaps suggests that children are carefree and irresponsible, and this impression is strengthened by the placing of a long, prominent headline to the left of the photograph.

The table within the text of the main article is also prominent, partly because colour is again used to highlight it, but also because it stands out from the print around it as it has its own headline and is within a frame.

The second article is less prominent than the first both because of its position and because the headline is shorter. However, when you have looked at the picture and read the first article, your eye naturally moves to the second article, so the layout as a whole is attractive and effective and engages the reader's interest.

The structure of the first article is straightforward; a number of short paragraphs explain the background to the feature, then essentially put into words what is set out in the table. In this way, both readers who prefer graphical information and those who prefer conventional written information are likely to understand the main points of the article. It ends with a quotation from a statistician, but otherwise relies on description and information.

The second article is structured quite differently, around an interview with a number of young people. Most of this article consists of direct quotations from them, including the headline.

The language interest in the feature relies on puns in the main headline and photograph caption to gain the reader's attention. Both puns are connected with the amount of money young people are reputed to spend on soft drinks: 'canny' (which refers to drinks containers, but is also a slang term meaning careful or thrifty), 'liquid assets' (which refers to drink as a liquid, but also means disposable income) and 'splashing out' (the drink in the photograph is splashing out of the can but this is also a slang term, meaning to spend in a carefree way).

In the articles themselves, the language is quite formal and some of the vocabulary would be challenging to weak readers. For example, words such as 'lucrative' (profitable), 'inducing' (tempting), 'expenditure' (spending) are used in the first article. In the second article there are words such as 'wary' (cautious), 'subsist' (live on), and 'adept' (skilled). However, because the second article contains a number of direct quotations from young people, the overall tone is less formal and more conversational.

Taken as a whole, this feature is interesting in its content and variety of language use, and attractive in its layout and presentation. It is likely to engage competent readers of teenage years or above.

Examiner's Comments

Q1 The answer to (a) uses the candidate's own words wherever possible (e.g. 'shoes', 'purchased') and successfully conveys the important difference between average and actual spends on certain items. This is the only point that needs to be made in (b), which is sufficient to gain full marks as it stands. The answer overall would also gain full marks, i.e. 6.

Q2 This is a quite difficult question, since points of comparison between the articles are not straightforward. The opening paragraph is therefore good, as it makes that point quite firmly, but then moves on in the second paragraph to contrast the approach and tone of the two articles – there is clearly more to say about this. The answer then proceeds coherently from the point about the more supportive tone of the second article to say what it adds to the first article. Not only does this response contain the necessary information to answer the question, it is also very logically presented. The candidate has shown sufficient understanding of the material and ability to express this clearly to gain the full 6 marks.

Q3 This is a long, detailed answer which starts sensibly with what the reader sees when he or she first looks at the feature, and describes how the eye moves about the page. The candidate has drawn usefully on her/his understanding of general aspects of reading media texts, such as looking at gender, composition of photographs, positioning of text and so on, and has carefully related these concepts to actual details in the given example. A particular strength of this answer is the close attention paid to the language, and how this is related back to other aspects of the feature (for example, the puns which tie in with the photograph). No examiner could ask for more than this! The candidate shows good knowledge of media techniques, excellent understanding of the source material, and an engaging style of writing. There is no doubt that this answer would gain the full 8 marks.

SECTION B

Sample Student's Answers

Q4

Dear Editor,

I am writing as the grandparent of two teenage children to add my opinions to those expressed in your feature on young people's spending habits.

I must agree with the statistician who was surprised at how much they have to spend these days. I never expected to buy food and drink or clothes when I was young – my parents provided what they thought was necessary, and if I wanted any more, that was hard luck. The small amount of pocket money I was given had to be used to buy birthday and Christmas presents for family and friends, and I was also taught to save for the future.

Now my grandson just seems to spend every penny he can get on computer games and football strips, while my granddaughter wastes a small fortune on nail varnish, clothes she only ever seems to wear once, and junk food – which is quite unnecessary, since she is fed very well at home.

My grandchildren insist on doing part-time jobs to support their spending habits. My grandson has a paper round, which means he does not get enough sleep, while my granddaughter stacks shelves in a local supermarket at the weekend when she should be doing her homework.

I'm sure they only behave like this because all their friends do. When I criticise them, they tell me I'm old-fashioned or go off in a sulk. Can anybody tell me how I can teach them to value money?

Yours,

A worried grandmother

Q5

CASH CONTROL
– or dosh disaster?

Feeling out of control when it comes to managing your money? Don't seem to know where it goes, or even where it comes from? Read on for top tips to turn torment into triumph!

Give us a job!
First, you need your money: so get out and earn some! Don't ask your aged parents all the time – they need it too! Part-time jobs are there if you look for them. Don't take no for an answer: beg, bribe, bully your way into:
● a paper round: not cool, maybe, but a steady earner – great exercise, too!
● helping in a shop: tough on the feet, but helps your maths no end!
● waiting on: customers can be so rude – but the tips make up for it!

Money, money, money
So now you've got some. How do you manage it?
For starters, know how much you should be paid – some people don't have a clue, they just take what they're given and spend it all.
If you know what you should be paid, you can:
● check you're getting what you're owed
● budget for what you can spend.

Chance to be Chancellor
What's that? you say. Budgets? Aren't they what boring politicians prattle about? But this is your budget – your breakthrough to billions!
● Make a list of what your lifestyle needs
● Decide how much you can afford to spend on each of them, each week
● Keep to it!

Savings success
If you don't spend all your CD cash one week, don't blow it on another – save it instead! Then have a bonanza blowout when funds allow!

It's easy – so do it – YOU KNOW IT MAKES SENSE!

Examiner's Comments

Q4 The layout and general tone of this answer is good. The candidate links the answer to the stimulus material by picking up on some details such as teenagers spending money on food, drink and clothes and skilfully relates this to the kind of comment the letter-writer might make about how this compares with her own upbringing. Note that the language is appropriately quite formal, but the use of a direct question to readers at the end is a good idea to give some immediacy to what might otherwise seem a rather 'distant' letter by an unsympathetic writer. This is a well-written answer which uses the material well and successfully creates the sense of a real person behind the letter. To gain the highest marks, a little more 'sparkle' throughout the letter would have been necessary. Nevertheless, as it stands, it would certainly gain 16 or 17 marks out of 20.

Q5 This candidate has revelled in the opportunity to show her/his understanding of various media techniques. The actual content of the article is fairly slender, but as this is a writing task, very high marks would be gained for showing such skills as:

- headline writing, using alliteration and repetition for effect;
- short, sharp sentences, with lots of question marks and exclamation marks to draw the reader into the text;
- short sections and bullet points to convey information clearly;
- use of slang to appeal to the target audience (e.g. 'dosh', 'cool', 'blow');
- use of upper-case letters for a strong visual (and linguistic) ending

Appropriateness to audience and purpose is the most important factor that an examiner takes into account when assessing an answer to a task of this type. This answer is full of the 'sparkle' which was lacking in the answer to Question 4. This, together with the display of skills listed above, indicates an answer of the highest quality which would gain 19 or even 20 marks out of 20.

Published by Collins Educational
An *imprint of* HarperCollins*Publishers* Ltd
77–85 Fulham Palace Road
London W6 8JB

© HarperCollins*Publishers* Ltd 1998

First Published 1998. Reprinted 2000

ISBN 0 00 323504 1

Andrew Bennett and Peter Thomas assert the moral right to be identified as the authors of this work.

British Library Cataloguing in Publication Data
A catalogue record for this book is available from the British Library.

Edited by Catriona Watson–Brown and Susan Millership
Production by James Graves, Anna Pauletti
Picture research by Tamsin Miller
Cover design by BCG Communications
Book design by Rupert Purcell and produced by Gecko Limited
Index compiled by Drusilla Calvert
Printed and bound in the UK by The Bath Press

Acknowledgements

The Authors and Publishers are grateful to the following for permission to reproduce copyright material: © Amnesty International, Amnesty International advertisement, pp. 179–80; © Au Pair in America, *Camp America publicity leaflet*, p. 241; © Binatone, 'Binatone' quick reference card, p. 85; Black Swan, *Notes from a Small Island* by Bill Bryson, pp. 107–108, 252; Ian Cave, 'Granary Wharf' leaflet, pp. 79, 103, 110; John Cleese & Connie Booth, *Fawlty Towers*, pp. 50–51, 53; *Countryside Magazine*, 'British Food is the Best by Far' by Alison Pratt, p. 121; Laurence Pollinger Ltd and the Estate of Frieda Lawrence Ravagli, 'Last Lesson of the Afternoon,' by D.H. Lawrence from *The Complete Poems of D.H. Lawrence*, p. 74; Department of the Environment © Crown copyright, *Helping the Earth Begins at Home;* 'Summertime Smog,' and 'Wintertime Smog,' Anti-drink-drive poster, pp. 99–100, 181, 172; Faber & Faber: 'The Trout' from *Death of a Naturalist* by Seamus Heaney, p. 34; 'Weeds' by Norman Nicholson from *Sea to West*, p. 39; *The Lord of the Flies,* by William Golding, pp. 9, 57; 'Thistles' by Ted Hughes from *Wodwo*, p. 41; *The Caretaker* by Harold Pinter, pp. 49, 52; *Lipstick on Your Collar* by Dennis Potter, pp. 47–48; Granta, *When did you Last See your Father?* by Blake Morrison, p. 118; *The Guardian:* 'London my London,' 1/8/95 by Sebastian Faulks, p. 186; 'Musical facts' graphs 9/5/95, p. 84; Heinemann, 'The Darkness Out There,' from *Pack of Cards* by Penelope Lively, pp. 14, 27; IDG, *Internet Explorer 3 for Windows 95 for Dummies*, p. 174; IPC Magazines Ltd, front cover of *Woman* magazine, p.124; *The Independent,* 'Canny kids splash out on food, drink and fashion with £8 in their pocket,' 23/7/97 by Glenda Cooper, p. 262; *The Lady*, cover of *The Lady*, p. 124; Macmillan, 'City Jungle' by Pie Corbett from *Sandwhich Poets Rice Corbett & Moses*; The Marvell Press 'Wires' by Philip Larkin, p. 36; Orion, *Under Milk Wood* by Dylan Thomas, p. 47; *The Observer*, 'The Lighthouse Keeper,' and 'The Seafront Attendant,' 6/7/97, p. 98; Oxfam, Oxfam leaflet, p. 93; Oxford/Chatto 'Dulce et Decorum est,' by Wilfred Owen from *The Complete Poems and Fragments*, p. 39; Penguin, *Animal Farm* by George Orwell, p. 208; *Jake's Thing* by Kingsley Amis, p. 15; *Going Solo* by Roald Dahl, p. 78; *The Catcher in the Rye* by J.D. Salinger, p. 20; *The Go Between* by L.P. Hartley, pp. 15–16; *Cider with Rosie* and *As I Walked out one Midsummer Morning* by Laurie Lee, pp. 17–18; *The Diary of Anne Frank* by Anne Frank, p. 152; *A Kestrel for a Knave* by Barry Hines, pp. 59, 199–200; *A View from the Bridge* by Arthur Miller, p. 46; *Pygmalion* by George Bernard Shaw, p. 45; *The Kingdom by the Sea* by Paul Theroux, pp. 77, 225; *I'm the King of the Castle* by Susan Hill, pp. 157–158; *St Joan* by George Bernard Shaw, pp. 204–205; Pergammon, 'Mastering the Craft' from *Mastering the Craft* by Vernon Scannell, p. 35; Phoenix, *The Siege of Krishnapur* by J.G. Farrell, p. 61; Puffin Books Ltd, *Daz 4 Zoe* by Robert Swindells, pp. 21–23; Random House: *The Commitments* by Roddy Doyle, William Heinemann/Minerva, p. 21; *The Last Enemy* by Richard Hillary, Pimlico, p. 188; *There was Once* by Margaret Attwood, p. 162; RNLI, 'Water Safety Code,' and 'Flags and Signs,' from *Beach Safety Guidelines*, p. 86; Routledge, 'The Dandelion,' from *Selected Poems* by Jon Silkin, pp. 32, 38; Scottish and Newcastle Retail, Lodge Inns publicity leaflet, p. 114; The Benefits Agency, Income support leaflet, p. 154; *The Daily Mirror,* 'It's Chelsea FC,' 6/8/97, p. 122; *The Daily Telegraph*, 'Obituary of Dame Violet Dickson,' 1/1/91, p. 94; Laurence S. Untermeyer, 'Portrait of a Machine,' by Laurence S. Untermeyer from *Roast Leviathan*, Harcourt Brace & Co., pp. 35, 60; Urathon Bike Tyres, Urathon bicycle tyres leaflet, pp. 89–90; The Women's Press, *Push Me, Pull Me* by Sandra Chick, p. 19; Chatto & Windus Ltd, 'Thistles' by Jon Stallworthy from *Root & Branch*, p. 68; 'Dress Sense' by David Kitchen, p. 40.

Photographs

The Archive Collection/Disney Corporation: p. 129; BBC Resources Centre: p. 213; BFI Stills/Canal + Image UK, Ltd: pp. 11, 133; BFI Stills/Imageworks: pp. 134, 208; BFI Stills/Kingworld: p. 204; BFI Stills/Polygram: p. 162; BFI Stills/United Artists: p. 199; BFI Stills/Universal Films: p. 150; BFI Stills/Warner Brothers: p. 45; Tim Booth: p. 210; Bridgeman Art Library/Fitzwilliam Museum: p. 158; John Cleese/Connie Booth: p. 51; © Babette Cole: p. 163; Collections/Anthea Sieveking: p. 156; Collections/Brian Shuel: p. 207; Collections/Michael St Maur Sheil: p. 77; Coral Cay Conservation: p. 216; Department of Health: p. 179; Department of the Environment, Transport and the Regions © Crown copyright 1997: p. 181; Holt Studios International/Nigel Cattlin: p. 69; Imperial War Museum: pp. 66 right, 188; Mary Evans Picture Library: pp. 23, 29, 48, 60, 63, 66, 74; Mary Evans/Jeffrey Morgan: p. 108; Michael O'Mara Books Ltd: p. 116; Minerva: pp. 21, 107; Christine Osborne Pictures: p. 147; P.A.L.: pp. 44, 47; Penguin: pp. 117, 135; Telegraph Colour Library: pp. 33, 191 bottom; Telegraph Colour Library/B. Losh: p. 171, Telegraph Colour Library/Larry Bray: p. 191 top.

Illustrations

Sally Artz, Nick Asher, Peter Byatt, Gecko Ltd, Madeleine Hardy, Michael Ogden, Dave Poole and Nick Ward.

Every effort has been made to contact the holders of copyright material, but if any have been inadvertently overlooked, the Publishers will be pleased to make the necessary arrangements at the first opportunity.

INDEX

A page number in **bold** is the most important reference to a subject.